Critique of Pure Music

Critique of Pure Music

James O. Young

UNIVERSITY PRESS

UNIVERSITY PRESS

Great Clarendon Street, Oxford, OX2 6DP,
United Kingdom

Oxford University Press is a department of the University of Oxford.
It furthers the University's objective of excellence in research, scholarship,
and education by publishing worldwide. Oxford is a registered trade mark of
Oxford University Press in the UK and in certain other countries

© James O. Young 2014

The moral rights of the author have been asserted

First Edition published in 2014

All rights reserved. No part of this publication may be reproduced, stored in
a retrieval system, or transmitted, in any form or by any means, without the
prior permission in writing of Oxford University Press, or as expressly permitted
by law, by licence or under terms agreed with the appropriate reprographics
rights organization. Enquiries concerning reproduction outside the scope of the
above should be sent to the Rights Department, Oxford University Press, at the
address above

You must not circulate this work in any other form
and you must impose this same condition on any acquirer

Published in the United States of America by Oxford University Press
198 Madison Avenue, New York, NY 10016, United States of America

British Library Cataloguing in Publication Data
Data available

Library of Congress Control Number: 2013941290

ISBN 978-0-19-968271-3

Links to third party websites are provided by Oxford in good faith and
for information only. Oxford disclaims any responsibility for the materials
contained in any third party website referenced in this work.

To the Fellows of the Spinnakers Academy

Preface

Formalism is the view that music is appreciated as pure form. On this view, music is not about anything, it does not represent and it has no content. At any rate, it has no weighty content. Some music may represent birdsong, bells, and a few other sounds, but it does not provide insight into the emotional lives of humans or other profound matters. Certainly it is not appreciated as the source of such insight. Prominent defenders of formalism (of one variety or another) have included Monroe Beardsley, Malcolm Budd, and Nick Zangwill, as well as the most influential contemporary philosopher of music, Peter Kivy. Other philosophers of music have been, without endorsing formalism, formalism's fellow travellers in that they are sceptical about the view that music has content. Stephen Davies is the most distinguished of these philosophers. This essay is designed to prove that formalism is false. (My opponents could, perhaps, best be described as anti-contentists and my view as contentism, but these terms seem awkward. My opponents will be described as formalists. My own view will be called anti-formalism.) Significant numbers of musical works, including some of the greatest masterpieces, are appreciated for their content.

While many philosophers have favoured formalism, or doubted that music has content, many musicians, music critics and ordinary music lovers have always believed that music can provide deep insight into the interior lives of humans. A recent book about Monteverdi, for example, contains this passage in the course of a discussion of *The Coronation of Poppea*:

> The languishing 'dying away' of Nerone's vocal line on 'affetti miei' extends over four bars. Three succeeding bars are left for the accompanimental instruments to bring this sequence to a musical period. The effect is one of great psychological insight: the human voice and words can no longer express the depths of Nerone's contentment.[1]

Similarly, Hermann Abert praises Mozart for his 'true psychological insight'[2] in his treatment of Donna Elvira, and Winton Dean speaks of

---

[1] Mark Ringer, *Opera's First Master: The Musical Dramas of Claudio Monteverdi* (Plompton Plains, N.J.: Amadeus Press, 2006), p. 303.
[2] Hermann Abert, *W.A. Mozart*, trans. Stewart Spencer (New Haven, C.T.: Yale University Press, 2007), p. 1101.

Handel's 'penetrating insight into human nature'.[3] The phrases 'psychological insight' and 'psychological depth' are used repeatedly to describe the achievements found in a wide range of compositions. Even the songs of Bruce Springsteen are described as providing 'psychological insight'[4] while the music of Led Zeppelin is said to have 'psychological depth'.[5]

All of the examples just given are of music with lyrics, but it is equally easy to find statements to the effect that instrumental music provides psychological insight. (In Chapter 4 I will argue that music with and without lyrics both have content in much the same way.) Many of these statements are by distinguished composers. Schumann admired the 'psychological' element of Schubert's compositions. Schumann wrote, with particular reference to Schubert's four-hand Rondeau, Op. 107, that 'nobody's compositions are such a psychological puzzle in the course and connection of their ideas as Schubert's, with their *apparently* logical progressions... What a diary is to those who jot down all their passing emotions, his music paper was to Schubert'.[6] Aaron Copland writes that, with Beethoven, 'music lost a certain innocence but gained instead a new dimension in psychological depth'.[7] Shostakovich held that his symphonies are about matters such as Stalin's character.

Formalists believe that anyone who speaks of music as having psychological depth or as providing psychological insight is confused. From the formalists' perspective, music is not the sort of thing that could provide psychological insight: patterns of sound can no more provide insight than the patterns of colour in a kaleidoscope can. Kivy calls the psychological depth of music an 'illusion'.[8] Davies is similarly sceptical about the view that music can provide psychological insight. He shares 'with Kivy the view that music is not profound as a result of revealing deep truths

---

[3] Winton Dean, *Handel and the Opera Seria* (Berkeley, C.A.: University of California Press, 1969), p. 24.

[4] Scott Calef, 'A Little of the Human Touch: Knowledge and Empathy in the Music of Bruce Springsteen', in Randall E. Auxier and Doug Anderson (eds.), *Bruce Springsteen and Philosophy* (Chicago, I.L.: Open Court, 2008), p. 225.

[5] Edward Macan, 'Bring Back the Balance', in Scott Calef (ed.), *Led Zeppelin and Philosophy: All Will be Revealed* (Chicago, I.L.: Open Court, 2009), p. 199.

[6] Robert Schumann, *Early Letters of Robert Schumann, Originally Published by his Wife*, trans. May Herbert (London: George Bell and Sons, 1888), p. 81.

[7] Aaron Copland, *Copland on Music* (Garden City, N.Y.: Doubleday, 1960), p. 39.

[8] Peter Kivy, *Osmin's Rage: Philosophical Reflections on Opera, Drama, and Text* (Ithaca, N.Y.: Cornell University Press, 1999), p. 268. In this passage he is speaking specifically about opera, but he believes that no music can provide psychological insight.

or ideas about emotions or their place in human life'.⁹ (This said, Davies's views on philosophy of music are much more nuanced than those of formalists.)

Anti-formalists are not so sure. Formalists would have us believe that listeners are systematically mistaken when they claim to have received psychological insights from music. An anti-formalist finds it difficult to believe that lots of people, many of them distinguished musicians or critics, regularly report receiving psychological insights from music when they do not. Some distinguished philosophers have taken a similar view: Aristotle anticipated some of the central arguments of this essay, and I find common ground with such eighteenth-century philosophers as Charles Batteux, Francis Hutcheson, Thomas Twining, Thomas Reid, and Jean-Jacques Rousseau. In recent years, several notable contemporary philosophers (including Jenefer Robinson, Jerrold Levinson, Charles O. Nussbaum and Kendall Walton) have also resisted formalism and the view that music has no content. This essay builds on the work of these philosophers and strengthens the case for anti-formalism.

This essay is intended as a comprehensive attack on formalism, but the principal contemporary advocate of formalism is Peter Kivy and no one comes in for more criticism in the course of these pages. His philosophy of music is the *bête noire* that is stalked on almost every page. I hope that this criticism will be regarded as a sincere form of flattery. Although I relentlessly criticize Kivy, I regard myself as, in an important sense, a member of his school. The questions that I address are the questions that he has posed. The methods that I adopt for addressing these questions (including reliance on the best psychological evidence, reflection on the musicological record, and a willingness to learn from the history of philosophy) are Kivy's methods. Even the title of this book is a kind of homage to Kivy. It is a title that he considered for *Music Alone*. (*Critique of Pure Music* is a much better title for my book.) I simply come to conclusions diametrically opposed to Kivy's. In particular, I come to the conclusion that a good deal of music is not simply appreciated as pure form.

In the course of writing this essay I have profited from the comments and criticisms of many people. I am particularly indebted to the philosophers who meet at the Spinnakers each Friday evening for a few pints

---

⁹ Stephen Davies, 'Profundity in Instrumental Music', in his *Musical Understandings and Other Essays on the Philosophy of Music* (Oxford: Oxford University Press, 2011), p. 190.

and some philosophical debate. While I was writing this book, these philosophers often included Sandy Bannikoff, Bob Bright, Craig Derksen, and Mike Raven. (One philosophical carpenter, Paul Jones, also regularly attends our gatherings at the Spinnakers.) Each week for a year they patiently listened to my latest ideas and helped me solve my latest problems. Mike Raven also read and provided careful and incisive comments on the complete manuscript. Members of the work in progress group in the Department of Philosophy of the University of Victoria also read the manuscript and discussed it with me. I would like to single out for thanks Margaret Cameron, Colin Macleod, Patrick Rysiew, and Audrey Yap. Two other members of my Department, Scott Woodcock and Klaus Jahn, also provided helpful suggestions. My old and dear friends Bill Barthelemy and Sheldon Wein read the earliest version of this essay and helped shape its evolution.

Two non-philosophers, the Revd Francis Dearman and my father-in-law the Honourable Donald Bowman, QC, read the manuscript. Their comments were useful in a number of ways but most importantly they have helped make the essay more accessible to non-specialists.

Many other people deserve thanks. Jeanette Bicknell helpfully commented on part of the essay when I presented it at the American Society for Aesthetics Eastern Division Conference in April 2011. Chris Bartel also had some helpful comments on this occasion. Peter Alward provided useful comments on a paper that I gave at the Western Canadian Philosophical Association in October 2011. I am grateful to Carolyn Swanson, one of my former students, for the opportunity to present part of this book at Vancouver Island University and for some valuable discussions. Similarly, I would like to thank Professor Oh Chong-hwan for the invitation to give the first three chapters as a series of lectures at Seoul National University in January 2012. These lectures were repeated, with emendations, at Beijing Normal University in April 2012. I am grateful to Professor Liao Shenbai for the invitation to speak in Beijing. I received valuable feedback from the audiences in both Seoul and Beijing. Julian Dodd provided helpful comments on an essay which formed the basis of Chapter 1 and which was included in an issue of *The Monist* devoted to philosophy of music. Similarly, Tomas McAuley provided useful comments on the version of Chapter 4 written for *The Journal of the Royal Musical Association*.

Thanks are owed to Dr Lisa Szeker-Madden, of the Victoria Conservatory of Music, for musicological advice. Thanks are also due to several psychologists. Carol L. Krumhansl kindly answered some questions I had about her research. Vladamir J. Konečni shared some of his forthcoming work with me, as did Jonna K. Vuoskoski. Tony Robertson took the trouble to provide thoughtful written comments after my presentation at Vancouver Island University.

Particular thanks are owed to Stephen Davies. He kindly provided me with a copy of the proofs of his *Musical Understandings* prior to its publication. Then, coincidentally, he ended up as one of the readers to whom Oxford University Press sent my manuscript. Davies's comments on my manuscript displayed the rigour and thoughtfulness that are the trademarks of all of his philosophical work. His comments have helped me make significant improvements to the essay. Tom Cochrane was the other reader and his comments were equally valuable and assisted me in improving this essay. He prompted me to take the difficult step of cutting passages that I had sweated over. Any author will tell you that cutting such passages is difficult, but it is sometimes necessary. I do not think that I cut as much as Cochrane would have liked, but cut I did. I would also like to thank Dr Eleanor Collins, the Oxford University Press editor responsible for my book, for her unfailing helpfulness and patience.

As I was preparing the final version of the manuscript, I was pleasantly surprised to find that I had profited at several points from the comments of my wife, Laurel Bowman. I am pleased to be able to offer to her my thanks as well as my love. My daughter Julia also made some valuable suggestions. Her younger brother (Piers) was still mainly a (pleasant) distraction.

Contents

1. Music and Expressiveness ... 1
   Connections Between Music and Emotion ... 1
   The Resemblance Theory ... 11
   Convention and Emotion ... 26

2. Music and the Arousal of Emotion ... 35
   Could Music Arouse Emotion? ... 35
   Does Music Arouse Emotion? ... 44
   How Music Arouses Emotion ... 58
   Which Emotions Can Music Arouse? ... 66
   Puzzles for the Arousalist ... 72
   The Formalist's Last Ditch ... 76
   A 'Special' Emotion ... 79

3. The Content of Music ... 87
   The Concept of Representation ... 87
   Representation in Music ... 97
   Anti-formalist Objections ... 112
   Formalist Arguments Against Representation in Music ... 117

4. Music and Lyrics ... 125
   Music and Lyrics: Allies or Antagonists? ... 125
   How Literature Works ... 132
   Music and the Arousal of Emotion, Again ... 137
   Music Plus Lyrics Equals Music Drama ... 143

5. The Value of Music ... 150
   The Value of Musical Form ... 150
   The Heresy of Substitutable Experience ... 154
   Sensory Pleasure and Valuable Emotions ... 158
   Profundity and Purism ... 167
   Music and Insight ... 174
   Envoi ... 182

Bibliography of Works Cited and Consulted ... 185
Index ... 197

At once the Passions to express and move;
We hear and straight we grieve or hate, rejoice or love:
In unseen Chains it does the Fancy bind;
At once it charms the Sense and captivates the Mind.

Nicholas Brady

There is more nonsense spoken and written about music than almost anything else I can think of.

Peter Kivy

1
Music and Expressiveness

Connections Between Music and Emotion

As long as philosophers have thought about music, many of them have thought that it has some important connection to ordinary emotions. Plato and Aristotle believed as much, though they disagreed about the nature of the connection. Their disagreement presaged the continuing debate about the connection between music and emotion. Some philosophers have held that music arouses emotion. Others have argued that music communicates or expresses emotion. Still others have maintained that music is expressive of emotion. From time to time, a few brave souls have suggested that music represents emotion. This chapter endorses the view that music is expressive of emotion. In particular, it argues for the view that music is expressive of emotion by resembling human expressive behaviour. A defence of the view that music is expressive of emotion by resembling human expressive behaviour is the first step towards demonstrating that music is not empty form and that music is valued in large part because of its content.

Formalism is currently a widely adopted approach to philosophy of music. Formalists believe that music is pure form without any extra-musical content. Listeners are held to delight in the patterns of tones, as one may delight in the abstract patterns of colour in a kaleidoscope or a Persian carpet. Formalists generally hold that music has no important link to emotion[1] or that it is linked only to some special aesthetic emotion that is attendant upon experience of patterns of sound.[2] The approach adopted in this essay is resolutely anti-formalist; on the view adopted here,

---

[1] Nick Zangwill is a typical formalist: 'What role...does emotion play in what music is, and in our experience of music? Answer: none of any significance.' 'Against Emotion: Hanslick Was Right About Music', *British Journal of Aesthetics*, 44 (2004), p. 42.

[2] Peter Kivy, *Music Alone* (Ithaca, N.Y.: Cornell University Press, 1990), ch. 8.

which may be called *anti-formalism* for want of a better name, music at least sometimes has extra-musical content. The case for anti-formalism begins with an examination of the link between music and emotion. Describing music in terms of emotion is commonplace. Poets, musicians, and philosophers all talk about music using emotion terms. John Dryden, in his *Ode on St Cecelia's Day*, wrote that,

> The soft complaining flute
> In dying notes discovers
> The woes of hopeless lovers,
> Whose dirge is whispered by the warbling lute.

Earlier, in the sixteenth century, Heinrich Glarean says of Josquin's *Planxit autem David* that in it

> ...has been preserved the mood appropriate to the mourner, who at first is wont to cry out frequently, and then, turning gradually to melancholy complaints, to murmur subduedly and presently to subside, when emotion breaks forth anew, to raise his voice again and to emit a cry.[3]

In the eighteenth century, Charles Avison, the talented English composer, wrote that:

> ...by the Musician's Art, we are often carried into the Fury of a Battle, or a Tempest, we are by turns elated with Joy, or sunk in pleasing Sorrow, roused to Courage, or quelled by grateful Terrors, melted into Pity, Tenderness, and Love, transported to the Regions of Bliss, in an Extacy of divine Praise.[4]

From an early period, philosophers made similar claims about music's power to arouse emotion. Francis Hutcheson noted that music can arouse in listeners 'Melancholy, Joy, Gravity, [and] Thoughtfulness'.[5]

Music critics also talk about music using emotion terms. In the nineteenth century, Otto Jahn described Mozart's Symphony No. 40, K. 550 as a work of 'sorrow and complaining' which 'rises...to a wild merriment'.[6] This way of talking about music is widespread and is a staple of music

---

[3] Heinrich Glarean, *Dodecachordon*, trans. Clement A. Miller (n.p.: American Institute of Musicology, 1965), vol. 2, pp. 271–2.
[4] Pierre Dubois (ed.), *Charles Avison's Essay on Musical Expression With Related Writings by William Hayes and Charles Avison* (Aldershot: Ashgate, 2004), p. 6.
[5] Francis Hutcheson, *An Inquiry into the Original of Our Ideas of Beauty and Virtue: In Two Treatises*, revised edn (Indianapolis, I.N.: Liberty Fund, 2008) p. 68.
[6] Otto Jahn, *Life of Mozart*, trans. Pauline D. Townsend (London: Novello, Ewer, and Co., 1882), vol. 3, p. 35.

criticism. Consider, for example, this passage from a review by Andrew Druckenbrod of a recent performance of Sibelius's Fifth Symphony:

The fast-moving string parts painted a nervousness, some of the many swells of the music had a touch of anger in them before... rising in glory, the bassoon solo was as desolate as can be, performed with an amazing, forlorn tone.[7]

Many more examples could easily be given of writers who link music and emotion. Give or take some Schenkerian analyses, it is difficult to find talk about music that does not employ emotion terms.

Talking about music in emotional terms gives rise to philosophical questions. Philosophers wonder about the meaning of statements that describe music in emotion terms, and whether or not these statements are true. I am inclined to think that when informed people are talking about music using emotion terms, they often say something true. I find it difficult to believe that skilled musicians and other informed people constantly make false statements about music. The real question is what statements about music employing musical terms mean. Several possible answers can be given to this question.

Some answers are completely implausible. One could take Jahn's comment to mean that Mozart's symphony is experiencing sorrow and merriment. This is an implausible interpretation since Jahn would then have made an obviously false statement. He might be wrong about Mozart's work, but Jahn has not said something obviously false. As I say, well-informed people are unlikely to make silly mistakes. Whatever Jahn meant, he was not attributing emotional states to music.

Another possibility is that people are speaking metaphorically when they describe music in emotional terms. On this view, the statement that music is sad has nothing to do with the emotional state of sadness. The suggestion that emotional descriptions of music are metaphors appeals primarily to formalists. Some formalists, such as Nick Zangwill,[8] believe that emotion statements about music are metaphors because they believe that our appreciation of music has little or no connection to emotion, and music has no features that would make emotional descriptions of music true. In particular, they believe that music does not arouse joy,

---

[7] Andrew Druckenbrod, 'PSO guest conductor finds strength, emotion in Sibelius', *Pittsburgh Post-Gazette*, 29 January 2011.
[8] Nick Zangwill, 'Music, Metaphor and Emotion', *Journal of Aesthetics and Art Criticism*, 65 (2007), 391–400.

melancholy, or other ordinary emotions. They believe that nothing about music is literally sad, joyful, or fearful. Still, they are aware that talk about music using emotion terms is commonplace. Indeed, Zangwill believes that almost all descriptions of music are metaphorical. When formalists say that statements about music that employ emotion terms are metaphors, they are saying that people do not really mean what they appear to mean when they make such statements. They mean something else. This strikes me as an implausible position for a couple of reasons.

For a start, it is unlikely that virtually all talk about music is metaphorical. A statement can only be a metaphorical use of language against a background of literal language use. A metaphor involves a departure from ordinary linguistic usage. In any realm of ordinary language use, most of the language is literal and metaphors are introduced from time to time and are easily distinguishable from literal language. So, for example, in talking about the weather we will sometimes speak metaphorically of brooding clouds, lashing rain, glorious sunshine, and so on. Most of the time, however, we speak literally: it is raining, we say, or we observe that the sun is shining. However, if the metaphorical analysis of emotional statements about music is correct, virtually every statement that people make about music is metaphorical. If our ordinary way of talking about music involves the use of emotion terms, then such terms are being used literally. Our ordinary ways of speaking are governed by conventions in a way that metaphors (which violate conventional usage) are not.

Consider this illustration of my point. Suppose whenever anyone wanted to talk about the weather they would use musical metaphors. So, for example, to say that it is raining someone would say, 'It is high-pitched today.' Or suppose that when it was sunny people always said, 'The weather has a dotted rhythm.' These would not be metaphors. Rather, they would be literal statements. 'High-pitched' would be ambiguous. It would refer both to rain and to high Hz. Similarly, if we always say, 'The music is sad' when the melodic line falls, the tempo is slow, and so on, then 'sad' has a new literal meaning and one does not speak metaphorically in calling music sad. Again, a statement is only a metaphor when it is a non-standard usage. (Dead metaphors are not an exception to this rule. When metaphors die, new literal meanings come into existence.) When we speak about music using emotion terms, we are not speaking metaphorically.

If emotional statements about music are not metaphors, we have a choice. The first possibility is that the use of emotion terms to describe music has something to do with the ordinary literal use of such terms. On this view, works of music have features that make the use of terms such as 'joyful', 'melancholy', or 'anxious' non-arbitrary. Alternatively, we can say that nothing about music makes its description as joyful or melancholy—as these terms are normally used—appropriate. On this view, we call music with slow tempi, minor tonality, and falling musical lines melancholy simply because we have established a new convention. This new convention has nothing in common with the old convention that governed the word 'melancholy'. Similar new conventions govern the description of music as joyful, triumphant, fearful, and so on. On this view, the words 'melancholy' and 'joyful' have been given additional, secondary literal meanings. To say that some music is sad is to say that it has certain formal characteristics.

A central hypothesis of this essay is that music has features that make its description in emotional terms non-arbitrary. When we apply emotion terms to music, we are doing so in a way that is related to the prior application of such terms to people and their mental states. (Stephen Davies and Malcolm Budd have defended this view.[9]) When listeners make an emotional statement about music they have detected a property of the music that is closely related to properties detected in other contexts in which they use emotion predicates. Empirical evidence, including evidence from psychology, will be presented later in this essay that strongly supports the hypothesis that the experience of music has much in common with the experience of ordinary emotions. Here I want only to make a preliminary attempt to clarify the relationship between music and emotion.

One might describe a work of music in emotional terms because it is an expression of emotion. Certainly the claim that music expresses emotion is a common one, but the claim that music expresses emotion can have different meanings. Often, when people say that music expresses emotion, they mean that composers' (or performers') emotions are manifested or displayed in some way in the music that they produce. Sometimes we express emotion by behaving in certain ways. I may dance for joy or droop because I am sad. Several arguments have been given for thinking that music is not usually in

---

[9] Stephen Davies, *Musical Meaning and Expression* (Ithaca, N.Y.: Cornell University Press, 1994), p. 228 and *Musical Understandings and Other Essays on the Philosophy of Music* (Oxford: Oxford University Press, 2011), ch. 2. For a similar view, see Malcolm Budd, *Aesthetic Essays* (Oxford: Oxford University Press, 2008), ch. 7 and ch. 8.

this way an expression of emotion. We have, in particular, good reason to believe that works of music do not express (in the sense just identified) emotions felt by the composers at the time of composition. Empirical evidence supports this view. For example, Mozart (among others) was distressed when writing some of his sunniest music. This music clearly does not manifest his emotional state at the time of composition. There are other reasons for thinking that music does not express emotion in the sense of manifesting it. It is hard to see how composers could write music expressing anguish if they were genuinely distressed. Someone in the grip of anguish is unlikely to write music worth hearing. And yet some music is properly described as anguished. For these and other reasons, the view that music generally manifests emotions a composer had at the time of composition is implausible.

It is more plausible to say that music expresses emotion in some other sense. Some composers likely intend their works to express emotions that they felt at some point, not necessarily at the time of composition. It seems likely, for example, that John Dowland expressed, in this sense of the word, some of his emotions in *Semper Dowland, semper dolens* and similar works. He may not have been doleful at the moment that he composed this work (versions exist for solo lute and for viol consort) but he seems to have been a melancholy man. Likely he wished to reveal something of his emotional life to listeners. In the Romantic period music was often intended to express emotion in this manner.

We do not, however, completely understand the relationship between music and emotion if we say that music expresses emotion in this broader sense of the term. For a start, it seems unlikely that all music that is described in emotional terms is an expression of some emotion its composer has felt. A work of music that is described in terms of martial ardour could have been composed by the most pacific soul. A congenitally cheerful composer could produce doleful music. As well, listeners can know nothing at all about a composer's intentions and, in particular, nothing about whether he intended to express his emotions, and yet describe a work of music as triumphant or doleful. In general, listeners cannot tell, just by listening to a work of music, that it expresses some particular emotion which the composer is experiencing. Even when this is so, listeners can hear that a piece of music is, for example, triumphant or doleful. Talk about music expressing emotion has not yet clarified the relationship between music and emotion. (There is another sense in which music may be said to express emotion, one to which I will return in Chapter 3.)

Peter Kivy and Stephen Davies have proposed another way of understanding the relationship between music and emotion. They defend the view (which can be traced back to the seventeenth century and beyond) that music is expressive of emotion. Kivy and Davies, in distinguishing between music expressing emotion and being expressive of emotion, made an enduring contribution to the philosophy of music. To say that music is expressive of emotion is to say that it has properties that resemble human expressive behaviour. A piece of music could be expressive of, say, joy without its composer (or performer) expressing joy. (Throughout this essay I will speak of composers and works. Talk of composers is understood to include talk of performing artists. Performances are included in the category of musical works.) So long as some feature of the music resembles the expression of joy, the music is expressive of that emotion. On Kivy's view, music that is expressive of some emotion need not be intended to be expressive of the emotion. It can just happen to resemble human expressive behaviour and in this way be expressive of some emotion. The extent to which music is intended to be expressive of emotion is an interesting question, one to which I will return in a later chapter.

If music is expressive of emotion, talk about music using emotion terms does not rely on completely new conventions about how to use emotion terms. We call music sad when it has features in common with human expressive behaviour. The next section will defend the view that music can be expressive of emotion and that it is so by resembling human expressive behaviour. (I will call this the *resemblance theory* of musical expressiveness.) Here I am only saying that, if this view is correct, we have an answer to the question about what emotional statements about music mean. They are elliptical statements. A statement such as 'The symphony is sorrowful and grieving' is a shorthand, or elliptical, way of saying 'The symphony is expressive of sorrow and grief'. Such a statement will be true if, as a matter of empirical fact, the symphony relevantly resembles human expressive behaviour.

Even if this is right, convention could play a role in musical expressiveness. Music could be expressive of some emotion simply because certain musical properties are conventionally associated with certain emotions. Kivy, for example, suggests that there is nothing inherently sad about music in the minor mode. Neither, he believes, is the major mode inherently expressive of positive emotions. Rather, he maintains, over the years, listeners (at least in the West) have come to associate negative emotions with minor keys and positive emotions with major keys. As a result of this association, minor keys are heard as expressive of negative emotions and major keys as expressive of positive emotions. This could be part of an explanation of how music becomes expressive of certain emotions. I will return to this question and investigate the extent to which convention plays a role in making music expressive of emotion. My conclusion will be that it plays a much smaller role than Kivy believes.

This brief survey of the ways in which music and emotion could be connected has thus far omitted the possibility that music arouses emotions in listeners. Music has been thought to arouse two sorts of emotion. For a start, it might arouse ordinary emotions, such as sadness, joy, and melancholy. Kivy calls these 'garden-variety' emotions and I will adopt his terminology. The other possibility is that music arouses a special emotion, one that we feel only in the context of the experience of music. Kivy defends the view that music arouses such a special emotion. In contrast, I believe that music arouses garden-variety emotions. (It may also arouse a special aesthetic emotion.) I will call the view that music arouses ordinary emotions *arousalism* and someone who defends this view an *arousalist*. Formalists deny that music arouses garden-variety emotions. Arousalism is a crucial part of the anti-formalism advocated in this essay.

Formalists deny that music can, by being expressive of emotions, arouse garden-variety emotions such as joy and melancholy, but this is not to say that they deny that music can arouse emotion. They may allow that a bad performance or a bad composition may arouse frustration or even anger. They typically will not deny that music with lyrics or a programme can arouse emotion. They will hold, however, that the emotion is being aroused by the semantic content associated with the music, not by the music. (Music with lyrics is discussed in Chapter 4, where I argue that such music arouses emotion very much as purely instrumental music does.) Formalists are also aware that works of music can have associations that enable them to arouse ordinary emotions. A piece of music that is expressive of sadness might arouse happiness in someone if it brings to mind an uncommonly happy time in his life. Finally, some formalists (for example, Kivy) believe that music can arouse a special musical emotion. The sheer beauty of a performance may elicit in listeners a sort of enthusiasm or excitement. (I will return to a consideration of special musical emotion in Chapter 2.)

As I have indicated, this essay is a defence of anti-formalism. Music has extra-musical content. The view that music is expressive of emotion is the first step in arguing for this hypothesis. Not all formalists deny that music is expressive of emotion. Indeed, Kivy, a committed formalist, is famous for defending the view that music can be expressive of emotion. (He calls his position 'enhanced formalism'.) Contrary to what Kivy believes, the view that music is expressive of emotion is the key to establishing that music arouses emotion. If music arouses emotion, formalism is untenable. Not for nothing have formalists so resolutely rejected arousalism. My strategy will be to defend the view that music is expressive of emotion. In particular, I will defend the view that music is expressive of emotion by resembling human expressive behaviour. I will then go on to argue (in the next chapter) that, by being expressive of emotion, music is able to arouse emotion. As we will see, the mechanisms by which music arouses emotion are diverse, but arousal starts with music being expressive of emotion.

Jerrold Levinson has articulated a theory of expressiveness in music that has much in common, as he notes, with the resemblance theory.[10] Levinson regards a work of music as expressive of some emotion when the work is readily perceived as a personal expression of that emotion. His theory falls within the general class of resemblance theories because a work can be perceived as the expression of an emotion only if it resembles the expression of emotion. Levinson does, however, have a worry about the resemblance theory. Everything resembles everything else in some respect. Indeed, everything resembles everything else in an infinite number of respects. Levinson wonders about how music resembles human expressive behaviour and to what degree it does. He hypothesizes that music can be heard as expressive of emotion only because humans have a disposition to hear certain features as expressive of emotion.[11] As we will see, there is good reason to believe that Levinson is right in hypothesizing the existence of this disposition. Our capacity to hear music as expressive of emotion is rooted in our evolutionary inheritance.

Levinson is also associated with the view that music can only be heard as expressive of emotion if it is heard as a personal expression, the expression of some persona. (Other philosophers have developed related theories

---

[10] Jerrold Levinson, 'Musical Expressiveness', in his *The Pleasures of Aesthetics: Philosophical Essays* (Ithaca, N.Y.: Cornell University Press, 1996), p. 102.
[11] Levinson, 'Musical Expressiveness', pp. 103–4.

according to which a theory of musical expressiveness involves reference to a persona.) Levinson's argument for this view turns on the premise that an expression of an emotion cannot exist independently of an expresser; that is, a person or persona who expresses the emotion.[12] This persona is 'minimal' in that it is 'characterized only by the emotion that we hear it to be expressing and the musical gesture through which it does so'.[13]

I have my doubts about Levinson's refinements of the resemblance theory and related refinements.[14] The claim that something can be expressive of some emotion only if it is experienced as the expression of some persona's emotion seems doubtful. The yellow on the kitchen walls together with William Morris-patterned curtains may be expressive of cheerfulness without being experienced as the expression of some persona's cheerfulness. Similarly, it seems that a musical work could be experienced as expressive of happiness without being experienced as some persona's happiness. Moreover, the empirical literature on musical expressiveness (to which I am about to turn) makes little or no reference to musical personae and suggests that expressiveness can be understood without reference to personae. I do not find myself positing a persona in my own experience of musical works (except works with lyrics or a programme). Even if this is not so, Levinson's conception of a persona seems so minimal as to add very little to the resemblance theory. Still, I will not take issue with Levinson's position or other persona theories. My aim is not to develop a detailed theory of musical expressiveness. Rather, my goal is to refute formalism. For this purpose, I need only defend a generic, lowest-common-denominator version of the resemblance theory. However, if it should turn out that the experience of music justifies the postulation of personae, then personae could be incorporated into my position on the experience of music.

---

[12] For a view similar to Levinson's see Tom Cochrane, 'Using the Persona to Express Complex Emotions in Music', *Music Analysis*, 29 (2010), 264–75. For a full and recent statement of this position see Jerrold Levinson, 'Musical Expressiveness as Hearability-as-expression', in Matthew Kieran (ed.), *Contemporary Debates in Aesthetics and the Philosophy of Art* (Malden, M.A.: Blackwell, 2006). Jenefer Robinson also defends a persona theory, most recently in Jenefer Robinson and Robert S. Hatten, 'Emotions in Music', *Music Theory Spectrum*, 34 (2012), 71–106.

[13] Levinson, 'Musical Expressiveness as Hearability-as-expression', p. 194.

[14] The persona theory has been criticized by Stephen Davies, 'Contra the Hypothetical Persona in Music', in his *Themes in the Philosophy of Music* (Oxford: Oxford University Press, 2003).

Although music can be expressive of emotion and can arouse emotion, not all music does either. Some music is interesting to us purely as musical form. The compositions of Babbitt, Schoenberg, and Webern are, I believe, such works. These compositions abandon many of the resources that have historically been used to express and arouse emotion, including melody and tonal harmony. Serialist compositions are created in accordance with a method (or theory) that specifies how the composition ought to unfold. Much if not all of the interest of such works lies in seeing how composers overcome the constraints imposed by the method and how they solve compositional problems. I will return to a discussion of such music in Chapter 5.

The Resemblance Theory

The resemblance theory, as the term is understood here, is the theory that music is expressive of an emotion because it resembles features of human expressive behaviour. (Some writers believe that music can resemble emotion itself.[15] This is an intriguing suggestion, but it currently lacks sufficient empirical support.) It should hardly be necessary to defend the resemblance theory of musical expressiveness. When Kivy first articulated his version of the resemblance theory (which he called the contour theory), he regarded it as 'commonplace, commonsensical, and well-known'.[16] Commonplace and commonsensical views are unlikely to turn out to be false. Nevertheless, Kivy, one of the resemblance theory's originators, now rejects the theory and other formalists are sceptical about the view that music is expressive of emotion. Consequently, the theory needs to be revisited. A good deal can be said in its favour.

Kivy used a typical expression on the face of a Saint Bernard dog to illustrate the resemblance theory. A normal Saint Bernard has a face expressive of sadness. This is not because this breed is especially given to sadness. It is not expressing, conveying, or communicating emotion by looking the way that it does. The dog's face is not expressive of sadness because one is made sad by looking at it. Rather, the droopy, jowly countenance resembles the face of a sad person. The dog's face has a resemblance

---

[15] See, for example, Robinson and Hatten, 'Emotions in Music'.
[16] Peter Kivy, *Sound Sentiment: An Essay on the Musical Emotions Including the Complete Text of The Corded Shell* (Philadelphia, P.A.: Temple University Press, 1989), p. 57.

to the expressive behaviour of a human who is sad and this resemblance (plus our recognition of the resemblance) makes the face expressive of sadness. A similar sort of resemblance makes possible expressiveness in music. Kivy uses an example from Monteverdi's work to illustrate the contour theory: 'We hear sadness in the opening phrase of the *Lamento d'Ariana* in that we hear the musical sounds as appropriate to the expression of sadness.'[17] We hear the work as expressive of sadness because we discern the resemblance between the musical line in the aria and the way a sad voice falls.

According to the resemblance theory, music's expressiveness depends on more than its resemblance to the human voice expressing emotion. We express our emotions in our bodily movements as well as in our voices. So the resemblance theory holds that music can also be expressive of some emotion by resembling human bodily movements that are associated with that emotion. Davies is the principal advocate of this view: the 'expressiveness of music depends mainly on a resemblance we perceive between the dynamic character of music and human movement'.[18] A person in the grip of melancholy will move in a slow, plodding manner. A happy person will move in a spritely manner: 'Just as someone who skips and leaps quickly and lightly, makes expansive gestures, and so on, has a happy bearing, so music with a similar vivacity and exuberance is happy sounding.'[19] The resemblance theory predicts that music expressive of sadness will move in a leaden manner while music expressive of joy will be brisk and lilting. Kivy sums up the resemblance theory by saying that, 'we hear music as speech, utterance, gesture, bodily movements, and so on'.[20] Whether listeners, when they hear music as expressive of emotion, are consciously aware of the similarity between music and expressive behaviour is a matter for debate. Likely some listeners are aware of the resemblance while others are not.

The resemblance theory receives a boost, Kivy believed, by a tendency of human beings to hear music as animate. The phenomenon of 'seeing as' is well known. For example, we see a few suitably arranged lines as a face. We see a bent stick as a snake. Kivy suggests that we have a similar

---

[17] Kivy, *Sound Sentiment*, p. 20.
[18] Davies, *Musical Meaning and Expression*, p. 229.
[19] Davies, *Musical Understandings*, p. 10.
[20] Kivy, *Sound Sentiment*, p. 58.

tendency to 'hear as'. We have, he writes, 'a strong tendency to hear music as "animate", as (at times) emotive utterance'. This tendency helps account for the fact that 'we perceive emotive properties in music'.[21]

Despite the considerations that he advanced in favour of the resemblance theory, Kivy now rejects the theory as false. Kivy's doubts about the theory began at an early date. In *Sound Sentiment* (1989) he already indicated that the theory of musical expressiveness presented in *The Corded Shell* (1980) 'has not entirely satisfied its author'.[22] While he was still certain that music is expressive of emotion, he described musical expressiveness as a 'divine mystery'.[23] In *Introduction to a Philosophy of Music* (2002), Kivy wrote that, 'Having vigorously defended the contour theory...I can no longer say that I am not without serious qualms'.[24] By 2006, he was emphatic: his version of the resemblance theory is 'a dead doggy'. (Jenefer Robinson had dubbed the theory 'the doggy theory', in reference to the Saint Bernard illustration.) Kivy has never provided arguments against the resemblance theory and he has not replaced the theory with another. He still believes that music is expressive of emotion, but now regards instrumental music as a ' "black box", as regards how these [expressive] properties get there'.[25] Other philosophers of music have been sceptical about the resemblance theory, at least as far as it posits resemblance between music and human vocal expression of emotion.[26]

The resemblance theory was adopted by enough musicians and philosophers for it to be commonplace. The Florentine Camerata developed the theory. Jacopo Peri (1601) noted the resemblance between music and the human voice: 'In our speech some words are so intoned that harmony can be based on them.... Having in mind those inflections and accents that serve us in our grief, in our joy, and in similar states, I caused the bass to move in time to these...following the passions'.[27] Kivy finds the

---

[21] Kivy, *Music Alone*, p. 6.
[22] Kivy, *Sound Sentiment*, p. 168.
[23] Kivy, *Sound Sentiment*, p. 258.
[24] Peter Kivy, *Introduction to a Philosophy of Music* (Oxford: Clarendon Press, 2002), p. 47.
[25] Peter Kivy, 'Critical Study: Deeper than Reason', *British Journal of Aesthetics*, 46 (2006), pp. 300–1.
[26] Davies, *Musical Meaning and Expression*, p. 229: 'To my ears, the likeness between music and the voice is slight.' See also Malcolm Budd, *Music and the Emotions* (London: Routledge and Kegan Paul, 1985), ch. 7.
[27] Oliver Strunk, *Source Readings in Music History* (New York: Norton, 1950), p. 374.

resemblance theory expressed in Johann Mattheson's *Der vollkommene Capellmeister* (1739). William Hayes, the eighteenth-century composer, wrote that, 'without *Imitation* there cannot possibly be any such Thing as true *musical expression*.'[28] Philosophers agreed with the musicians. Hutcheson wrote, 'The human Voice is obviously vary'd by all the stronger Passions.' He added that we can discern 'resemblance between the Air of a Tune, whether sung or play'd upon an Instrument...to the sound of the human voice.'[29] According to Thomas Reid, a melody can be 'an imitation of the tones of the human voice in the expression of some sentiment or passion'.[30] Elsewhere Reid called the art of the musician 'nothing else but the language of nature' since it can resemble 'modulations of the voice' and 'gestures'.[31]

The resemblance theory is not only commonplace, it is commonsensical. As Hayes suggests, it is hard to see what other account of musical expressiveness is tenable. The only other available account of musical expressiveness is the arousal theory, according to which music is expressive of emotion because it arouses emotion. The problem with the arousal theory of musical expressiveness is that it is parasitic on the resemblance theory.[32] As I will argue below, music arouses emotion in large part because it is expressive of emotion in the manner described by the resemblance theory. There just does not seem to be a viable alternative to the resemblance theory. The fact that Kivy has not replaced the resemblance theory with another (though he continues to believe that music is expressive of emotion) suggests as much.

Even though the resemblance theory is commonplace and commonsensical, formalists continue to doubt it. We need arguments that will convince the sceptics. Fortunately, the resemblance theory is an empirical theory and psychologists have marshalled an impressive body of experimental evidence in its favour.

---

[28] Dubois (ed.), *Charles Avison's* Essay on Musical Expression *With Related Writings by William Hayes and Charles Avison*, p. 97.
[29] Hutcheson, *An Inquiry into the Original of Our Ideas of Beauty and Virtue*, p. 68.
[30] Thomas Reid, *The Works of Thomas Reid, D.D.*, third edn (Edinburgh: McLachlan and Stewart, 1852), p. 504.
[31] Reid, *Works*, p. 118.
[32] For this point, see Tom Cochrane, 'A Simulation Theory of Musical Expressivity', *Australasian Journal of Philosophy*, 88 (2010), 191–207.

The resemblance theory and vocal expression

In rejecting the resemblance theory, Kivy has asked what 'evidence, if any, is there for the claim that listeners subliminally hear the analogy, if indeed it exists, between the contour of music and human emotion?'[33] It turns out that there is quite a lot. There is also evidence that music can resemble features of expressive behaviour besides its contour. I will begin by looking at some empirical evidence that supports the view that music is expressive because it resembles emotionally charged speech. The resemblance theory is an empirical theory. The theory will be confirmed to the extent that features of the human voice and human behaviour expressive of some emotion are found to resemble features of music expressive of the same emotion. Unfortunately, Kivy has given up on the resemblance theory precisely when psychology is providing an impressive amount of empirical evidence for the theory. The theoretical basis for thinking about parallels between different sensory modalities is also now available, particularly in the work of Mark Johnson.

Empirical evidence for resemblance between music and vocal expression is marshalled in a review article by Patrik N. Juslin and Petri Laukka. These authors reviewed 140 studies of the human ability to 'decode' the expression of emotion in vocal expression and in musical performance. The first conclusion to be drawn from these studies (one that some formalists would likely not challenge) is that people are nearly equally good at determining the emotion expressed in a musical performance as they are at discerning what emotion is expressed in spoken words.[34] For example, people are approximately equally good at determining that a speaker's mode of speaking expresses sadness as they are at detecting that a musical performance is expressive of sadness. Even more strikingly, a good deal of evidence suggests that people pick up on the same features of speech and music when they judge that either is expressive of a given emotion.

Speech and musical performances can resemble each other in a variety of ways. For example, they can share common pitches. They can have similar pitch contours (rising or falling). Music and speech can have similar dynamics; that is, they can be loud or soft. Music and speech can

---

[33] Kivy, *Introduction to a Philosophy of Music*, p. 46.
[34] Patrik N. Juslin and Petri Laukka, 'Communication of Emotions in Vocal Expression and Music Performance: Different Channels, Same Code?' *Psychological Bulletin*, 129 (2003), p. 786. For a critical discussion of this article, see Davies, *Musical Understandings*, p. 39.

share a similar tempo. (Speech tempo is calculated in terms of words per minute. Music tempo is a function of beats per minute.) In both speech and music, dynamics can vary or remain constant. In addition, pauses in speech correspond to articulation in music and there can be similarities in timbre and attack. (Attack refers to the rise time or rise rate of the amplitude of notes or speech segments.) These features, which appear in both speech and music, are the features that people detect when they discern the expressive content of utterances and music.

Many parallels can be found between the expression of emotion in speech and in music. In both speech and musical performances, slow tempi are found to be expressive of sadness or tenderness. In both speech and musical performances, quick tempi are found to be expressive of anger (think of the 'Queen of the Night' aria from Mozart's *Magic Flute*) and happiness. In both the verbal and the musical cases, high sound volumes and timbres marked by high frequencies are heard as expressive of happiness and anger while low sound levels and timbres characterized by low frequencies are heard as expressive of sadness or tenderness. Low pitch contributes to both speech and music being experienced as expressive of sadness. (In Renaissance musical theory low voices were associated with the expression of melancholy.) In both speech and music, variation of dynamic levels contributes to music being heard as expressive of anger and fear. Consistent dynamic levels are associated in both contexts with sadness and tenderness. A fast attack is associated with anger, fear, and happiness in both music and the spoken word. In contrast, a slow attack is interpreted as expressive of sadness or tenderness. In general, in both speech and music irregularities in pitch and dynamics are heard as expressive of negative emotions. More research is needed to establish conclusively these and other similarities between how speech and music are expressive of emotion, but the evidence is already quite compelling.

Some psychologists, such as Juslin, have suggested that music owes its high capacity for expressiveness to its intensification of the expressive features of the human voice.[35] For example, human speech is expressive of anger when characterized by quick, loud, and harsh tones. Musical instruments have the capacity to produce sounds louder, faster, and harsher in

---

[35] Patrick N. Juslin and Daniel Västfjäll, 'Emotional responses to music: The need to consider underlying mechanisms', *Behavioral and Brain Sciences*, 31 (2008), p. 566.

timbre than the human voice can produce. Juslin suggests that this makes music particularly suited to the expression of emotion.

Interestingly, psychological research bears out one of Kivy's key illustrations of the contour theory, the drooping opening measures of Monteverdi's *Lamento d'Arianna*. The falling line, Kivy once believed, mirrors the fall of a voice expressing grief. The evidence is not absolutely conclusive, but Juslin and Laukka note that falling contours seem to be associated with emotions such as sadness in both vocal expression and musical performance.[36]

Jaak Panksepp has identified another possible source of the resemblance between expressive properties of the human voice and the expressive features of music. Panksepp believes that an evolutionary account of our experience of music is available. Our experience of music is shaped by inherited adaptations of the mammalian brain. This could help explain why listeners often find a high-pitched crescendo (played on a violin or sung by a soprano) to be expressive of piercing grief or fear. Panksepp hypothesizes that such musical passages resemble separation calls of young animals, including young children. He goes on to argue that this sort of musical passage will arouse emotion, but one can argue that the passage is also expressive of grief or fear because the resemblance of musical passages to the heartbreaking separation calls of young children becomes apparent as a result of some deep-seated hard-wiring.

Panksepp's suggestion strikes me as rather speculative, but it seems clear that certain musical performances have features expressive of grief or terror because they resemble wailing or cries. (I have in mind, for example, the solo treble part in Allegri's *Miserere* or the first statement of 'Ad te clamamus' (To thee we do cry) in Handel's *Salve Regina*, HWV 241.) Other psychologists have noted that music can resemble the expression of fear by employing a quick attack, high pitch, loudness, and so on.[37] It is no accident that the theremin is used in the soundtracks of scary movies. Its characteristic timbre is reminiscent of moaning.

---

[36] Juslin and Laukka, 'Communication of Emotions in Vocal Expression and Music Performance', p. 796.
[37] Scherer, Klaus R. and Marcel R. Zentner, 'Emotional Effects of Music: Production Rules', in Patrik N. Juslin and John A. Sloboda (eds.), *Music and Emotion: Theory and Research* (Oxford: Oxford University Press, 2001), p. 367.

Another part of our evolutionary inheritance makes possible another way in which music can be expressive of emotion. Mammals and birds signal dominance, aggression, and strength using low-pitched and falling vocalizations. Think, for example, of the roar of a male lion. In contrast, high and rising vocalizations signal weakness, submission, and defeat.[38] Accidentally step on your dog's tail and you will have an example of such a signal. Human vocalizations follow this pattern. Low voices are used to threaten and our voices become squeaky with fear. Hayes is a composer who takes advantage of the expressive possibilities opened up by this aspect of our evolutionary inheritance. The aria 'He threw his blood-stained sword' from *The Passions* is given to a bass voice. Similarly, Polyphemus in Handel's *Acis and Galatea* (HWV 49) is sung by a bass. Sung by a countertenor, the same music would be much less expressive of a sense of menace.

Likely our capacity to recognize the expressive properties of music is in another way rooted in a basic biological ability. Infants respond positively to the expressive features—including contour, volume, and rhythm—of 'motherese'. This is the expressive, song-like vocalization that mothers use in communicating with their newborn children. As any parent can tell you, and as psychologists have confirmed,[39] neonates favour songs with low volume, regular rhythm, and smooth contour. This indicates that children are able to detect expressive properties. Infants prefer infant-directed singing of caregivers to singing directed at adults. This preference is even found in two-day-old infants born to congenitally deaf parents who, presumably, have had very limited exposure in the womb to music.[40]

The resemblance theory and bodily motion

The resemblance theory predicts that the expressive properties of music depend on resemblance to bodily behaviour expressive of emotions as

---

[38] Norman D. Cook, 'The Sound Symbolism of Major and Minor Harmonies', *Music Perception*, 24 (2007), p. 316.

[39] Sandra E. Trehub, Anna M. Unyk, and Laurel J. Trainor, 'Adults Identify Infant-Directed Music Across Cultures', *Infant Behavior and Development*, 16 (1993), p. 195.

[40] Jamshed J. Bharucha, Meagan Curtis, and Kaivon Paroo, 'Varieties of musical experience', *Cognition*, 100 (2006), p. 155. The experiment to which I refer here addresses, at least to a large extent, the concerns expressed by Stephen Davies about whether neonates are 'musical innocents'. See *Musical Understandings*, p. 40.

well as to expressive features of the voice. Davies has defended the view that music resembles the expressive motions of the body, as have other philosophers. Davies writes that, 'Our experience of music is like our experience of the kinds of behavior which, in human beings, gives rise to emotion characteristics in appearances.'[41] I regard Davies's view as commonplace, commonsensical, and well known but we need an argument that will convince a sceptic who does not find the position to be commonsensical. Ideally, one would hope to find psychological evidence that confirms that the expressive properties of music result (in part) from a resemblance between these properties and human expressive movement. Such evidence is available, but it has not been so systematically assembled as the evidence for the resemblance between music and the human voice expressing emotion. Nevertheless, a good deal of empirical evidence can be marshalled in favour of the hypothesis that some of the expressiveness of music is the result of resemblance to bodily expressive behaviour.

For a start, the psychological evidence strongly supports the conclusion that music 'often elicits an experience of motion'.[42] Some philosophers[43] have doubted that the experience of music involves the experience of motion. After all, music does not literally move through space. Most philosophers have, however, accepted the commonsensical view, supported by psychology, that the experience of music involves an experience of motion.[44] It is commonplace to describe music as swooping, soaring, inexorable, dancing, dragging, skipping, lilting, limping, darting, quavering, static, and so on. The question is why music is experienced as being in motion. The answer is that we experience music as moving as a result of cross-domain mapping, a pervasive feature of our experience of the world. Cross-domain mapping is the transfer of concepts derived from one sensory modality to experiences derived from another sensory modality. In the case of music, concepts derived from our visual and tactile modalities are applied to experiences derived from the auditory modality. Once

---

[41] Davies, *Musical Meaning and Expression*, p. 239.
[42] Bharucha et al., 'Varieties of musical experience', p. 157.
[43] Malcolm Budd, 'Motion and Emotion in Music: How Music Sounds', *British Journal of Aesthetics*, 23 (1983), 209–21.
[44] For a recent discussion, see Andy Hamilton, 'Rhythm and Stasis: A Major and Almost Entirely Neglected Philosophical Problem', *Proceedings of the Aristotelian Society*, 109 (2011), 25–42.

music is experienced as involving motion, new ways in which it can resemble human expressive behaviour emerge.

Many philosophers and psychologists have argued that our perception of music is shaped by concepts derived from the experience of bodies in motion. Mark Johnson focuses on three fundamental ways in which we experience motion: (1) we see objects move; (2) we move our bodies; and (3) we feel our bodies moved by forces.[45] He argues that these three fundamental experiences of motion lead us to develop three fundamental ways of conceiving of music. (In his early work, Johnson characterized these ways of conceiving as 'image schemas' that we acquire as our bodies interact with our environments.[46]) The first sort of experience leads us to conceive of music as moving, as when we say that music accelerates or (in a final retard, for example) slows. This sort of experience also leads us to say that music leaps, floats, meanders, and so on. In response to the second sort of experience of emotion we are led to conceive of music as movement through a terrain.[47] We say that we 'come' to a passage, that the recapitulation is 'ahead' of us, that a voice 'enters', and so on. Finally, we say that music can 'carry us along', 'transport us', 'lift our spirits', and 'take us for a ride'. Psychologists have similarly argued that we apply to music concepts that we derive from experience of objects in motion. In the musical case, we think about sound using concepts derived from experience of the motion of objects.[48]

Even if all this is true we are not quite to the conclusion we want: music is expressive because it resembles motions of our bodies that express emotions. Arnie Cox argues that when we hear music we hear it as the sort of bodily motions in which we would need to engage in order to produce similar sounds.[49] This may be part of the story, but a good deal of

---

[45] Mark Johnson, *The Meaning of the Body* (Chicago, I.L.: University of Chicago Press, 2007), p. 247.

[46] Mark Johnson, *Body in the Mind: The Bodily Basis of Meaning, Imagination, and Reason* (Chicago, I.L.: University of Chicago Press, 1987), p. xiv: an image schema is 'a recurring, dynamic pattern of perceptual interactions and motor programs that gives coherence and structure to our experience'.

[47] For examination of this sort of motion, and its relation to music, see Charles O. Nussbaum, *The Musical Representation: Meaning, Ontology, and Emotion* (Cambridge, M.A.: MIT Press, 2007).

[48] Lawrence M. Zbikowski, 'Conceptual Models and Cross-Doman Mapping: New Perspectives on Theory of Music and Hierarchy', *Journal of Music Theory*, 41 (1997), p. 200.

[49] Arnie Cox, 'The mimetic hypothesis and embodied musical meaning', *Musicae Scientiae*, 5 (2001), 195–212.

expressive behaviour does not have associated sounds. For example, no sounds are associated with leaden trudging, yet such behaviour can be highly expressive.

Fortunately, an experiment by Manfred Clynes and Nigel Nettheim makes the final connection between music and bodily expressive movement. The experimenters began by determining the contours of motion associated with seven emotions: anger, hate, grief, love, sexual attraction, joy, and reverence.[50] This was done by measuring patterns of finger pressure and asking test subjects which patterns of finger pressure were associated with each emotion. Anger, for example, was characterized by a strong, abrupt spike in pressure followed by an equally abrupt release of pressure. Grief is associated with a gradual decline in finger pressure, and so on. The researchers then generated patterns of sound with the same contours as the patterns of finger pressure. So, for example, it was hypothesized that an abrupt upward jump of a minor sixth would be heard as expressive of anger, while a gradual decline of about four semi-tones would be experienced as expressive of grief. And so it proved. Recordings were made of simple melodies with abrupt leaps, gradually falling pitch, and so on. Test subjects were reliably able to determine, on the basis of contour, the emotion that a recording expressed. There was some confusion between love and reverence, as well as between anger and hate, but overall subjects were able to discern the emotion each recording expressed.

This evidence supports Davies's version of the resemblance theory. Just as abrupt, violent motion is expressive of anger, so is it the case that music characterized by abrupt jumps in pitch, with a strong attack, is experienced as expressive of anger. Gradually declining musical lines, like gradually drooping motions, are experienced as expressive of sadness. Other expressive motions neatly correlate with musical motions in the way that Kivy and Davies initially hypothesized without the benefit of the latest psychological research. Even if the resemblance theory were not commonsensical, it would still be well supported by empirical science.

Another, very different, experiment also leads to the conclusion that there is a cross-domain resemblance between music and bodily motion. In this experiment, test subjects were provided with both visual and

---

[50] Manfred Clynes and Nigel Nettheim, 'The Living Quality of Music: Neurobiologic Basis of Communicating Feeling', in Manfred Clynes (ed.), *Music, Mind, and Brain: The Neuropsychology of Music* (New York and London: Plenum Press, 1982), 47–82.

auditory stimuli. The visual stimuli consisted of an animated ball bouncing up and down on a screen. The tempo and height of the bounce was varied. Subjects reported that the higher the ball bounced and the faster it bounced, the more the ball was expressive of happiness. The auditory stimuli consisted of a single repeated note. The pitch height and the tempo of the note were varied. Subjects reported that the higher the pitch and the faster the tempo, the more the music was expressive of happiness.

The cross-domain parallels are striking. In both the visual and auditory experiments, tempo and relative height influence judgements about the emotions of which the stimuli are expressive.[51] It seems likely that the perception of expressiveness of the auditory stimuli is linked to the expressiveness of certain sorts of bodily movements. Humans move slowly and in a leaden fashion when sad. They move briskly and with a bounce in their steps when happy. Similarly, music that moves slowly and in a step-wise fashion is experienced as expressive of sadness while quick music (with certain other characteristics) is experienced as expressive of happiness.

One would predict, on the basis of the psychological evidence, that listeners should be able to detect the emotional expressiveness of music regardless of culture. After all, all musical styles have 'psychophysical' features (as some psychologists call them) such as tempo, timbre, contour, and attack rate. If these are the features of music on the basis of which listeners determine the expressive characteristics of music (and if these characteristics co-relate with the same features of human expressive behaviour across cultures), it should be possible to determine the expressive features of music from any culture. Kivy disagrees. He thinks, for example, that, 'To the uninitiated ear, every *rāga* presents about the same mood: a kind of exotic stupor.'[52]

Psychologists have tested this prediction for which, as they note, 'Kivy offered no empirical evidence.'[53] The test involved playing *rāgas* to a group of thirty Canadian undergraduates (twenty-eight of whom were

---

[51] Annabel J. Cohen, 'How Music Influences the Interpretation of Film and Video: Approaches from Experimental Psychology', in Roger A. Kendall and Roger W.H. Savage (eds.), *Perspectives in Systematic Musicology* (Los Angeles, C.A.: Department of Ethnomusicology, University of California, Los Angeles, 2005), pp. 19–21.

[52] Kivy, *Sound Sentiment*, p. 89.

[53] Laura-Lee Balkwill and William Forde Thompson, 'A Cross-Cultural Investigation of Perception of Emotion in Music: Psychophysical and Cultural Cues', *Music Perception*, 17 (1999), p. 61.

completely unfamiliar with Indian music and two of whom had a passing acquaintance with the genre). Classical Hindustani music presents an interesting test case since each *rāga* (or mode) has an associated *rasa* (or emotional state). The test subjects, contrary to what Kivy predicts, were able to determine, with a high degree of reliability, the *rasa* expressed by the Hindustani music they heard. In particular, they were able to determine that individual performances were expressive of joy, sadness, and anger. Even more strikingly, the researchers were able to co-relate reports that music is expressive of a given emotion with psychophysical features of the music. For example, judgements that a *rāga* expressed joy were co-related with brisk tempi. There was a strong negative co-relation between reports that a performance was expressive of sadness and quick tempi. Another study showed that Japanese listeners performed well at determining the emotions of which Western and Hindustani musical works are expressive.[54]

The experiment conducted by Clynes and Nettheim also found that the ability to recognize the emotion expressed in sound is independent of culture. They repeated at a remote Australian Aboriginal settlement the experiment described above. Exposure to Western culture of the test subjects was very limited. There was no television and no local radio in the Aboriginal community, though the subjects had periodic contact with Western culture via occasional movie showings and shortwave radio. Most of the test subjects did not speak English. (The experiment was conducted in the early 1980s.) Yet the performance of the Aboriginal subjects in detecting the emotion expressed in the recording was very similar to the performance of their Western counterparts. In one case (joy), the Aboriginal subjects detected the expressed emotion more reliably than did the subjects in the university context. These results indicate that detecting the expressive properties of music relies on detecting similarities to human expressive behaviour that is common to a variety of cultures. In case the matter still admits of any doubt, another study showed that the Mafa people of Northern Cameroon, who are completely ignorant

[54] Laura-Lee Balkwill, William Forde Thompson, and Rie Matsunaga, 'Recognition of emotion in Japanese, Western, and Hindustani music by Japanese listeners', *Japanese Psychological Research*, 46 (2004), 337–49. Other studies are less compelling. See, for example, Davies, *Musical Understandings*, p. 45, for a criticism of the methodology of Andrew H. Gregory and Nicholas Varney, 'Cross-cultural Comparisons in the Affective Response to Music', *Psychology of Music*, 24 (1996), 47–52.

of Western music, were able to recognize that excerpts of Western music are expressive of happiness, sadness, and fear.[55] There is no mystery about what makes a performance expressive of emotion. There is a 'code' that musicians can learn that will make their playing more expressive of emotion. This code is based on human expressive behaviour, both vocal and bodily.

In one experiment, eight amateur guitarists were, in a single lesson, taught to play in a manner that was more expressive of emotion. They played a piece of music, with the intention of making a performance expressive of certain emotions. Listeners then rated the expressiveness of each performance. In the second part of the experiment, half of the guitarists were coached on how to make their performances more expressive of certain emotions. The instructions they were given were based on what psychologists had found to make a performance expressive of certain emotions. So, for example, the players were told that, if they wished to produce a performance expressive of sadness, they needed to play with more legato. In the final stage of the experiment, the guitarists performed again and listeners were asked to rate the degree to which their performances were expressive of certain emotions. A single coaching session resulted in an approximately 50% increase in the success listeners had in determining the emotion of which the performance was intended to be expressive. In the first stage, approximately 50% of listeners discerned the emotion of which the playing was intended to be expressive. After the coaching session, this number increased to about 75%. The control group of four guitarists (who had not received coaching) continued to receive the previous results.[56]

The features that make music expressive of emotion are so well understood that it is possible to programme a computer to produce music whose expressive properties are as easily recognized by listeners as the expressive properties of performances by humans.[57] A computer need only be

[55] Thomas Fritz, Sebastian Jentschke, Nathalie Gosselin, Daniela Sammler, Isabelle Peretz, Robert Turner, Angela D. Friederici, and Stefan Koelsch, 'Universal Recognition of Three Basic Emotions in Music', *Current Biology*, 19 (2009), 573–6.

[56] Patrik N. Juslin and Roland S. Persson, 'Emotional Communication', in Richard Parncutt and Gary E. McPherson (eds.), *The Science and Psychology of Music Performance: Creative Strategies for Teaching and Learning* (Oxford: Oxford University Press, 2002), pp. 230ff.

[57] Patrik N. Juslin, 'Emotion in music performance', in Susan Hallam, Ian Cross, and Michael Thaut (eds.), *The Oxford Handbook of Music Psychology* (Oxford: Oxford University Press, 2009), p. 384.

programmed to produce music that has the features that have been found to resemble human expressive behaviour. Listeners have no trouble determining the emotions of which the computer-generated music is expressive. This is not to suggest that there is a recipe for producing expressive performances of the highest aesthetic value. Listeners prefer the expressive music produced by humans, likely because these performances have the subtle variations typical of human expressiveness. Performance is an art as musicians need to choose the particular expressive features that are, in any given case, expressive of some emotion.

Composition is also an art. The composer can achieve the same expressive results in a variety of ways. As noted above, certain expressive features are associated with more than one emotion (for example, quick tempi are associated with both happiness and anger). More than one expressive feature is associated with a single emotion (for example, slow tempi, legato articulation, and falling lines are associated with sadness). Part of the art of composition is combining expressive features of music in intelligent and effective ways. In doing so, the composer can produce music expressive of precise shapes of emotion. Skilful combination can produce music expressive of what Kivy calls 'the exuberant joy' found in 'Pleni sunt coeli' in Bach's Mass in B minor or 'the confident but more subdued joy' of 'I know that my Redeemer liveth' from Handel's *Messiah*.[58]

The skill of the composer is also manifested in the way that a composition can be expressive of a series of emotions. A work of any considerable length may be expressive of a range of emotions. The skilful composer, in creating such a work, creates a coherent whole. In addition, the contrasts between passages expressive of differing emotions can contribute to the overall expressive character of the work. For example, a passage in a work will be expressive of a particular shade of happiness in part because it follows on from another passage expressive of a certain sort of sadness. It is hard to see how composers and musicians are going to be replaced by computers any time soon.

Defending the resemblance theory should hardly be necessary. It really is commonsensical and commonplace. That it should need to be defended against Kivy is even more remarkable. The only remotely plausible alternative to the resemblance theory is some sort of arousal theory, according

---

[58] Kivy, *Sound Sentiment*, p. 53.

to which music is expressive of emotion because it arouses emotions in us. Such a theory is anathema to any formalist. In any case, as we have seen, the psychological evidence in favour of the resemblance theory is compelling, even if the commonsense case fails to convince. The resemblance theory may not, however, be the full story about musical expressiveness. We need to turn now to a consideration of the extent to which musical expressiveness depends on convention.

Convention and Emotion

At the outset we identified two ways in which music could be expressive of some emotion. The first was the resemblance theory. According to this theory, the application of emotion predicates to music is semantically related to the application of such predicates to human expressive behaviour. The other possibility is that new conventions are developed that govern the application of emotion predicates to music. On this view, a piece of music with certain formal features is expressive of some emotion by convention. Convention almost certainly plays a role in making music expressive of emotion. Recent psychological evidence suggests, however, that the role is smaller than Kivy and others have believed.

Thus far, in considering how music could be expressive of emotion by resembling human expressive behaviour, we have focused on features of music that can be possessed by a melody or even a single note. We have seen how the rise or fall of a melodic line can resemble human expressive behaviour. We have seen how attack, dynamics, and tempo play a role in making music expressive of emotion. This cannot, however, provide a complete account of how music is expressive of emotion. Relations between tones also contribute a great deal to the expressive character of music. Consider, for example, the distinction between major and minor modes. Music in minor keys tends to be expressive of sadness more than is music in major keys. This is well known to the average music lover, and was long ago confirmed by psychologists.[59] Yet it is not immediately clear why the use of the minor mode makes music expressive of sadness while the major mode tends to make music expressive of positive emotions. It is tempting to say that the differing expressive characters of the major and

---

[59] Kate Hevner, 'The Affective Character of the Major and Minor Modes in Music', *American Journal of Psychology*, 47 (1935), 103–18.

minor modes are simply the result of convention. I will call this position *conventionalism*.

Kivy endorses conventionalism. He holds that music in minor keys has no intrinsic features that make it expressive of sadness. That is, nothing in the contour of music in the minor mode resembles the expression of sadness any more than the contour of music in the major mode does. In the West, at least, a convention has simply evolved of regarding music in minor keys as sad. Similarly, Kivy maintains, major modes and diatonic composition 'are merely the customary accompaniments of happy emotions'. Consequently, 'they are recognized as such where they occur'.[60] On Kivy's view, certain chords have come to be regarded as having an unstable or restless character as a result of compositional convention. A diminished triad (such as B-D-F) is an example of such a chord. In the syntax of Western music, it requires resolution and its use imparts a tension to the music. This syntax is, however, completely conventional. In Kivy's view, 'a static event like the sounding of a chord' cannot be similar to 'any expressive behaviour' which involves movement.[61]

Evidence can be marshalled in favour of conventionalism. Defences of conventionalism turn on two key points. The first is that the minor third is no more dissonant than a major third. The second is that the minor triad (the triad formed on the tonic in minor keys) is inherently not less stable or associated with sad emotions than is the major triad. We can grant that the minor third is not more dissonant than the major third. It is also true that in non-Western music and some folk music, the minor triad is not regarded as expressive of sadness.[62] Only for a comparatively short period of Western musical history, from the Renaissance until about 1900, was the minor triad considered active and dissonant.[63] This certainly suggests that minor thirds and minor triads are only conventionally associated with sadness and other negative emotions.

Several reasons can be given for thinking that the arguments in favour of conventionalism are not conclusive. The first is that, as Leonard B. Meyer noted, we need to look at the expressive character of the entire minor mode and not just the character of minor thirds and minor triads. Meyer

[60] Kivy, *Sound Sentiment*, p. 80.
[61] Kivy, *Sound Sentiment*, p. 80.
[62] Leonard B. Meyer, *Emotion and Meaning in Music* (Chicago, I.L.: University of Chicago Press, 1956), p. 231.
[63] Kivy, *Sound Sentiment*, p. 82.

noted that the minor mode inherently tends towards chromaticism. He believed that this chromaticism contributes to the expressive character of the minor mode by introducing ambiguity and uncertainty into minor mode compositions.[64] Meyer did not discuss the possibility that this chromaticism introduces greater dissonance into the minor mode. Likely this is because he regarded dissonance as largely the result of convention. Later some evidence will be provided that indicates that dissonance is not the result of convention and that the presence of dissonance makes music expressive of negative emotions.

Conventionalism faces another challenge. Suppose it is the case that minor mode music is considered expressive of sadness only in some cultures. It does not follow from this that minor mode music does not resemble some feature of human expressive behaviour. Minor triads and minor mode music could resemble a feature of human expressive behaviour that is found only, or found more often, in some culture or cultures. If this is the case, then the association of the minor mode and some expressive character (sadness) is not the result of arbitrary musical convention. I will return to this point below. Evidence is available that indicates that the minor mode resembles vocal expression in American English. (It may also resemble vocal expression in other languages. If so, then the association of minor mode music and sadness could exist across cultures.)

Let us turn now to a consideration of evidence against conventionalism. Recent psychological research indicates that the expressiveness of major and minor modes is not completely conventional. (This research was not available to Meyer in the 1950s or Kivy in the 1980s.) Evidence is now available that suggests that musical mode can contribute to similarities between music and the human voice under the influence of emotion. In one series of experiments, actresses (all participants were female) were presented with a series of four emotionally charged scenarios. The actresses were given scripted two syllable lines (such as 'Okay' and 'Let's go') to be uttered in response to these scenarios. One line was to be uttered in an angry manner, another was to be given a happy expression, a third was to be pleasantly expressed, and finally one was to be expressive of sadness. The experimenters recorded the recitals of the lines and then subjected them to acoustical analysis. Lines uttered in a manner expressive

---

[64] Meyer, *Emotion and Meaning in Music*, pp. 224ff.

of sadness typically dropped a minor third from the first syllable to the second. Lines uttered in a manner expressive of anger often (the correlation was less marked than the association of sadness with the minor third) rose by a minor second.[65]

Another set of test subjects then listened to recordings generated in the first part of the experiment. A fall of a minor third was significantly correlated with the perception of an utterance being expressive of sadness. A rise of a minor second was significantly correlated with the perception that an utterance is expressive of anger. Other subjects listened to a series of melodic intervals and were asked about the emotions of which each interval is expressive. The minor second was evaluated as expressive of anger and sadness. The minor third was strongly perceived as expressive of sadness. The perfect fifth was strongly identified as an interval expressive of happiness. These findings are significant because minor thirds and minor seconds occur significantly more frequently in music written in the minor mode than they do in major mode compositions.

A statistical analysis of Western classical music and Finnish folk songs shows that compositions in the major and minor modes have strikingly different distributions of tonic and melodic intervals.[66] (A tonic interval is the interval between a melody note and the tonic of the key in which the composition is written. A melodic interval is the interval between adjacent notes of a melody. Classical music and Finnish folk music were chosen for analysis because digital databases make representative classical and Finnish folk compositions easily searchable.) In classical music written in the major mode 18.2% of the tonic intervals are major thirds, while only 0.8% of the tonic intervals are minor thirds. In Finnish folk songs the percentages are 16.8% and 0%, respectively. In classical music written in the minor mode, these percentages are almost reversed. Minor thirds are 15.8% of the tonic intervals and 0.8% are major thirds. In Finnish folk songs the percentages are nearly identical: 15.6% of the tonic intervals are minor thirds and 0.2% are major thirds. When we look at melodic intervals, we find more minor seconds in music composed in minor keys than

[65] Meagan E. Curtis and Jamshed J. Bharucha, 'The Minor Third Communicates Sadness in Speech, Mirroring Its Use in Music', *Emotion*, 10 (2010), 335–48.
[66] Daniel L. Bowling, Kamraan Gill, Jonathan D. Choi, Joseph Prinz, and Dale Purves, 'Major and minor music compared to excited and subdued speech', *Journal of the Acoustical Society of America*, 127 (2010), p. 496.

we find in major mode music. In major mode classical music, 20.8% of the melodic intervals are minor seconds, while in major mode Finnish folk music 13.3% of the melodic intervals are minor seconds. In contrast, minor seconds account for 28.2% of the melodic intervals in minor mode classical music and 19.9% of the melodic intervals in minor mode Finnish folk songs. These distributions of melodic and tonic intervals are not accidents. Rather, the distributions are the result of the differing distributions of intervals within the two modes.

We can conclude from this that music in the minor mode will, due to the comparative frequency of minor thirds and minor seconds, resemble the human voice expressing negative emotions such as sadness and anger. This conclusion should be regarded as preliminary. The experiment on which I am drawing was conducted only with speakers of American English. It remains to be seen whether similar results can be found for speakers of other languages. There is some evidence. The Kaluli of Papua New Guinea, for example, associate the descending minor third with 'sadness, isolation, and loss'.[67] Very recent research indicates that the musical scales preferred in a culture are linked to the tonal characteristics of the culture's language.[68] Even with a cautionary note about extending the results to members of other linguistic groups, the experiment still indicates that there is a resemblance between music in the minor mode and some human vocal expression.

Major and minor scales may resemble expressive speech in another way. It is well established that when a human voice is expressive of excited, happy emotions it will have a higher fundamental frequency (F_0) than it has when it is expressive of negative emotions such as sadness. (F_0 is the lowest frequency of a periodic waveform. The F_0 for two notes is the greatest common divisor of the harmonic series of the two notes.) The F_0 for tonic thirds is significantly higher in major mode music than it is for tonic thirds in minor mode music. This is a consequence of the ratios that define intervals and the different distributions of intervals within the two modes. For example, as already noted, a high percentage of the thirds in major mode compositions are major thirds and a high percentage of the thirds in

---

[67] Steven Feld, ' "Flow Like a Waterfall": The Metaphors of Kaluki Musical Theory', *Yearbook for Traditional Music*, 13 (1981), p. 30.
[68] Shul' er Han, Janani Sundararajan, Daniel Liu Bowling, Jessica Lake, and Dale Purves, 'Co-Variation of Tonality in the Music and Speech of Different Cultures', *PLoS ONE* 6(5) (2010), e20160. doi:10.1371/journal.pone.0020160.

minor mode music are minor thirds. Major thirds are defined by a ratio of 5:4 while minor thirds are defined by a ratio of 6:5. Consequently, the F_0 of thirds in major mode music is higher than the F_0 of thirds in minor mode compositions. In classical music the difference is 21Hz. In Finnish folk music the difference is 15Hz.[69] A similar pattern is found for tonic sixths. The F_0 for tonic sixths in major mode classical music is 46Hz higher than in minor mode music. The difference is 13Hz in Finnish folk music. In the musical data on which this research is based, compositions in the minor mode are, on average, pitched slightly higher than those in major keys. Despite this, the mean F_0 of tonic thirds, sixths, and melodic seconds in major mode compositions is higher than the mean F_0 for the same intervals in minor mode compositions.[70]

These features of major and minor mode music indicate another way in which mode can contribute to being expressive of emotion. Music in major keys resembles the vocal expression of happy emotions while minor key music resembles sad, subdued vocal expression. In a variety of cultures, low F_0 is common when speech is expressive of negative emotion. Consequently, minor mode music will resemble subdued vocal expression in many cultures. I am not suggesting that the lower F_0 of minor key compositions is enough to make music in minor keys expressive of negative emotions. It seems reasonable, however, that a resemblance between the acoustic spectra of minor key music and the spectra of voices in the grip of negative emotions contributes to the expressive character of music in the minor mode.

Psychologists have not discussed modulation from key to key, but I hypothesize that it too contributes to the expressive properties of music by increasing or decreasing F_0. Most listeners have noticed how the mood of a composition can brighten as it modulates into a higher key, say from the tonic into the dominant. Similarly, the expressive character of a work can darken when it modulates into a lower key. Given the results that psychologists have found with the difference between major and minor keys, changes in expressiveness attendant upon modulation seem plausibly attributed, at least in part, to changes in F_0.

---

[69] Bowling et al., 'Major and minor music compared to excited and subdued speech', p. 497.
[70] Bowling et al., 'Major and minor music compared to excited and subdued speech', p. 501.

Let us turn now to a consideration of dissonance and consonance. It is well established that dissonance and consonance contribute to the expressive properties of music. One might wonder whether this contribution is the result of convention or some other factor. The contribution that consonant and dissonant intervals make to musical expressiveness has never seemed to be entirely the result of convention. In all cultures, the octave, fourth, and fifth are consonant intervals.[71] Nevertheless, it has appeared that certain intervals are regarded as dissonant in some cultures but not in others. Recent empirical research seems to indicate, however, that the perception of dissonance has a biological basis.

An experiment with six-month-old infants demonstrated a preference for consonant intervals over dissonant ones. The stimuli in the experiment consisted of perfect fifths, perfect octaves, tri-tones, and minor ninths. When the infants turned away from the source of the stimulus, the stimulus stopped. Eleven of the twelve infants involved in the experiment listened longer to the consonant intervals.[72] In another experiment, four-month-old infants were played dissonant and consonant versions of a melody. One version of the melody was harmonized with minor seconds. In the other version, the harmony was in parallel thirds. Infants fretted and turned away when presented with the dissonant harmonization of the melody.[73] A similar result has even been found in two-day-old infants of children born to congenitally deaf parents. Such infants, as with the other children of congenitally deaf parents mentioned above, would presumably have had extremely limited exposure to music while *in utero*.[74] (When deaf parents give birth, psychologists must descend in hordes.) These experiments indicate that there is a biological basis for the distinction between consonant and dissonant intervals.

Experiments that employ magnetic resonance imaging seem to indicate a hardwired negative emotional response to dissonant and minor chords. Experiments have found that different sorts of chords arouse different BOLD (blood-oxygen-level dependence) in the limbic system, including

---

[71] Meyer, *Emotion and Meaning in Music*, p. 231.

[72] Laurel J. Trainor and Becky M. Heinmiller, 'The Development of Evaluative Responses to Music: Infants Prefer to Listen to Consonance Over Dissonance', *Infant Behavior and Development*, 21 (1998), 77–88.

[73] Scherer, Klaus R. and Marcel R. Zentner, 'Emotional Effects of Music: Production Rules', p. 367.

[74] Nobuo Masataka, 'Preference for consonance over dissonance by hearing newborns of deaf parents and of hearing parents', *Developmental Science*, 9 (2006), 46–50.

the amygdala. An experiment which began by confirming that test subjects perceived minor and dissonant chords as sadder than major chords found that the minor and dissonant chords produced higher BOLD responses in the limbic system than did major chords.[75] Half of the individuals in this experiment were trained in classical music, while half were non-musicians. The experiment found no difference in the MRI results for the two groups.

Let us put this evidence together. The perception that minor keys and dissonant intervals (such as minor seconds) are expressive of negative emotions and major keys expressive of positive emotions does not seem to be entirely conventional. (The perception of certain intervals as dissonant, and expressive of negative emotion, is linked to the perception of minor keys as expressive of negative emotions: the intervals we hear as dissonant are more commonly found in minor mode music.) Contemporary psychology provides reason to believe that something in human hardwiring leads us to regard certain intervals as expressive of negative emotions. A reasonable hypothesis is that certain audible signals are processed as alarm calls. When music resembles these alarm calls, emotion centres in the limbic system are activated and the music is heard as expressive of negative emotions such as sadness and anger. In contrast, the consonant intervals typically found in major keys are experienced as expressive of positive emotions. Our preference for motherese and other parts of our evolutionary inheritance are likely to be part of the explanation of this experience. In addition, the experience of certain intervals (which have different distributions in major and minor modes) as resembling vocal behaviour expressive of emotion has a cultural, if not a biological, basis.

I conclude that the current best psychological evidence strongly indicates that the resemblance theory, as originally defended by Kivy and Davies, is correct. Kivy was unwise to abandon the theory. The best currently available empirical evidence also suggests that musical expressiveness depends less on convention than originally seemed to be the case. In particular, the contribution of modes and intervals to

[75] Karen Johanne Pallesen, Elvira Brattico, Christopher Bailey, Antti Korvenoja, Juha Koivisto, Albert Bjedde, and Synnöve Carlson, 'Emotion Processing of Major, Minor, and Dissonant Chords: A Functional Magnetic Resonance Imaging Study', *Annals of the New York Academy of Sciences*, 1060 (2006), p. 452. See also Anders C. Green, Klaus B. Baerentsen, Hans Stødkilde-Jørgensen, Mikkel Wallentin, Andreas Roepstorff, and Peter Vuust, 'Music in minor activates limbic structures: a relationship with dissonance', *NeuroReport*, 19 (2008), 711–15.

musical expressiveness is not completely conventional, but is the result of similarities between music and the vocal expression of emotion. The appeal to the psychological literature has only been necessary because some philosophers profess themselves unable to hear any resemblance between music and human expressive behaviour. Perhaps, however, the strongest evidence for the resemblance theory is made available when we listen to music. Caccini and, most successfully, Monteverdi put the theories of the Florentine Camerata into practice. It is hard to listen to their music and not hear the resemblance to the human voice under the influence of various emotions. Similarly, the music of Bach and Handel reflects the theories of Matthesson. The music of Hayes provides another excellent illustration of the resemblance theory. His oratorio, *The Passions*, is a masterpiece of hypotyposis. Music that resembles human expressiveness is not limited to the Western art music tradition. I recently had occasion to hear, for the first time, a live performance of Korean *pansori* (theatrical narrative songs). The resemblance of the singing to the human voice moved by passions was immediately apparent. A variety of other non-Western traditions similarly resemble human expressive behaviour, vocal and non-vocal. African musicians and their descendants in North America and elsewhere imitate speech and other sounds in their music.[76]

Nothing that has been established to this point is incompatible with certain versions of formalism. The view that music is expressive of emotion because it resembles human vocal and non-vocal expressive behaviour was, for a time, part of Kivy's enhanced formalism. The resemblance theory of musical expressiveness can, however, be used as a premise in an argument for the conclusion that music arouses emotion. The formalist must oppose the view that music arouses ordinary emotions since, if it does, the door is opened to the conclusion that music represents emotion and is not pure, contentless form.

---

[76] Learthen Dorsey, "'And All that Jazz" Has African Roots!' in James L. Conyers (ed.), *African American Jazz and Rap: Social and Philosophical Examinations of Black Expressive Behavior* (Jefferson, N.C.: McFarland, 2001), p. 50.

2

Music and the Arousal of Emotion

Could Music Arouse Emotion?

Having established that music is expressive of emotion, we can turn to the question of whether it also arouses emotion. Ordinary music lovers are often astounded to find that there is any question about music's capacity to arouse garden-variety emotions, but *arousalism* (as I will call the view that music arouses ordinary emotions by means of its expressive properties) remains highly contested in philosophy of music circles. Some of the most influential figures in philosophy of music deny that music can arouse ordinary emotions. In my view, the empirical evidence strongly supports the arousalist position. I also believe that psychology has made considerable progress in explaining how music arouses emotion. Some philosophers[1] have already begun to marshal this evidence and I will continue the attempt to integrate psychological results into a philosophical understanding of music.

Before I do so I will address some preliminary concerns. In particular, I will make a couple of methodological observations. Next, I will examine some a priori arguments for believing that music could not arouse ordinary emotions. These arguments are unsuccessful.

The first preliminary point is methodological: even if a complete account of how music arouses emotion is currently unavailable, we can know that music arouses emotion. In general, we can know that A causes B without being able to explain how A causes B. For example, not even the

---

[1] For example, Jenefer Robinson, *Deeper than Reason: Emotion and its Role in Literature, Music, and Art* (Oxford: Clarendon Press, 2005), ch. 13 and Tom Cochrane, 'A Simulation Theory of Musical Expressivity', *Australasian Journal of Philosophy*, 88 (2010), 191–207.

CEO of Philip Morris seriously doubts that smoking causes cancer, but an explanation of how smoking causes cancer remains elusive. That there is a causal relationship between smoking and cancer is the best explanation of the constant conjunction. Similarly, if the empirical evidence shows that listening to music is constantly conjoined with the arousal of garden-variety emotions, then we are justified in concluding that listening to music arouses the emotions. This said, I believe that an explanation of how music arouses emotion is beginning to emerge. Even if, however, everything I say about how music arouses emotion is false, it does not follow that music does not arouse garden-variety emotions.

This brings us to the second methodological point: any explanation of how music arouses emotions will be in large part a psychological explanation. I regard this as good because we can reasonably hope that with the progress of empirical science, our understanding of how music arouses emotions will improve. Progress has already been made and we can extrapolate to future progress. A sceptic about arousalism such as Kivy does not share my optimism about the prospects of psychology being able to explain how music arouses emotion. Worse, he does not believe that a psychological explanation could ever be forthcoming.

Kivy looks at the history of psychological attempts to explain the arousal of emotion by music and is unimpressed. He believes that these attempts 'range from the wildly false through the uselessly true to the highly controversial'.[2] It must be admitted that psychological efforts to understand how music arouses emotions are at a relatively early stage. Worse, philosophers whose arguments depend on preliminary psychological results run the risk of having their views empirically refuted. In a worst case, they will end up looking as silly as Hegel does when he endorses phrenology, in his day the cutting edge of psychological research. With Hegel's unfortunate example before me, I will nevertheless suggest that a reasonably well-confirmed account of how music arouses emotion is beginning to emerge and that psychology has contributed to this account. While depending on empirical results is risky, the alternative is worse: an anti-scientific a priorism.[3] Kivy, in contrast, believes that he has at least three a priori arguments for why a psychological explanation can never be forthcoming.

---

[2] Peter Kivy, *Music Alone* (Ithaca, N.Y.: Cornell University Press, 1990), p. 149.
[3] For a similar sentiment, see Charles O. Nussbaum, *The Musical Representation: Meaning, Ontology, and Emotion* (Cambridge, M.A.: MIT Press, 2007), p. 204.

The first argument begins with the claim that we have a satisfactory explanation of how ordinary emotions are aroused in non-musical contexts. Kivy tells the story of his fatuous Uncle Charlie who arouses anger by telling insensitive lies about poor Aunt Bella. We understand perfectly well how Uncle Charlie arouses Kivy's anger. This explanation is folk-psychological: we just need to know that Kivy believes that Uncle Charlie is cruelly mendacious and we understand why Kivy is incensed. We have, in contrast, no folk-psychological explanation of the arousal of affects by music. On the face of it, he believes, the arousal of emotion by music is completely puzzling. Kivy writes that, 'for *music* we don't have the Uncle Charlie explanation at all. We are in need of "psychology" right from the start.'[4]

Yet, Kivy believes, an 'Uncle Charlie explanation' ought to be available for the arousal of emotion by music. He reasons that music 'is a perfectly ordinary part of our culture's furniture and of the furniture of every other culture we know anything about.'[5] Given that music is such a ubiquitous phenomenon, Kivy finds it astounding that there should be no commonsensical explanation of its power to arouse emotion by means of its expressive properties. Kivy does not believe that there has to be a commonsensical explanation of everything. Rather, such an explanation is to be expected just because 'emotive arousal is a common, everyday affair and the ordinary conditions under which ordinary human beings have emotions aroused in them are familiar to us all, well understood on the commonsensical level, part of our "informal psychology"'. Kivy believes that this argument is 'convincing if not, perhaps, absolutely conclusive.'[6] The argument seems to be this:

(1) If music arouses emotion, then this arousal has a commonsense explanation (since it is an everyday affair).
(2) There is no commonsensical explanation of the arousal of emotion by music.
∴ (C) Music does not arouse emotion.

Obviously the key to the argument is the first premise. The second premise could be questioned. Indeed, the explanations of the arousal of emotion

---

[4] Kivy, *Music Alone*, p. 150.
[5] Kivy, *Music Alone*, pp. 150–1.
[6] Kivy, *Music Alone*, p. 152.

that I shall offer below are versions of explanations that have long been offered by non-psychologists. For the moment, however, I will grant (2). Kivy's argument initially seems to depend on us accepting the principle that:

(P) Any commonplace event has a commonsense explanation.

The argument seems, however, to be about probabilities. (This would explain why the argument is held to be convincing but not absolutely conclusive.) Given that the argument is probabilistic, a more charitable account of the principle underlying the first premise would be:

(P') Any commonplace event likely has a commonsense explanation.

So stated, the first premise is implausible. Nothing is more common than the fall of unsupported massive objects. Yet commonsense failed to explain such events. They were not explained until Newton's laws of motion were discovered. But Kivy likely does not have such cases in mind. When he is talking about 'affairs' he seems to have in mind events in human mental lives. In particular, he is thinking about causal relations between mental events and other events. An even more charitable reading of the principle would be:

(P") Any ordinary mental event likely has a commonsensical explanation.

This principle is certainly not obviously true.

In fact, I suggest that it is not. Nothing is more common in the mental lives of humans than the causal relation between willing that one's hand move and the movement of one's hand. And yet, as Princess Elisabeth of Bohemia pointed out to Descartes, there is no commonsense explanation of the causal relation between our acts of will and the motions of our hands. If there is an explanation of this causal relation, it is a psychological explanation. A good deal else in the mental lives of humans also requires scientific explanation. There does not seem to be a strong correlation between causal relations involving mental events and the availability of commonsense explanations.

Perhaps, however, I have not been charitable enough in my interpretation of Kivy's vague word 'affair'. Perhaps he meant to speak only about emotions. Perhaps he believes only that all emotions can be given a commonsensical explanation. If this is his view, however, his argument faces a more serious difficulty. The claim about emotions owes whatever plausibility it may possess to the claim that it is an instance of a more general principle. Now it appears that emotions are *sui generis* in requiring commonsensical explanation. In other words, Kivy is simply stipulating that a commonsense explanation must be available for any emotion. It follows that commonsense explanation of the arousal of emotion by music ought to be available. It is not, so Kivy concludes that music does not arouse emotion. He has simply arbitrarily decided that the only explanation can be a commonsense explanation. In any case, Kivy simply does not have a 'convincing', let alone an 'absolutely conclusive', argument against the view that music arouses emotions.

Kivy's argument faces another difficulty. Although psychology can contribute to our understanding of how music arouses emotions, psychological inquiry only confirms and expands upon what commonsense had already suggested. People already understood to a large extent how music arouses emotions long before psychologists came along and systematically confirmed what people believed. For example, people understood long before psychologists came along that the arousal of emotion by music was to be explained, at least in part, by the somatic effects of music and by the process of emotional contagion. I will return to this point, but first let us consider a second argument against the availability of a psychological explanation of the arousal of music by emotion.

Again, Kivy provides the classic statement of this argument designed to show that music cannot arouse emotion in the way that the arousalist believes it does. He has argued that music does not arouse garden-variety emotions since, when listening to music, we do not behave as we do when in the grip of emotion: 'Normally emotions are associated with modes of behavior: they are not merely psychological episodes with no behavioral implications. When I am angry, I strike out; when I am melancholy, my head droops and my appetite wanes.'[7] We do not, when listening to music expressive of fear or anger, engage in typical flight or fight behaviour. When listening to sad music we do not try to remove the source of sadness. Instead, we usually continue listening raptly to the music. Kivy concludes that we do not experience garden-variety emotions while listening to music.

---

[7] Peter Kivy, *Sound Sentiment: An Essay on the Musical Emotions Including the Complete Text of The Corded Shell* (Philadelphia, P.A.: Temple University Press, 1989), p. 155.

The first response to this argument is that Kivy admits that emotions can be aroused without being accompanied by their normal behavioural correlates. Kivy freely allows that literature arouses garden-variety emotions.[8] Yet one does not run screaming after reading *War of the Worlds* even though it is frightening. Kivy can scarcely deny that we are moved to sadness and feel fear when watching a good production of *Othello, Romeo and Juliet*, or even a horror movie. Normally, if one is afraid that some tragic event will occur that one can avert, one will take steps to prevent the tragedy. Yet we do not run onto the stage and pull the pillow away from the actor playing Othello. We do not seize the poison before Romeo can drink it. Neither does one run from the movie theatre when the aliens start shooting their ray guns. The conclusion to draw from these cases is that we can feel garden-variety emotions without displaying the behaviour normally associated with these emotions (and without having the beliefs we often have when feeling emotions).

The second response is that we do have behavioural responses when music arouses emotion. Physiological changes, which occur in response to music, are behavioural responses. Overt behaviour can also accompany emotional responses to music. When we hear certain forms of music we are moved to dance for joy or to play air guitar. If we happen to be in a concert hall, we will be discreet and quietly tap our toes or nod our heads.[9] In the privacy of our own homes we may be a little more exuberant. I do not think that I am the only one who air conducts and otherwise moves around to the music in the privacy of my living room. Listening to other music that arouses more sombre emotions we become still. Perhaps we cry. Sometimes we are so moved that our appetites wane. The fact is that our emotional responses to music do have a behavioural aspect. They are not always precisely the behavioural responses we have when we feel emotions in the ordinary course of our lives, but the emotions are not precisely the same in other respects either (a point that I will elaborate below).

A final argument for believing that arousalism is mistaken remains to be considered. This argument, which can be traced to Hanslick's *The Beautiful in Music*, turns on adoption of the cognitive theory of emotions.

---

[8] Kivy, *Sound Sentiment*, p. 214.
[9] For a similar point, see Derek Matravers, *Art and Emotion* (Oxford: Clarendon Press, 1998), p. 155 and Roger Scruton, *The Aesthetics of Music* (Oxford: Clarendon Press, 1997), pp. 355–6.

According to this theory, several conditions must be met in order for someone to be in an emotional state. Most importantly, in order to be in an emotional state, a person must have certain beliefs about some object. So, for example, in order to experience fear, a person must believe that some object is a serious threat. Similarly, in order to experience sadness one must believe that some unfortunate event has occurred. To be joyful, one must believe that some happy event has occurred, and so on. One cannot have beliefs about music, the argument continues, that would make possible fear, joy, or sadness. One cannot believe that music is threatening, so it cannot arouse fear. Listening to music expressive of sadness, one does not believe that some unfortunate event has occurred, so it cannot arouse sadness. In general, the conditions for the arousal of garden-variety emotions are not present when one listens to music. Therefore, music cannot arouse garden-variety emotions. Part and parcel of this position is the view that emotions are more than phenomenological states and emotions cannot be distinguished by reference to their phenomenological characters alone. The distinction between, for example, sadness and tenderness lies not in the 'feel' of the emotional state, but in the object towards which it is directed and the beliefs the agent has about that object.

Some authors have taken issue with this claim, arguing that emotions can be distinguished without reference to their cognitive aspects.[10] Others have noted that objectless emotions are possible.[11] For example, sometimes adolescents feel sad without knowing why they are sad or having anything to be sad about. On other occasions people are cheerful without being cheerful about something in particular. I will not become unduly embroiled in these debates nor will I defend an alternative theory of emotion. Instead I will draw attention to well-established empirical facts about listeners' reactions to music. All anecdotal reports of the arousal of emotion and all self-reports from experimental studies are unlikely to be false. Moreover, physiological evidence from experimental contexts also indicates that emotions are aroused by music.[12] I will turn to this task in

---

[10] Jerrold Levinson, 'Hope in the Hebrides', in his *Music, Art, and Metaphysics* (Ithaca, N.Y.: Cornell University Press, 1990), p. 334.
[11] Stephen Davies, *Musical Meaning and Expression* (Ithaca, N.Y.: Cornell University Press, 1994), p. 301; Daniel Putnam, 'Why Instrumental Music Has No Shame', *British Journal of Aesthetics*, 27 (1987), p. 56.
[12] Dale L. Bartlett, 'Physiological Responses to Music and Sound Stimuli', in Donald A. Hodges (ed.), *Handbook of Music Psychology*, second edn (San Antonio, T.X.: IMR Press, 1996), 343–85.

the next section. In the meantime, we can make considerable progress in understanding how music arouses emotion simply by becoming clear about what is meant by the claim that music arouses emotions. Many doubts about arousalism can be overcome by becoming clear about what the position involves.

From the very beginning of the contemporary debate over whether music arouses emotion, defenders of arousalism have maintained that whatever affects music arouses, they are not precisely the emotions people feel in the course of their ordinary lives. That is, to say that music arouses sadness is not to say that it makes people feel precisely as they do when they are moved by some tragic event in their lives.[13] Instead, music is said to arouse a 'faint recall' of an emotion. Arousalists maintain that music arouses something less than 'full-fledged' or 'full-blooded' emotions. Formalists have sometimes treated this sort of statement by arousalists as a major concession.[14] It is, however, nothing of the sort. Suppose that music arouses emotions that are not full-fledged or full-blooded. That is, suppose that it arouses affects that differ from the emotions that we feel in the ordinary course of life. On this supposition, music would still arouse something that formalists do not believe is aroused by music. Debates about what to call the affects aroused by music are bootless. The real question is whether affects (other than special musical emotions) are aroused by music. If such affects are aroused, we might as well call them emotions since 'emotion' is the term used by the vast majority of writers.

I will not argue against the cognitive theory of emotions (such an argument is beyond the scope of this essay). It is only fair, however, that I be forthcoming about the theory of emotions that I favour: a perceptual theory of emotion, according to which emotions are perceptions of certain kinds of bodily states. This is a view of emotions that originated with William James, who observed that 'bodily changes follow directly the perception of the exciting fact'. He went on to say that 'our feeling of the same changes as they occur *is* the emotion.'[15] More recently Jesse J. Prinz has

---

[13] For example, John Nolt, 'Expression and Emotion', *British Journal of Aesthetics*, 21 (1981), 139–150 and Jerrold Levinson, 'Music and Negative Emotion', in his *Music, Art, and Metaphysics*, p. 298. For a similar point, see Matravers, *Art and Emotion*, p. 146. Aaron Ridley describes this sort of position as a 'weak arousal' theory: *Music, Value and the Passions* (Ithaca, N.Y.: Cornell University Press, 1995), ch. 6.

[14] For example, Kivy, *Sound Sentiment*, p. 217.

[15] Quoted in Robinson, *Deeper than Reason*, p. 28.

defended the view that emotions are perceptions of certain types of bodily states.[16] These bodily states often track certain sorts of conditions in the environment of the person feeling the emotion. For example, in the face of an immediate and serious physical threat, certain bodily states occur. Fear is the perception of these states. Other bodily states track the obtaining of unfortunate conditions in the environment that affect a person's interests or the interests of a person's fellows. Sadness is the perception of these states.

Having said this, I need to say something more about why I propose to say that the affects aroused by music are emotions. After all, the bodily states aroused by music are not tracking, for example, immediate serious physical threats or unfortunate conditions in listeners' environments. To say that music arouses emotions is to say that music gives rise to bodily states akin to those caused by conditions encountered by people in the course of their interaction with their non-musical environment, the perception of which is characterized as an emotion. Moreover, perceptions of the bodily states aroused by music are phenomenologically similar to perceptions of bodily states that track conditions in the environment. So, for example, some music arouses bodily states that are similar to states that track serious threats in the environment. (These states include posture, blood pressure, respiration, finger temperature, and so on.) When listeners are in these bodily states they report that they have feelings similar to those they have when threats in the environment are tracked by their bodily states. In general, experimental evidence indicates that, when they listen to music, listeners have bodily states similar to those that they have when in the grip of emotions in other contexts.

The phenomenological character of the affects aroused by music is not identical to the phenomenological character of emotions aroused in other contexts. Neither are the bodily states identical. These facts are, however, precisely what one would expect given the view that the emotions aroused by music are not full-fledged. While the experience of music gives rise to physiological states, and emotions, the physiological states that result from the experience of music are less pronounced than those that can occur in the course of everyday life. The physiological changes that result from the experience of music are related (as Carol L. Krumhansl's results,

---

[16] Jesse J. Prinz, *Gut Reactions: A Perceptual Theory of Emotion* (Oxford: Oxford University Press, 2006).

to be considered in some detail below, indicate) to the changes associated with garden-variety emotions aroused in ordinary life. For example, when people experience sadness in the course of their quotidian experience, they will experience certain changes to respiration, posture, pulse, and so forth. When listeners report having sadness aroused by music, they will have similar but less marked changes to respiration, posture, pulse, and so on. Given that the physiological states we experience in response are less pronounced than in other contexts, we would expect that the phenomenological character of affects aroused will also be less pronounced. The psychological evidence in this way seems to support the practice, long adopted by philosophers and music lovers, of describing as emotions the states aroused by music.

Although I am persuaded by the arguments for a perceptual theory of emotions, the arguments presented in this chapter are designed to be independent of this theory. The reader need only grant that the occurrence of bodily states and perceptions of these bodily states is compelling evidence that emotions have occurred. If these states and perceptions occur while a person is listening to music, then we have evidence that emotions occur while listening to music. Readers need not accept that the occurrence of these bodily states and perceptions *constitutes* emotions.

Does Music Arouse Emotion?

The anecdotal and experimental evidence for the arousal of emotion by music alone strikes me as completely compelling. In large numbers, people report that they have emotion aroused in them by music. These reports are both anecdotal and collected in experimental contexts. Nevertheless, it is important to examine these reports since some philosophers, musicologists, and psychologists continue to be sceptical about arousalism. These sceptics have one crucial reason for thinking that music does not arouse emotion. They believe that listeners who report the arousal of emotion are systematically mistaken about what they experience when listening to music. I will argue that such systematic error is highly unlikely.

Formalists believe that reports that music (by itself) arouses emotion are false. For over thirty years, Kivy has led the charge against arousalism. Kivy is explicitly committed to disregarding people's claims about their experience of music.[17] He believes that people can be systematically mistaken in reporting their subjective states. He offers an analogy to motivate this suggestion. Hume thought that people were mistaken when they believed that 'beautiful' refers to an objective feature of objects. He believed that the term really refers to sentiments in the mind of a person making an aesthetic judgement. Similarly, Kivy believes that listeners make a mistake when they believe that they are moved to an emotion by music. Really, the emotion is in the music as an expressive property, not in the listener. Sometimes, Kivy insists, people do not know what they are talking about. According to Kivy, when a philosopher says that people do not know what they are talking about, the philosopher has adopted an error theory, in J.L. Mackie's sense of the term.[18]

Unfortunately, Kivy is mistaken about error theories. As Mackie uses the term, it does not refer to the view that some people are mistaken about the referent of a term. Rather, an error theory is the view that the statements in some class, although they are the sorts of things that could be true, are all false. The class of statements with which Mackie was concerned is the class of ethical judgements. On Mackie's view, all ethical judgements, though truth-apt, are false. In adopting an error theory about such judgements, he held that, 'although most people in making moral judgements implicitly claim, among other things, to be pointing to something objectively prescriptive, these claims are all false'.[19] They are false because the world contains no ethical facts to make them true. Kivy is, of course, free to use the expression 'error theory' in any way that he pleases, but he ought not to attribute to Mackie a position that he did not hold.

More importantly, Kivy is guilty of another confusion. It is possible that people make a mistake when they believe that music arouses emotion in them. But it is not the same sort of mistake that Hume identifies when he says that 'beauty' refers to something subjective or that a behaviourist has made when claiming that 'pain' refers to a sort of behaviour. If Hume is right and I use the term 'beauty' thinking that it refers to something objective, I have made a conceptual error. In particular, I have made a mistake about how to conceive of the referent of the term 'beauty'. If, however,

---

[17] Kivy grants that he 'is going to have to insist that some people are... genuinely mistaken when they report that sad music has saddened them'. *Sound Sentiment*, p. 160.

[18] Peter Kivy, 'Moodophilia: A Response to Noël Carroll and Margaret Moore', *Journal of Aesthetics and Art Criticism*, 65 (2007), p. 323.

[19] J.L. Mackie, *Ethics: Inventing Right and Wrong* (Harmondsworth: Penguin, 1977), p. 35.

I maintain that I have had a mood or emotion aroused in me, when no such mood or emotion has been aroused, I have made an empirical error. I do not know what my own feelings are.

While widespread conceptual error is possible, perhaps even common, systematic error about one's experience is much less likely.[20] It is possible that we all think that 'chair' refers to a physical object but it really refers to a sense datum or an idea in the mind of God. There is no empirical way to determine that someone has made such an error. It is much less likely that many people often judge, for example, that they feel warm or see red when they do not. Similarly, it seems unlikely that many people are often mistaken about their own affective states. Arousalists are not committed to saying, as Kivy charges, that reports about affective states are 'incorrigible'.[21] They are simply saying that it is implausible that people are wrong all of the time about their affective states. It is Kivy who is saddled with an implausible view. He must hold that the very many sensitive listeners who report that they have had emotions aroused in them by musical works have repeatedly made an empirical error about their experiential states.

Nevertheless, Kivy continues to defend this view. He gives another argument for why we should be unmoved by listeners' reports of having had emotions aroused in them. He suggests an analogy between these reports and the reports given by defenders of astrology. 'Clearly, astrology works,' someone might reason. After all, 'Why else would so many of us say that it does? Why else would we resort to astrology and astrologers, sometimes at considerable expense, if astrology did not work?'[22] Kivy's suggestion is that the arousalist ought to be given no more credit than the astrologer. The analogy fails, however. The astrologer's argument is relevantly different from the argument for the thesis that music arouses emotion.

Consider this argument:

(1) Many people say that astrology works.
∴ (C) Astrology works.

---

[20] Stephen Davies makes this point about those who report that music arouses emotions in them: 'It would be very surprising if their self-reports were systematically mistaken.' 'Artistic Expression and the Hard Case of Pure Music', in his *Musical Understandings and Other Essays on the Philosophy of Music* (Oxford: Oxford University Press, 2011), p. 15.

[21] Kivy, *Sound Sentiment*, p. 160.

[22] Peter Kivy, 'Mood and Music: Some Reflections for Noël Carroll', *Journal of Aesthetics and Art Criticism*, 64 (2006), p. 276.

The argument is clearly invalid, but Kivy may be supposed to have had in mind a suppressed premise:

(2) If many people say that astrology works, then astrology works.

Now the argument is valid (by modus ponens), but (2) is false so the argument is unsound. Consider now this argument:

(1*) Many listeners report that music arouses emotion in them.
(2*) If many listeners report that music arouses emotions in them, then music arouses emotions in many listeners.
∴ (C*) Music arouses emotions in many listeners.

This argument is valid. The only question is whether it is sound. Premise (1*) is uncontroversially true. Even Kivy will admit that it is. I suggest that (2*) is also true. The second premise of Kivy's parody argument (2) is false because people are not reliable judges of the effects of celestial bodies. In the second argument, however, (2*) is true. As I have already suggested, people are good judges of their occurrent subjective states. Again, people sometimes make mistakes about their subjective states, but most people most of the time will not make a mistake of this sort.

I am not suggesting that music arouses garden-variety emotions in everyone. On the contrary, first-person reports of experience indicate that music arouses garden-variety emotions in some people and not in others. The reasonable position to take is that both formalists and arousalists sincerely and, for the most part, accurately report the effects that music has on them. The experimental evidence supports this conclusion. Music seems to have different physiological effects on different listeners.[23] This suggests that its emotional effects also vary from listener to listener.

It seems that we need to take seriously subjective reports to the effect that music arouses emotions in at least some listeners. The evidence that music arouses emotion in listeners is not, however, limited to anecdotal reports. An increasingly large psychological literature also suggests that music arouses emotion. Kivy is as unpersuaded by the psychological literature as he is by the anecdotal evidence.

---

[23] Jaak Panksepp and Günther Bernatzky, 'Emotional sounds and the brain: the neuro-affective foundations of musical appreciation', *Behavioural Processes*, 60 (2002), p. 142.

Problems with psychology: self-reports

Kivy is not only sceptical about first-person testimony about the effects of music. He is also sceptical about the results of psychological experiments that appear to indicate that music arouses affects in listeners. By his own admission, Kivy has spent little time studying the psychological literature, but he has read and been critical of results of an experiment reported in a paper by Krumhansl[24] that have been cited in Jenefer Robinson's philosophy of music.[25] Krumhansl and Robinson believe that the experiment provides evidence, in the form of self-reports and physiological data, that suggests that emotions are aroused by music. Kivy and other formalists are not convinced.

Consider for a start the self-reports of the arousal of emotions. Kivy suggests that the experiment's subjects were 'really just recognizing the emotions in the music and reporting them as *felt* emotions'.[26] That is, he re-asserts his 'error theory'. In support of this theory, he adds that the experiment's subjects may have been improperly influenced by psychologists: 'an authority figure, the experimenter, has planted in the subjects' minds the thought that they *will, should,* are *expected to* feel an emotion, and an emotion of a certain kind, and their task is to tell the experimenter how much'.[27] Kivy hypothesizes that subjects duly reported that some degree of that emotion had been aroused.

Kivy here raises a serious concern. Empirical evidence suggests that the results experimenters obtain depend on the questions they ask. Experimenters are, however, highly sensitive to the possibility that subjects will confuse emotion aroused by music and emotions of which music is expressive.[28] In one experiment, psychologists asked subjects both about the emotions they felt and the emotions they perceived in music. Subjects were less likely to report feeling most emotions when asked about what

---

[24] Carol L. Krumhansl, 'An Exploratory Study of Musical Emotions and Psychophysiology', *Canadian Journal of Experimental Psychology*, 51 (1997), 336–52.

[25] Robinson, *Deeper than Reason*, pp. 369–76.

[26] Peter Kivy, 'Critical Study: Deeper than Reason', *British Journal of Aesthetics*, 46 (2006), p. 306.

[27] Kivy, 'Critical Study: Deeper than Reason', p. 306. This concern about leading questions is also found, for example, in Kivy, *Sound Sentiment*, p. 161.

[28] See, for example, Alf Gabrielsson, 'Emotion Perceived and Emotion Felt: Same or Different?' *Musicae Scientiae*, Special Issue 2001–2002, 123–47.

they perceived in the music than when they were asked to report what they felt.[29] We should not conclude from this that emotions are not aroused by music. Many subjects still reported that they felt emotions while listening to music. In fact, the experimenters found that, for some emotions, subjects were more likely to report that an emotion was aroused by some music than that an emotion was expressed in the music, when asked about both. Moreover, no one who believes that emotions are aroused by music need deny that music is also expressive of emotions. Still, the results of this experiment indicate that we need to be cautious when interpreting the results of psychological experiments. We should, as Kivy reminds us, be suspicious when philosophers uncritically assert that psychologists have proved some point.

At the same time, we ought to remember that psychologists know their business. They know how to design experiments and Krumhansl's experiment, in particular, is cleverly designed. She was aware, in designing the experiment, of Kivy's view that musical performances are expressive of emotion without arousing emotions. She designed an experiment to distinguish between emotions being expressed and emotions being aroused. The subjects were specifically asked 'to judge their own emotional reactions to the music, not the emotion expressed by the music'.[30] This might be thought to incline subjects to report the arousal of emotion. The real cleverness of the experiment is only apparent, however, when we look at its details. Krumhansl selected music expressive of sadness (adagios by Albinoni and Barber), fear (Mars from Holst's *Planets* and Mussorgsky's *Night on Bare Mountain*), and happiness (a movement from Vivaldi's Spring Concerto and Hugo Alfvén's *Midsommarvaka*). She then divided her test subjects into four groups. One group used a slider to indicate how much sadness they felt when listening to these recordings; the second group was asked to indicate how much fear was aroused; the third judged happiness; and the fourth was asked to assess the degree of tension they felt. (The tension results were not material since all of the music samples generated similar self-reports about tension.)

---

[29] Klaus R. Scherer and Marcel R. Zentner, 'Emotional Effects of Music: Production Rules', in Patrik N. Juslin and John A. Sloboda (eds.), *Music and Emotion: Theory and Research* (Oxford: Oxford University Press, 2001), p. 380.

[30] Krumhansl, 'An Exploratory Study of Musical Emotions and Psychophysiology', p. 347.

So Kivy has somewhat misrepresented the design of the experiment. The experiment did not ask people listening only to music expressive of some emotion to report how deeply they felt that emotion. One group of people listening to the six selections were asked how sad they felt, but three other groups, listening to the same recordings, were asked about a completely different affect. What is striking is that the subjects in the sadness group, for example, reported feeling sad when listening to music expressive of sadness, but not when listening to music expressive of other emotions. If a leading question were responsible for the subjects reporting sadness, then the question should have elicited reports of sadness regardless of the expressive properties of the music. But the question did not elicit this response except in the case of music expressive of sadness.

Krumhansl's experiment had additional features that were designed to guard against the effects of leading questions. After listening to each excerpt and reporting the extent to which it elicited the emotion corresponding to their group, test subjects completed a questionnaire that gave them a choice of affects. They were asked about the extent to which each composition made them feel afraid, amused, angry, anxious, contemptuous, contented, disgusted, embarrassed, happy, interested, relieved, sad, and surprised. Statistically significant increases in reports of sadness followed hearing the Albinoni and the Barber selections. Similar correlations were found between reports of anxiousness after hearing the Holst and the Mussorgsky, and reports of happiness after listening to the Vivaldi and the Alfvén. It is true that there may have been a presumption that some emotion would be elicited, but subjects were given the opportunity to report that no emotion of any sort was aroused. The reasonable conclusion to draw from this data is Krumhansl's: 'the six selections did, as indicated by self-report measures, produce the intended emotions'.[31]

One might still think, however, that the design of the experiment was flawed. One could hold that the very fact that subjects were asked to report the emotion that they experienced while listening suggested to the subjects that they should be feeling some garden-variety emotion. Empirical evidence is available that supports this position. These are the instructions Krumhansl gave to participants in her experiment:

Music is thought to have many effects on people, including influencing their emotions. Indicate how much fear you are experiencing from moment to moment by

[31] Krumhansl, 'An Exploratory Study of Musical Emotions and Psychophysiology', p. 347.

moving the slider from left to right. The slider should be at the far left if you feel none of that emotion, and at the far right if you feel that emotion as strongly as you have in response to music in the past.

Vladimir Konečni, a psychologist sceptical about the view that music induces emotions, maintains that 'the first sentence of the instructions *asserts* that music influences emotions; this may create an emotion-inflating "response set"'. Konečni repeated Krumhansl's experiment, but gave participants different instructions. He replaced the first sentence of the instructions with 'Researchers disagree on whether or not music has an effect on emotion'. The result was that subjects listening to the selections by Albinoni and Barber reported that they felt significantly lower degrees of sadness.[32]

At least two reasons can be given for thinking that Konečni does not undermine the view that music arouses emotions. For a start, there is a question about which instructions to listeners are better. Contrary to what Konečni states, Krumhansl's instructions do not assert that music influences emotions. To say, 'It is thought that *p*' is not to assert that *p*. Konečni's own instructions are arguably more likely to influence test subjects than Krumhansl's. His instructions plant a seed of doubt in the listener's mind. There is disagreement about what researchers believe, they suggest. Given such instructions, the test subject may well be hesitant to report any significant degree of emotion. After all, researchers disagree. But there is a more fundamental reason why Konečni does not refute the view that music arouses emotion. His test subjects still report, albeit to a lesser degree than Krumhansl's, that music arouses emotions in them.

By Konečni's own admission, even his experiment reveals 'a residual reported emotion, or "emotion", that was significantly greater than zero'. He needs to explain how this would be and offers three possible hypotheses. The first is that participants feel foolish reporting zero emotion. It is hard to see why this would be the case, particularly when Konečni chose instructions that were designed not to make subjects believe that emotions are aroused by music. (It is one thing to suggest that others have

---

[32] Vladimir J. Konečni, 'Does Music Induce Emotion? A Theoretical and Methodological Analysis', *Psychology of Aesthetics, Creativity, and the Arts*, 2 (2008), p. 121. Konečni quotes the instructions to test subjects from personal correspondence with Krumhansl.

designed their experiments poorly. It is quite another to suggest that one's own experiments are flawed.) The second hypothesis falls back on a move that Kivy has made familiar: 'Participants neglect to look "inside themselves" and misattribute the expressive features of the stimulus music to their own state.'[33] That is, listeners have confused emotions expressed by the music with emotions they feel. Again, we are asked to believe that large numbers of listeners are consistently unable to tell the difference between intellectually apprehending the expressive properties of music and being in an affective state. Finally, Konečni hypothesizes that listeners have confused garden-variety emotions with aesthetic emotion. I will return to this third possibility. Suffice it to say for now that we are asked to believe that many listeners are systematically mistaken about their affective states and that the third hypothesis, like the others, is pure speculation. No reason is provided for believing any of them.

One way to filter out the effect of researcher's expectations is to ask listeners about both the emotions they feel and the emotions they perceive. Several experiments have done precisely this and the results are instructive. An experiment conducted by Marcel Zentner, Didier Grandjean, and Klaus R. Scherer gave subjects two instructions: 'Please indicate the frequency at which you *feel* the emotion states described by the terms listed below' and 'Please rate the frequency at which you *perceive* the emotional state described by the terms listed below'.[34] Interestingly, large numbers of the students who participated in this study reported both that they felt emotion when listening to music and that they perceived that musical works were expressive of emotion. This is evidence that the participants in this experiment both felt and perceived emotions. Zentner and his colleagues are not the only psychologists to ask subjects about both felt and perceived emotions. Kari Kallinen and Niklas Ravaja also asked subjects to make judgements about emotions perceived and emotions aroused. They found that subjects report that music is perceived to have properties expressive of emotion and that it arouses emotion. Interestingly, these researchers report that participants in the

---

[33] Konečni, 'Does Music Induce Emotion?', p. 122.
[34] Marcel Zentner, Didier Grandjean, and Klaus R. Scherer, 'Emotions Evoked by the Sound of Music: Characterization, Classification and Measurement', *Emotion*, 8 (2008), p. 498.

experiment had no difficulty distinguishing between the two sorts of judgements.[35]

Zentner and his colleagues drew another striking conclusion from their data. They explicitly asked whether Kivy's 'error theory' is compatible with the empirical evidence. The experimenters note that, if listeners systematically mistake emotion perceived for emotion felt, the question they are asked should not make a difference. Ask them whether they feel an emotion or ask them whether they perceive it, and the answer will be the same: they will report that they feel the emotion. This is, however, not the result that the experimenters found.[36] For certain pieces of music, the test subjects were more likely to report that they had emotions aroused in them. Listening to other pieces, the listeners were more likely to report that they perceived emotion. (Asked both questions, for most emotion terms they were more likely overall to report that they perceived the emotion than that they felt it, but reports of the arousal of emotion were still common.) This indicates that the subjects were aware of the difference between felt and perceived emotion and that they could distinguish between feeling and perceiving emotion. Like Krumhansl, however, these psychologists take the large number of reports of the arousal of a variety of affects to be strong evidence that music arouses emotion.

A final concern about the reports of test subjects remains to be considered. Someone might argue as follows. Psychologists have found that subjects can have one emotion aroused in them, but be induced to report that it is a very different emotion. For example, in a famous experiment conducted by Dutton and Aron, male subjects on a fear-arousing bridge were interviewed by an attractive female interviewer. The subjects confused the fear aroused by the bridge for sexual attraction to the interviewer.[37] Perhaps, similarly, a single emotion (perhaps excitement) is aroused by works of music, and subjects (prompted perhaps by the expressive properties of musical works) systematically take themselves to have distinct garden-variety emotions aroused by the music.

[35] Kari Kallinen and Niklas Ravaja, 'Emotion perceived and emotion felt: Same and different', *Musicae Scientiae*, 10 (2006), p. 206.
[36] Zentner et al., 'Emotions Evoked by the Sound of Music', p. 501.
[37] Donald G. Dutton and Arthur P. Aron, 'Some evidence for heightened sexual attraction under conditions of high anxiety', *Journal of Personality and Social Psychology*, 30 (1974), 510–17.

I find this conclusion improbable. The argument has the advantage, it must be admitted, of positing a possible mechanism that accounts for the systematic error listeners supposedly make in reporting their emotions. I remain sceptical, however, about the suggestion that subjects are systematically mistaken about their emotional states. While it is possible that listeners are systemically mistaken about the emotion they are feeling, there is no evidence that they are. Moreover, the argument slides from the claim that listeners may be mistaken about their emotional state in any given situation to the claim that listeners may be mistaken in all situations. My grounds for scepticism about this argument will, however, only fully emerge in the next section where I discuss another reason for thinking that music arouses emotions. This reason is provided by the fact that music has an effect on the bodily states of listeners. When listeners report experiencing a given emotion, and they are put into physiological states that are associated with that emotion in non-musical contexts, the conclusion that emotions have been aroused is better supported than the conclusion that listeners are somehow confused.

If only a few experimenters had found that subjects report the arousal of emotion by music, we would be wise to be careful about uncritically accepting that music arouses emotions. However, the body of psychological literature which has found that test subjects report the arousal of emotion is now huge. Experimenters have taken steps to ensure that subjects do not confuse emotions of which music is expressive and emotions which music arouses. The only way to resist the conclusion that music arouses emotion is to maintain that test subjects are systematically mistaken and, as I have argued, this view is simply not plausible. If, however, any doubts remain about the capacity of music to arouse emotion, additional evidence can be provided.

Problems with psychology: physiological results

Self-reports are not the only available evidence for the hypothesis that music can arouse a range of garden-variety emotions. Psychologists have also collected a large amount of physiological evidence. Krumhansl, for example, has monitored physiological changes in subjects listening to the six recordings already mentioned. While subjects were listening to the excerpts, instruments measured such factors as blood pressure, finger temperature, pulse rate, pulse amplitude, respiration rates, and respiration depth. This experiment 'indicated that the physiological measures were different for the intended Sad (Albinoni-Barber), intended Fear (Holst-Mussorgsky), and intended Happy (Vivaldi-Alfven) excerpts'.[38] Krumhansl takes this result to confirm that the emotional states of the test subjects varied with the expressive character of the recordings they heard.

Again, some formalists are not buying it. Kivy concedes that the test subjects experienced physiological changes while listening to the various excerpts. He denies that these changes indicate that garden-variety emotions were aroused in the subjects. Kivy indicates that other possible interpretations are compatible with the physiological data. The first is that garden-variety emotions are being aroused, but they are not being aroused by the music alone. Alternatively the data may indicate that the subjects experience aesthetic emotion while listening to music. Finally, Krumhansl may be detecting physiological changes that have no correlated emotion. Kivy is only exercising due diligence questioning Krumhansl's conclusions. On balance, however, the empirical evidence best supports Krumhansl's conclusions.

Let us begin by considering the possibility that the music's associations (rather than the music itself) may be arousing emotions and the associated physiological changes. This is, of course, possible. Robinson worried that 'the pieces that Krumhansl chose have marked cultural associations, at least for Americans... Some of the emotions that listeners feel may... be partly due to these associations.'[39] Kivy thinks that this concession undermines the results of the experiment. He also worries that the titles of the pieces may contribute to the emotions that the excerpts arouse. Four of the pieces have titles: *Mars, Night on Bare Mountain, Spring,* and *Midsommarvaka.*

Let us consider the possibility that the titles of the excerpts aroused emotions. For a start, both of the sad selections (the Albinoni and Barber) lack descriptive titles. Yet the subjective reports and physiological data indicate no less conclusively for these selections than for the others that emotion has been aroused. The absence or presence of descriptive titles seems to be irrelevant. Still, Kivy believes that descriptive titles are bound to inspire flights of fancy, and these flights of fancy could arouse emotion.

---

[38] Krumhansl, 'An Exploratory Study of Musical Emotions and Psychophysiology', p. 343.
[39] Robinson, *Deeper than Reason,* p. 461, n. 66. Kivy cites this passage, 'Critical Study: Deeper than Reason', p. 307.

It seems unlikely, however, that such a vague title as *Spring* or *Mars* would inspire the same sort of imaginings, with the same associations and same emotions, for all or many of the test subjects. That is why a well-designed experiment uses a large group of subjects (in this case, forty subjects were asked for their subjective reports and another thirty-eight had their physiological responses measured).

In any case, Kivy's point is moot since the test subjects were not told the titles of the pieces. The test subjects were asked, after they listened to the excerpts, which of them they recognized. Holst's *Mars* was the only composition recognized by more than a few of the participants in the experiment.[40] Consequently, the test subjects were, for the most part, ignorant of the titles of the composition while they were listening to them, and knowledge of the titles could not have had a significant impact on the results of the experiment.

Similar considerations apply to the suggestion that cultural associations account for the experimental results. It is unlikely that the excerpts would have the same cultural or individual associations for all of the almost eighty subjects. Consequently, we cannot account for similar emotions by appeal to similar associations. In any case, the music used in the experiment had no associations of any kind for most of the test subjects since they had not heard the music before or, at least, did not recognize it.

Turn now to the possibility that music arouses emotion, but this is aesthetic emotion. Kivy notes Krumhansl's observation that, 'Emotion-specific changes in physiology did not clearly map onto those found in studies of non-musical emotions.'[41] While there was no clear mapping, some similarities were observed between physiological states associated with emotions aroused by music and the states found when the same emotion is aroused by non-musical events. Other experimenters, as will be noted below, have also found that such similarities exist. Still, Kivy is right that differences exist between the physiological states of listeners reporting the arousal by music of, say, sadness and people aroused to sadness in non-musical contexts. Certainly, if such a mapping were found, we would have reason to believe that music was evoking garden-variety emotions in listeners. The failure to find a close mapping does not, however,

---

[40] Personal correspondence from Carol Lynne Krumhansl, 30 December 2010.
[41] Krumhansl, 'An Exploratory Study of Musical Emotions and Psychophysiology', p. 351; quoted in Kivy, 'Critical Study: Deeper than Reason', p. 306.

show that sadness and fear were not aroused in listeners. No one believes that a person listening to music expressive of fear is in precisely the same state as someone facing a genuinely dangerous situation. Consequently, we should expect to find differences between the physiological states of someone experiencing fear in a threatening situation and those of someone experiencing an affect aroused by music expressive of fear.

Still, it is possible that the emotion being detected in Krumhansl's experiment is the musical emotion that Kivy believes that music can arouse. Let us consider this possibility. Kivy writes that 'great music in the Western, absolute music canon, moves us to a kind of enthusiasm, or excitement, or ecstasy directed at the music as its intentional object'.[42] It seems that, on Kivy's account, there is a single sort of emotion (variously describable as enthusiasm, excitement or ecstasy) that can be aroused by music qua aesthetic object. Kivy believes that this emotion is aroused by a wide variety of musical compositions, expressive of a wide variety of emotions. The aesthetic emotion might be aroused by a composition expressive of sadness, fear, triumph, joy, or many other emotions. (It could also be aroused by music expressive of no emotions.) If a correlation exists between emotions and physiological states, we would expect that there would be a single sort of physiological state that corresponds to the type of emotion aroused by music. Someone hearing a musical performance expressive of sadness, and experiencing aesthetic emotion, would be in one physiological state. The same (or another) listener hearing a work expressive of another emotion, and experiencing aesthetic emotion, would be in the same physiological state. The empirical evidence indicates, however, that listeners are in a variety of physiological states as they listen to music. So I conclude that listeners are not in a single emotional state.

This conclusion may seem too quick. An objector could argue that the experiential state of aesthetic emotion is a functional state realizable by very different underlying physiological states. If so, the listeners in Krumhansl's experiment (and other experiments) may be in a variety of physiological states yet be in a single emotional state (namely, the state of experiencing aesthetic emotion). I am unmoved by this objection. I do not deny that it is possible that two listeners (or the same listener on different occasions) can be in different physiological states but in the same

[42] Kivy, 'Mood and Music', p. 280.

emotional state. I simply maintain that, as a matter of psychological fact, emotional states are closely correlated with particular physiological states. We know from many experiments, including Krumhansl's, that musical excerpts are associated with a variety of physiological changes. Excerpts that are expressive of sadness (and that elicit self-reports of sadness) are correlated with one sort of physiological change, while excerpts that are expressive of another affect (and that elicit different emotional self-reports) are correlated with other sorts of changes. In other words, the physiological states of listeners vary with the expressive properties of music. This is precisely what we would not expect, if Kivy is right and music—regardless of its expressive properties—elicits a single sort of emotion. I conclude that, if physiological changes indicate that music has aroused emotion, the emotions aroused are garden-variety emotions. It is possible that some aesthetic emotion is also aroused. There is empirical evidence that it is. But the psychological evidence suggests that ordinary emotions are also aroused.

Finally there is the possibility that the experiment is detecting physiological changes without any accompanying affective state. This is possible, but highly unlikely. In Krumhansl's experiment, ninety seconds of silence preceded the hearing of each musical excerpt. During this period of silence baseline physiological measurers were established. Once the recordings began, physiological changes began to occur in the test subjects. Simultaneously, the subjects began to report changes in their affective states. The strong correlation between reports of emotions being aroused and the onset of physiological changes strongly suggests that the physiological changes were not occurring independently of the correlated emotions. This conclusion is reinforced by the fact that emotions and other affects are accompanied by physiological changes.

How Music Arouses Emotion

Now we need to ask how music gives rise to physiological changes, and emotions, in listeners. There is good reason to believe that music can initiate such changes in a variety of ways. It is doubtful that we are currently in a position to provide an exhaustive account of the ways in which music arouses emotions in listeners, but several ways seem to be relatively well supported by the experimental evidence. I will focus on four reasonably well-established ways in which music arouses emotion: automatic brain reflexes, emotional contagion, somatic effects, and the frustration and realization of musical expectations. Interestingly, in many cases psychologists are arriving at conclusions that philosophers reached a good while ago.

Here I will ignore some of the ways that music arouses emotion. I will concentrate for the time being on instrumental music. Few people deny that music with associated words (either lyrics or a programme) can arouse emotion, but some writers believe that the words are doing all of the arousing. I will return to a consideration of music with lyrics in Chapter 4. Here I will ask if music can, without the assistance of words, arouse emotion. As well, I am concerned only with how music can arouse emotion qua aesthetic object. Everyone, even formalists, allows that a piece of music can arouse emotions in virtue of its associations. The question at issue is whether music can arouse emotion when listeners pay close attention to it as an aesthetic object and to nothing else.

I will also discount another mechanism for the arousal of emotion by music. Quite commonly people imagine visual images (for example, images of landscapes) while listening to music.[43] These images can trigger emotions. I will ignore this mechanism because the properties of musical performances do not lead, in any systematic way, to the images some listeners form. That is, nothing in a performance makes some image more appropriate than any other. Rather, the images seem to be the result of a listener's imagination more than the result of any feature of the music. The images are, in short, the product of what Kivy calls 'wool gathering'[44] and not the product of attention to features of the music.

Let us turn now to a consideration of the first way in which music arouses emotions. Sometimes emotional states aroused by music appear to be the result of automatic brain reflexes. Features of music can resemble potentially dangerous events or warning calls. These features include abrupt, loud, and dissonant sound events. These events generate reflex responses that result in emotions. There is some difference of opinion about the parts of the brain where these reflexes occur. Some psychologists maintain that it is in the brain stem.[45] Others maintain that the limbic system is the site of the reflexes. Some

---

[43] Patrik N. Juslin and Daniel Västfjäll, 'Emotional responses to music: The need to consider underlying mechanisms', *Behavioral and Brain Sciences*, 31 (2008), p. 564.
[44] Kivy, 'Moodophilia', p. 324.
[45] Juslin and Västfjäll, 'Emotional responses to music', p. 564.

authorities believe that the reflexes occur more specifically in the amygdala. MRI results indicate that the amygdala is stimulated by dissonance and by minor keys.[46] In any case, it appears that elements of musical performances can, by resembling dangerous events, trigger reflexes in deep-seated parts of the brain. Sometimes these reflexes may be a simple startle response. There is debate about whether such responses are emotions.[47] On other occasions, it seems clear that the reflexes are full-fledged emotions.

The emotions aroused by means of brain reflex seem mainly to be negative emotions such as fear and sadness. The study of patients with damage to the amygdala seems to support this conclusion. A female patient (S.M.) with complete bilateral damage to her amygdala has, when judged against a control group of women of similar age and educational background, difficulty determining that music is expressive of sadness and fear. S.M. frequently judges that music is expressive of peacefulness when normal control subjects judge that it is scary. Normal subjects never make this mistake. S.M. also reports a lower arousal of emotion by scary music than normal subjects report.[48] When judging whether music is expressive of happiness, and in making judgements about the emotion aroused by happy music, S.M.'s responses were normal.

The evolutionary advantage of a hair trigger reflex for negative emotions is readily apparent. The thalamus (perhaps activated by the amygdala) is an early warning system that detects potential dangers faster than the cortex. False positives (such as our reflex responses to music) are a small price to pay for the ability to quickly appraise and respond to danger in the environment. It seems clear that some of the emotions aroused by music are the result of brain reflexes.

Let us turn now to a consideration of emotional contagion as one of the ways in which music arouses emotion. Emotional contagion is a phenomenon familiar both to psychologists and to ordinary observers of human experience. Most of us are aware that the company of happy people often raises a person's spirits and engenders happiness. Similarly, if one spends

---

[46] Karen Johanne Pallesen, Elvira Brattico, Christopher Bailey, Antti Korvenoja, Juha Koivisto, Albert Bjedde, and Synnöve Carlson, 'Emotion Processing of Major, Minor, and Dissonant Chords: A Functional Magnetic Resonance Imaging Study', *Annals of the New York Academy of Sciences*, 1060 (2006), p. 452.

[47] Jenefer Robinson, 'Startle', *Journal of Philosophy*, 92 (1995), 53–74.

[48] Nathalie Gosselin, Isabelle Peretz, Erica Johnsen, Ralph Adolphs, 'Amygdala damage impairs emotion recognition from music', *Neuropsychologia*, 45 (2007), 236–44.

time in the presence of melancholy people, one can feel one's spirits dampened. Adam Smith was among the first philosophers to note the phenomenon of emotional contagion, writing that,

When we see a stroke aimed and just ready to fall upon the leg or arm of another person, we naturally shrink and draw back our own leg or our own arm; and when it does fall, we feel it in some measure, and are hurt by it as well as the sufferer.[49]

Psychologists have studied this familiar experience of emotional contagion. They have concluded that people tend to mimic the expressive behaviour, including facial expressions, postures, and ways of moving, of the people around them. The adoption of this behaviour in turn induces, likely via the process of proprioception (awareness of the relative positions of the parts of our bodies), physiological changes and, consequently, emotions.[50]

It is a commonplace that emotions are not only communicated from person to person. Emotional contagion can occur without the belief that someone is experiencing an emotion. For example, emotional contagion occurs in response to movies and plays, where the belief that someone is experiencing an emotion is lacking.[51] Emotional contagion can also occur in response to expressive properties. Colin Radford observed that people may feel their spirits rise after experience of a cheerful shade of yellow.[52] Similarly, the use of a dreary shade of grey in a painting could depress the spirits of observers. It seems that we can catch emotions from items that are expressive of emotions as well as directly from the expressive behaviour of others.

Philosophers, beginning with Hutcheson in the eighteenth century, have maintained that emotional 'Sympathy or Contagion'[53] can occur when music is expressive of emotion. More recently others, notably

---

[49] Adam Smith, *Theory of the Moral Sentiments*, third edn (London: A. Miller, 1767), p. 3.

[50] For a discussion, see Jamshed J. Bharucha, Meagan Curtis, and Kaivon Paroo, 'Varieties of musical experience', *Cognition*, 100 (2006), p. 158.

[51] Klaus R. Scherer, 'Which Emotions Can be Induced by Music? What Are the Underlying Mechanisms? And How Can We Measure Them?' *Journal of New Music Research*, 33 (2004), p. 245.

[52] Colin Radford, 'Emotions and Music: A Reply to the Cognitivists', *Journal of Aesthetics and Art Criticism*, 47 (1989), pp. 69–76.

[53] Francis Hutcheson, *An Inquiry into the Original of Our Ideas of Beauty and Virtue*, revised edn (Indianapolis, I.N.: Liberty Fund, 2008), p. 68.

Davies,[54] have developed the sort of commonsensical point advanced by Radford and Hutcheson. On the basis of empirical evidence, many psychologists now agree with the philosophical hypothesis. Music can induce changes in facial expression and posture just as the company of other people in the grip of various emotions can. The plausible psychological explanation of these changes is that emotional contagion occurs when listeners recognize (consciously or unconsciously) that music resembles human expressive behaviour, as the resemblance theory holds.[55] These changes in turn give rise to physiological changes, the proprioception of which leads to emotion.

The process of emotional contagion may be facilitated by the presence of mirror neurons in the brain. Mirror neurons were discovered in monkey brains twenty years ago. These neurons fire both when a monkey engaged in an activity and when it perceived another monkey or a human engage in that activity. More recently evidence for the existence of mirror neurons in the human brain has emerged.[56] The mirror neuron hypothesis is still controversial but it may help explain the familiar experience of emotional contagion while listening to music.

Music arouses emotion in a third way: it affects bodily movements and rhythms. This third way is related to emotional contagion. Both contagion and the somatic mechanism arouse emotion by affecting the body. The somatic mechanism has an impact on bodily rhythms. Many listeners find it difficult to remain still while listening to music.[57] (Oscar Levant was once stopped for speeding and told the traffic cop, 'You can't possibly hear the last movement of Beethoven's Seventh and go slow.'[58]) Even in a concert hall they will move subtly in time to the music. In recent years, philosophers have increasingly noted the tendency of music to inspire the body to movement. Again, Davies was among the first to note this effect of

---

[54] Davies, *Musical Meaning and Expression*, pp. 279–307; for a more recent statement by Davies, see *Musical Understandings*, p. 55.

[55] Juslin and Västfjäll, 'Emotional responses to music', p. 566; Scherer and Zentner, 'Emotional Effects of Music', pp. 367ff. Some philosophers have come to this same conclusion: see Cochrane, 'A Simulation Theory of Musical Expressivity', p. 198, and Davies, *Musical Understandings*, pp. 60–4.

[56] Gordy Slack, 'Source of human empathy directly observed', *New Scientist*, vol. 196, no. 2629 (2007), p. 12.

[57] Scherer, 'Which Emotions Can be Induced by Music?' p. 245.

[58] Quoted in Sheila E. Anderson, *The Quotable Musician from Bach to Tupac* (New York: Allwork Press, 2009), p. 29.

music on the body.[59] More recently, Robinson (who talks of the 'Jazzercise effect'[60]) and Noël Carroll[61] have argued that music's inspiration of bodily movement contributes to the arousal of affects in listeners. (Carroll prefers to talk about the arousal of moods, rather than the arousal of emotion.)

As we listen to music, we move in a variety of ways. We dance, sway, air conduct, and tap our toes. Even in the confining atmosphere of the concert hall we engage in subtle movement. This movement could be a response to the expressiveness perceived in music but it can also be the result of a direct effect on human physiology. Rhythm affects listeners' respiration and heartbeat. This is so even when audience members are listening passively (i.e., without overt movements) as audiences do in the modern concert hall. These physiological changes lead to a range of neurophysiological changes similar to those associated with emotions experienced in daily life.[62] Again, this movement has an effect on listeners' physiological states and, consequently, their emotions. Different motions are associated with sadness, joy, triumph, and so on. Expressive properties are perceived in music, bodily motion is inspired, physiological change ensues, and garden-variety emotions result. This conclusion is a confirmation of folk-psychological reflection on the emotional effects of music.

Leonard B. Meyer posited a fourth way in which music can arouse emotions. Within the system of tonal harmony, certain events and series of events are typical or atypical. For example, certain chords are experienced as unstable and are typically resolved into other stable chords. (Often we describe the movement from the unstable to the stable as a movement from tension to rest.) As a result, music can lead us to form expectations and these expectations can be realized, realized after a delay, frustrated, and so on. According to Meyer, the experience of the realization or frustration of musical expectations can lead listeners to be surprised, frustrated, and expectant. Perhaps music can even move us to be hopeful or to yearn for some musical outcome. I will talk of this mechanism for arousing emotions as the Meyer mechanism.

---

[59] Davies, *Musical Meaning and Expression*, p. 291.
[60] Robinson, *Deeper than Reason*, p. 392.
[61] Noël Carroll, 'Art and Mood: Preliminary Notes and Conjectures', in his *Art in Three Dimensions* (Oxford: Oxford University Press, 2010).
[62] Scherer, 'Which Emotions Can be Induced by Music?' p. 245.

A recent study has provided empirical support for the hypothesis that music arouses emotion in the manner described by Meyer.[63] An experiment employed six chorales by J.S. Bach, each of them with an unexpected chord. For example, these works will have an unexpected minor chord in place of an expected major chord. The experiment involved reworking these chorales in two ways. In the first way, the unexpected chord was replaced with one more common. So, for example, a major chord replaced an unexpected minor chord. In the second way, the unexpected chord was replaced by one even more unexpected: a Neapolitan sixth. Test subjects—a group of well-trained musicians and an equally large group of non-musicians—listened to all eighteen versions of the chorales. While they listened, the experimenters recorded subjective reports of emotional arousal and perception of tension, as well as finger temperature and electroencephalography (EEG) results. The experiment found that perception of tension, subjective reports of emotion, finger temperature, and EEG results were all correlated with the increase of harmonic unexpectedness. Trained musicians, more familiar with the conventions of tonal harmony, had more marked responses to the degree of unexpectedness, but the non-musicians also responded. This suggests that the Meyer mechanism is an effective method of arousing emotion. Unexpected musical events, which introduce tension into music, initiate physiological changes and, consequently, arouse emotion. Unfortunately, the experiment does not show which particular garden-variety emotions are associated with unexpected harmonic events.

Philosophers have often wondered whether our responses to music are the result of conscious apprehension or a sort of automatic reflex. A constant in Kivy's thought about music has been his rejection of the view that we respond to music automatically, the way that we respond to a drug. That is, he rejects the view (which he traces to Descartes) that music is a stimulus that arouses emotions in listeners without the listeners engaging in any cognition. Kivy calls this the 'stimulation model' of music and believes that it is 'utterly hopeless'. According to the stimulation model, music is a 'physical stimulus that, by interacting with our sense organs and, through them, the rest of our auditory apparatus, puts us in a pleasurable

---

[63] Nikolaus Steinbeis, Stefan Koelsch, and John A. Sloboda, 'The Role of Harmonic Expectancy Violations in Musical Emotions: Evidence from Subjective, Physiological, and Neural Responses', *Journal of Cognitive Neuroscience*, 18 (2006), 1380–93.

state'.⁶⁴ Suitably tweaked (pleasure may not be our sole object in listening to music), the stimulation model is not as hopeless as Kivy would have us believe. The available evidence suggests that some part of our emotional responses to music is automatic. Other responses depend on our consciously apprehending music.

A good deal of evidence supports the hypothesis that some emotional reactions occur reflexively and without conscious thought or appraisal of the musical work. Some of this evidence has already been noted. Consider, for example, the fact that dissonant chords induce the same BOLD effects in trained musicians and other people. Since trained musicians consciously appraise music to a higher degree than non-musicians, these MRI results indicate that emotional responses are independent of conscious appraisal. As well, we have noted that emotional reactions to music occur in very young infants. Other evidence that some emotional responses to music are automatic can be provided. The emotional responses to music happen more quickly than they could if high cognitive processing were involved. The fact that emotions can be induced in listeners who are not attending to music also indicates that some emotional responses to music are automatic.⁶⁵

On the other hand, some arousal of emotion by music does seem to involve conscious appraisal of the music. There is evidence that the degree to which music arouses emotion in listeners is linked to their extent of familiarity with a piece of music and the style in which it is composed. This seems particularly well established in the case of emotions that are aroused by responses to the formal properties of music by the Meyer mechanism. These expectations are, in large part, the result of convention, and the extent to which music arouses emotion depends in part on familiarity with these conventions. Young children do not respond as adults do to unexpected chords and, as noted above, trained musicians have more marked emotional responses to unexpected musical events than do non-musicians. It seems reasonable to suppose that listeners are first consciously aware of musical events, and then have emotional responses.

It seems likely that all, or virtually all, of our emotional responses to music as an aesthetic object involve some cognition. When we listen to

[64] Kivy, *Music Alone*, p. 31.
[65] Daniel Västfjäll, 'A review of the musical mood induction procedure', *Musicae Scientiae*, Special Issue 2001–2002, 173–211.

most music, all of the arousal mechanisms will be operating simultaneously. Consequently, there is no reason to worry that arousalism is guilty of Budd's 'heresy of the separable experience'.[66] According to this heresy, the same type of emotional experience listeners have while listening to some piece of music could be had without listening to the music. The heresy allows the possibility that people could take some drug and experience the same emotions they have while listening to some musical performance. The arousalism considered here does not subscribe to this heresy since the full range of emotional responses to music is unavailable without cognition of the musical performance.

Which Emotions Can Music Arouse?

Having established that music can arouse emotions, and given a sketch of how it does so, we need to ask which emotions music can arouse. The psychological literature has focused on a small range of emotions: happiness, sadness, anger, fear, and a few others. We can say with a high degree of confidence that these emotions are aroused. One might wonder about whether shades of each of these emotions are aroused and one might also wonder about emotions other than those psychologists have investigated. There is no point trying to determine a priori which emotions music can arouse. We need to examine each of the ways in which music can arouse emotions and ask which emotions are aroused by each of them. In the absence of more empirical evidence we cannot be certain, but it seems that music can arouse a broad palette of emotions.

The emotions resulting from brain reflex are easily enumerated. The emotions aroused by means of brain reflex will likely be limited in number and basic. Basic emotions are usually thought to include anger, fear, sadness, joy, surprise, and perhaps a few others. These emotions have obvious survival value and we seem to have evolved deep-seated detection mechanisms that, when triggered, produce these basic emotions. There is, however, no reason to suppose that we have similar detection mechanisms corresponding to other, more complex, emotions such as yearning, ennui, triumph, and so on. If music arouses such emotions, it probably does not

---

[66] Malcolm Budd, *Music and the Emotions: The Philosophical Theories* (London: Routledge & Kegan Paul, 1985), p. 125.

do so by means of brain reflex. It seems plausible, however, that in combination with other mechanisms, brain reflex can be used to arouse various shades of the emotions that it can arouse.

The emotions that can be aroused by the somatic effects of music can also be briefly considered. Music can apparently, by inspiring boisterous movement, arouse elation and jollity. Music also seems to be able to arouse sombreness by slowing down the bodily movements of listeners. It is unclear, however, precisely how many emotions music can arouse by means of its somatic effects. It is unclear, for example, what motions of the body, aroused by music, would give rise to emotions such as fear, anger, love, and so on. Careful observation and, ideally, experimentation are needed before any definitive answer can be given to questions about which emotions music can arouse by its effects on the body. For now, however, it seems likely that music arouses a fairly limited number of emotions by means of its somatic effects.

It is more difficult to determine which emotions music can arouse by emotional contagion. The number of emotions that music can arouse by contagion will presumably closely correspond to the number of emotions of which music can be expressive. There is considerable difference of opinion about the range of emotions of which music can be expressive. Some writers believe that music can be expressive of subtle grades of emotion. Others think that it can only be expressive of grossly differentiated emotions. There is also disagreement about the types of emotion of which music can be expressive. Budd believes that the list is 'embarrassingly short'.[67] Others think that the list is quite extensive. If the list is short, then the number of emotions aroused by emotional contagion will be correspondingly small.[68] I will return shortly to the question of whether music is expressive of shades of emotion. I will begin by considering whether there are some emotions of which it cannot be expressive. Two main arguments have been given for thinking that music cannot be expressive of certain emotions. Both of these arguments concern the so-called Platonic emotions: hope, shame, pride, love, embarrassment, and so on.

---

[67] Malcolm Budd, 'Music and the Communication of Emotion', *Journal of Aesthetics and Art Criticism*, 47 (1989), p. 129. Kivy is similarly sceptical about the capacity of music to be expressive of fine-grained emotions: *Sound Sentiment*, p. 183.

[68] Derek Matravers embraces this conclusion: *Art and Emotion*, p. 153.

The first of the two arguments turns on the claim that Platonic emotions always have an object. They are about something.[69] Perhaps one can be anxious, cheerful, or sad without being anxious, cheerful, or sad about something, but the Platonic emotions are held to be different. It is suggested, for example, that one cannot be proud without being proud of some particular accomplishment. Similarly, one cannot feel ashamed without feeling ashamed of some act one has performed or that is performed by someone (for example, a family member or a compatriot) with whom one is associated. Add to this point the premise that music lacks propositional content and cannot be about anything, and one can conclude that music cannot be expressive of Platonic emotions. Music cannot be about any object so it cannot be expressive of an emotion that is essentially directed towards an object.

This argument is inconclusive. There is more to any emotion than its cognitive components.[70] An emotion, even a Platonic emotion, has a phenomenological character, associated desires, physiological correlates, patterns of behaviour, and so on. If the resemblance theory is correct, music could in principle be expressive of even a Platonic emotion by resembling the characteristic verbal or non-verbal behaviour associated with the emotion. There is no difference, from the perspective of the resemblance theory, between Platonic emotions and others. There is no reason, moreover, why music could not arouse the feelings of some emotion without someone having a belief normally associated with that emotion. It happens, as I have argued above, with emotions such as sadness and joy. We have no reason to suppose that it cannot happen with pride and love.

This said, we come to the second reason for thinking that music cannot be expressive of Platonic emotions: there is no characteristic behaviour associated with Platonic emotions.[71] If not, then music cannot be expressive of such an emotion by resembling its associated behaviour. Consider, for example, pride. The suggestion is that there is no standard and distinctive behaviour associated with this emotion. As Kivy notes, pride can be manifested in a wide variety of ways.[72] Examples of behaviour manifesting

---

[69] Julius Moravcsik, 'Understanding and the Emotions', *Dialectica*, 36 (1982), 207–24.
[70] Levinson, 'Hope in the Hebrides', p. 344.
[71] Stephen Davies adopts the view that music cannot be expressive of an emotion that lacks 'characteristic behavioral expression'. *Musical Meaning and Expression*, p. 235.
[72] Kivy, *Music Alone*, p. 177.

pride include wearing one's *Légion d'honneur* on one's lapel, clapping wildly at one's child's piano recital, parading through the streets of San Francisco dressed in spandex, and so on. It is hard to see how music can be expressive of any of these behaviours. In any case, it seems that there has to be a standard way of manifesting an emotion if music is to be expressive of that emotion. Only by resembling a standard way of manifesting an emotion could music be heard as expressive of that emotion. If music cannot be expressive of an emotion, then it cannot arouse that emotion by emotional contagion.

This argument appears to be convincing, but only up to a point. Music cannot be expressive of emotions, in the manner identified by the resemblance theory, without a standard associated behaviour. I cannot think of any music that I would characterize as expressive of shame. The reason I cannot think of any such music may well be that people in the grip of shame do not behave in a typical manner. This argument does not, however, show that music cannot be expressive of any Platonic emotions. Some may have associated standard behaviour. Consider, for example, pride. Perhaps no expressive behaviour is a standard expression of pride, but perhaps we must cast the net more narrowly. Perhaps certain sorts of pride have standard associated behaviours.

Kivy considers the case of pomposity. A certain sort of strutting and posturing is characteristic of the pompous individual. By strutting and posturing, Kivy holds, music can be expressive of pomposity. Pomposity is not exactly an emotion, one might think. (Kivy calls it a Platonic attitude.) The pompous individual does, however, experience certain emotions. Interestingly, excessive pride (a Platonic emotion) is among them. The reason that music cannot be expressive of pride may be that it cannot be expressive of any emotion so coarse-grained. Perhaps it can only be expressive of certain shades of pride: pompous pride, dignified pride, nobility, and so on, each of which arguably is associated with certain forms of behaviour. Dignified pride, for example, is associated with stately motion. If so, then it is possible that music arouses such emotions by emotional contagion.

This point brings us to the question of whether music can arouse shades of an emotion by means of contagion. One might wonder whether music arouses only generic sadness or whether it can arouse melancholy, despair, desolation, grief, and so on. Some philosophers have thought that music can arouse only generic sadness and other generic emotions. I suggest that the shades of emotion that music can arouse by emotional contagion will be commensurate with the shades of emotion of which music can be expressive. There is no agreement on the question of whether music's expressiveness is fine- or coarse-grained. Some people believe that music is expressive of only a limited range of emotion shades. Others believe that music's expressiveness is very precise. This view can be traced back at least as far as the sixteenth century. Adrian Petit Coclico, a student of Josquin, wrote that 'the most outstanding musicians... truly know how to embellish melodies, to express in them all the emotions of all kinds'.[73] Mendelssohn is in the same camp. He famously wrote:

> Music... fills the soul with a thousand things better than words. What the music I love expresses to me, is not thought too indefinite to be put into words, but, on the contrary, too *definite*.[74]

Debussy said something similar: 'music begins where speech fails. Music is intended to convey the inexpressible.'[75] Anecdotal evidence supports this view, as does reflection on the mechanisms by which music arouses emotion.

Certainly anecdotal reports from knowledgeable commentators suggest that music's expressiveness can be quite fine-grained. Consider two works that have been thought to be expressive of sadness: Tchaikovsky's Symphony No. 6, Op. 74 (*Pathétique*) and Mozart's Symphony No. 40. While both of these works are expressive of sadness, to say that they are expressive of the same sort of sadness is implausible. Deryk Cooke is typical of commentators on Tchaikovsky's final symphony when he states that it is expressive of 'fierce despair'.[76] The adjectives 'despairing' and 'inconsolable' are constantly used in describing this work, particularly the final movement. In contrast, Abert writes of a passage in Mozart's symphony that it 'assumes an air of deepest resignation within the somber mood of G minor, thereby affording affecting proof of the profound human

---

[73] Adrian Petit Coclico, *Musical Compendium*, trans. Albert Seay (Colorado Springs, C.O.: Colorado College Music Press, 1973), p. 8.
[74] Felix Mendelssohn, *Letters of Felix Mendelssohn Bartholdy From 1833 to 1847*, trans. Lady Wallace (Boston, M.D.: Oliver Ditson, 1863), pp. 269–70.
[75] Quoted in Bernard Williams, *On Opera* (New Haven, C.T.: Yale University Press, 2006), p. 14.
[76] Deryk Cooke, *The Language of Music* (Oxford: Oxford University Press, 1959), p. 106.

emotions that lie concealed within this movement'.[77] Writing of a passage in Mozart's *Masonic Funeral Music*, Jahn states that it is 'expressive of grief in all its varied shades'.[78] Dowland's *Lachrimae Pavan* expresses yet another shade of sadness. It is clear to me, moreover, that these works leave the listener feeling quite different. That is, they arouse different emotions. The emotions listeners feel, I suggest, correspond to the different varieties of sadness of which the works are expressive.

The empirical evidence suggests that composers have at their disposal a range of mechanisms that make music expressive of, and able to arouse, fine gradations of emotion. If music could only be expressive of some emotion in a single way, then one might expect that its expressive range would be limited. But, as we have seen, music can be expressive of an emotion in a variety of ways. Pitch, attack, melodic shape, dynamics, tonality, harmony, and a variety of other factors can all be manipulated to the end of making a piece of music expressive of a given emotion. The various combinations of expressive mechanisms available to the composer can be expected to have subtly different physiological effects. The perception of each different physiological state will result in a somewhat different emotional state. For example, low pitch, slow attack, drooping melodies, minor tonality, dissonant harmony, and other factors can be used in different combinations to make music expressive of sadness. To my ear, at least, harsh dissonance imparts a note of angry grief, while drooping melodies and slow attack make a piece expressive of melancholy rather than generic sadness.

Finally, emotions can be aroused by means of response to musical form. The empirical evidence on the range of emotions aroused by response to musical form is limited. However, this is, perhaps, a promising mechanism from the perspective of those who believe that music can arouse a full gamut of emotions. Meyer suggests that our cognition of musical patterns can lead us to become anxious or apprehensive (when we doubt that a desired outcome will ensue), hopeful (when we look forward to a desired outcome), or disappointed (when our expectations are frustrated).[79] (When Levinson argues that Mendelssohn's *Hebrides Overture* is

---

[77] Hermann Abert, *W.A. Mozart*, trans. Stewart Spencer (New Haven, C.T.: Yale University Press, 2007), p. 1124.

[78] Otto Jahn, *Life of Mozart*, trans. Pauline D. Townsend (London: Novello, Ewer, and Co., 1882), vol. 2, p. 411.

[79] Leonard B. Meyer, *Emotion and Meaning in Music* (Chicago, I.L.: University of Chicago Press, 1956), pp. 27, 29, 182.

expressive of hope, he did so by drawing attention to patterns in the music. He argues that we hear certain patterns of sound as aspiring to achieve certain goals. Aspiration is, of course, part and parcel of hope. Levinson is concerned with the expression of hope, but perhaps the same patterns arouse hopefulness.) Anxiety, hopefulness, and disappointment all are (or can be) Platonic emotions, the sort of complex emotions which some people doubt that music can arouse.

When all of the mechanisms for arousing emotion are considered together, it seems likely that music can arouse a wide range of emotions and fine gradations of each one. The evidence for this conclusion, I have already acknowledged, is not decisive. When, however, we consider the anecdotal reports of listeners (who often report that music arouses fine shades of emotion[80] and a variety of emotions) and the various mechanisms by which music can arouse emotion, the conclusion seems likely. This said, the arousalist position seems to give rise to several puzzles, some of which will be considered in the next section.

Puzzles for the Arousalist

By this point it is clear that music arouses emotion, but the fact that music arouses emotion gives rise to some puzzles. This section will consider two of these puzzles. The first puzzle turns on the arousalist's claim that music expressive of some emotion arouses that emotion (by contagion, or some other means). Kivy has claimed that some music is expressive of emotion and yet, because it is an aesthetic failure, completely fails to move us. The second puzzle for arousalism is also posed by Kivy. He has wondered how it is possible that listeners could possibly be moved by all of the emotions of which a lengthy piece of music is expressive. It seems that we simply cannot change our emotional state quite so quickly.

Arousalism gives rise to a third puzzle. Music is often expressive of unpleasant emotions, such as sadness and fear. Suppose that music that is expressive of these emotions also arouses these emotions. There is then a question about why anyone would willingly listen to music expressive of unpleasant or negative emotions. I will defer consideration of this question until Chapter 5.

---

[80] This seems to be the view of Jerrold Levinson, 'Music and Negative Emotion'.

Consider first the problem of bad music that is expressive of emotion. A poor work of music could still be expressive of, say, sadness. That is, poor music can have properties expressive of sadness: it can be slow, with a falling melody, in a minor key, and so on. The arousalist seems required to maintain that such music will arouse sadness in listeners. This strikes Kivy as wrong: 'Music can be very sad, or very cheerful [that is, expressive of sadness or of cheerfulness], while leaving the listener quite apathetic, completely unmoved emotionally.'[81] Bad composers (Kivy mentions Telemann) have composed 'yards of mournful music, but it would be bizarre to describe very much of it as "moving". Yet on the emotivist's [i.e., the arousalist's] account, that is just what we would have to say, for on that account the music is mournful in virtue of arousing mournfulness in listeners, and moving for the same reason.'[82] Kivy, on the other hand, is not committed to believing that bad sad music will move listeners. Music moves us to feel musical emotion by virtue of its beauty. Bad sad music is not beautiful, therefore it is not moving. Call this the *bad sad music argument*.

As the argument is formulated, it is not an argument against the arousalism advocated here. Kivy believes that anyone who thinks that music arouses some emotion also thinks that music is expressive of that emotion because it arouses emotion. Here I have adopted the view that music is expressive of emotion because it resembles human expressive behaviour. This view is independent of the view that music also arouses emotion. Nevertheless, even for the version of arousalism advocated here the bad sad music argument is potentially worrisome. It could be that there is music expressive of sadness that is bad music. If music arouses emotion by contagion, then music expressive of sadness, even if the music is bad, should move listeners to sadness. But, Kivy says, bad music does not move listeners.

Let us consider some bad sad music. Telemann is an odd example of someone who writes reams of bad and mournful music. For a start, he is a very good composer. He is not, perhaps, in the same league as contemporaries such as Bach, Handel, and Rameau, but Telemann's music is often first rate and deeply moving. Also, his musical style is pretty squarely *galant* and not much given to mournfulness. Let us consider a more

---

[81] Peter Kivy, 'Experiencing the Musical Emotions', in *New Essays on Musical Understanding* (Oxford: Clarendon Press, 2002), p. 117.
[82] Kivy, *Music Alone*, p. 162.

uncontroversial example. I take it that a muzak rendition of the Beatles song 'She's leaving home' is an instance of bad sad music. It might seem that one is more likely to be moved to hilarity than melancholy by such music. Similarly, a poor performance of 'Jingle bells' has features that are expressive of cheerfulness, but one might think that it does not arouse cheerfulness in us. This seems to count against the arousalist position.

The bad sad music argument is successful only if works such as the muzak version of 'She's leaving home' do not arouse sadness. It is not clear to me that it does not. I have just listened to it, and I think that it does arouse sadness, likely because of responses to its expressive features: the slow tempo and droopy musical lines. (Of course, the words likely also contribute to the emotional effect, though they are rather trite.) Similarly, it is not clear to me that even a muzak version of 'Jingle bells' does not arouse cheerfulness. Despite myself, I am likely to find myself tapping my toes, humming along and feeling rather cheery. My guess is that if you hooked me up to an MRI, you would find evidence that emotion is being aroused. I doubt that I am the only one. Muzak (including 'Jingle bells' each Christmas) is played in shops precisely because it puts shoppers into a cheerful state of mind (so they will spend money). This is well established in the psychological literature.

This is not, however, the whole story about our responses to bad sad (and bad cheerful) music. I am also irritated by the schmaltz of a muzak version of a Beatles song. It is maudlin. The piece arouses emotion, but it does not do so in a novel or striking way. The edges of the song have been filed off. Any value the music has as a source of the arousal of emotion is outweighed by my boredom and irritation. All things considered, most listeners will not have a valuable aesthetic response to the muzak version of 'She's leaving home' when they listen to it carefully. It is possible that, when listeners pay careful attention to the muzak performance, their irritation interferes with its capacity to arouse an emotion by means of its expressive properties.

The fact that some piece of music arouses some emotion does not entail that it is aesthetically valuable. Being able to arouse some emotion is not a sufficient condition of being an aesthetically worthwhile piece of music. (It is probably not a necessary condition either.) Arousalists are not committed to saying that the fact that some piece of music arouses emotion makes it aesthetically valuable. On the contrary, they will certainly maintain that the mere fact that a piece of music is expressive of certain emotions, and arouses them, does not make the piece of music aesthetically valuable. Aesthetic value will depend, at least in part, on how music arouses emotion and what emotions are aroused. When a work of music arouses emotions in an interesting and insightful way then it may very well be aesthetically valuable.

Let us turn now to consideration of another problem for arousalism. It has been suggested that we cannot possibly experience, in the course of listening to a composition, the gamut of emotions of which it is expressive. A large-scale Romantic symphony (such as the works of Schumann, Brahms, Tchaikovsky, and Mahler) is successively expressive of a wide range of emotions. In the course of an hour or so such a symphony may be expressive of triumph, despair, joy, and melancholy. Anyone who actually had these emotions aroused in him, Kivy maintains, would be unusually 'susceptible to mood swings' and 'a man with a problem'.[83] He would be 'some kind of supercharged manic-depressive'.[84] Since it is unlikely that affective states can swing so quickly in well-adjusted listeners, Kivy thinks he has another reason to be sceptical about the view that the emotions of listeners correspond to the states of which music is expressive. Even if occasional listeners experience wild emotional swings, Kivy believes, they cannot count as audience members who are listening to music in a way that is typical of those who appreciate music as an aesthetic object.

This argument is much less compelling than Kivy believes. A little reflection reveals that, in the course of daily life, we can feel a wide range of emotions in a short period of time. Derek Matravers notes that in the course of reading the morning newspaper a reader 'can be amused, indignant, heartened, disheartened, saddened, and so on'.[85] This seems right. Reading the front page I am angry at the latest cutbacks to healthcare and postsecondary education. A human-interest story catches my eye and I am glad that an old lady's cat was rescued from poachers. I turn to the sports page and I am despondent: my favourite team's losing streak has been extended and the team's star player is injured again. The feelings I have as I read the paper are, perhaps, not as intense as those one experienced when one's canary died or one lost one's favourite sweater. They are

---

[83] Kivy, 'Mood and Music', p. 279.
[84] Kivy, *Sound Sentiment*, p. 23.
[85] Matravers, *Art and Emotion*, p. 155.

nevertheless emotions. Psychological research confirms that certain affective responses can arise and dissipate very quickly.[86]

The experience of art can also lead us to experience several emotions in a short period of time. Consider, for example, typical experiences of films and plays. In viewing such works, audience members commonly report experiencing in the course of ninety or so minutes (or not much more time than a large-scale symphony lasts) a wide range of affective states. As evidence that this sort of experience is common, consider the phrase, 'I laughed, I cried.' This phrase has become such a cliché in movie reviews that a Google search (together with the search terms 'movie' and 'review') yielded almost 50,000 hits. We would regard as a poor judge of aesthetic value someone incapable of feeling a wide range of emotions in the course of watching a movie or play. If the affective states of moviegoers and theatre audiences can swing so wildly, the affective states of concertgoers could demonstrate similar rapid variation. Of course, perhaps it is unlikely that a single individual could, in the course of an hour or two, feel a wide range of emotional states such as are aroused in the course of ordinary life, but a wide range of affective states of the sort aroused by works of art seems well within the capacity of most people.

The Formalist's Last Ditch

Some formalists continue to deny that music arouses emotion, at least in some listeners some of the time. Kivy has, in recent writings, moved from the claim that music does not arouse affects to the more modest view that music does not arouse emotion if one is listening to it in a particular way. In particular, he doubts that music will arouse emotion when 'people are listening to music the way it is supposed to be listened to in its status *as a fine art*'. He denies that affective responses are 'relevant to our appreciation and enjoyment of absolute music as *music*; that is, as *art*'.[87] Formalists listen to music as a fine art and, Kivy believes, no emotions are aroused in them. Formalists are canonical listeners. There may be, Kivy allows, other ways of listening to music, perhaps even other canonical ways of listening,

---

[86] Roy F. Baumeister, Kathleen D. Vohs, C. Nathan DeWall, and Liqing Zhang, 'How Emotion Shapes Behavior: Feedback, Anticipation, and Reflection, Rather Than Direct Causation', *Personality and Social Psychology Review*, 11 (2007), 167–203.

[87] Kivy, 'Mood and Music', p. 275.

which arouse emotion. But Kivy is not interested in these ways of listening. His last ditch is the claim that there is at least one way of listening that does not arouse emotion.

Before addressing the last ditch defence of formalism, it should be acknowledged again that music affects listeners in a variety of ways. Kivy is adamant that he does not have garden-variety emotions aroused in him by music: 'by the dog, I swear that sad music does not make me sad, nor happy music happy'.[88] There is no reason to doubt his sincerity or veracity. I wish only to maintain that many listeners who pay close attention to music as an aesthetic object can have emotions aroused. I also want to suggest that this is by no means an unusual reaction to music among well-informed listeners.

In his most recent writings, Kivy holds that music arouses emotion in some listeners but not others. People who listen to music as an aesthetic object do not have emotions aroused. He holds that such people are the 'informed' and 'devoted' music lovers.[89] Music arouses emotion in people who listen to music in another way. It may, for example, arouse emotion in a child whose mother sings to it in a soothing tone of voice. Perhaps music arouses emotion in dancers. In neither case is music arousing emotions in listeners who are paying close attention to it as an aesthetic object and nothing else. I have two responses to this position.

The first is that the position comes perilously close to being tautological, if it is not outright tautological. Kivy seems to be saying that listening that does not arouse emotion does not arouse emotion. That is certainly true, but completely uninformative.

The second is that it is not clear that one has fully appreciated music if one has failed to have emotion aroused. Likely one can listen to music in a way that minimizes one's emotional response. Similarly one can read a novel in a way that minimizes one's emotional response. People can, for example, read a book while focusing on finding instances of metonymy or synecdoche while ignoring, to the greatest extent possible, all other aspects of the novel. Such readers may not have emotions aroused in them. We would hardly say, however, that such people have had the fullest

---

[88] Kivy, 'Auditor's Emotions: Contention, Concession, Compromise', in *New Essays on Musical Understanding*, p. 76.
[89] Peter Kivy, 'Moodology: A Response to Laura Sizer', *Journal of Aesthetics and Art Criticism*, 65 (2007), p. 313.

aesthetic appreciation of the novel. We might even doubt that they have had an aesthetic experience at all. If the book in question is, say, *Bleak House* and readers do not feel pity and anger, one would hardly say that they have appreciated the book in the least. We would not do so even if they can tell us how many instances of metonymy are to be found in the novel. Similarly, if listeners know that 'Ave vera virginatus' from Josquin's *Ave Maria* is written as a canon at the fifth, but do not feel a quiet joy or serenity while listening to it, they have not had the fullest possible aesthetic appreciation of the work.

There is no reason to suppose that to listen in a way that results in emotional arousal is not to listen to music as an aesthetic object. Listeners who have emotion aroused by music need not be wool gathering. That is, they need not be allowing their attention to the music to lapse and, instead, paying attention to their imaginings. On the contrary, some empirical evidence suggests that those who pay closest attention to musical form have more intense emotions aroused than those who do not. This is a conclusion to be drawn from the experiment that showed that trained musicians had more marked emotional responses to unexpected musical events, such as minor chords where major chords are expected.[90] The trained musicians appear to have had more intense emotion precisely because they are trained to be aware of musical form. Kivy has stated that, 'until the psychologists hook up their electrodes and brain scans to [informed listeners who pay careful attention to music]... I will remain skeptical about *what psychology has shown* about the artistic experience of music'.[91] This is precisely what psychologists have done and the results do not support his view.

Kivy has suggested that psychologists would get different (and more informative) results if they studied listeners in concert halls rather than undergraduates in laboratories. He believes that they would find that music does not arouse emotion. I find this difficult to believe. It seems unlikely that a laboratory provides better conditions for aesthetic experience of music than does the concert hall. When listeners are comfortable and able to concentrate fully on music, as they (ideally) are able to do in a concert hall, the various mechanisms by which music arouses emotion should be able to function more smoothly. At least some of the

---

[90] Steinbeis et al., 'The Role of Harmonic Expectancy Violations in Musical Emotions'.
[91] Kivy, 'Moodology', p. 317.

mechanisms seem to function independently of a listener's location. For example, listeners cannot somehow turn off their brain reflexes when they sit down in a concert hall. Listeners cannot stop the somatic effects of music from occurring or from emotional contagion from happening. The closer attention listeners pay to music, the more music is likely to affect them.

Music does not arouse emotion in all listeners and some music arouses no emotion in anyone. Sometimes music arouses emotion even when listeners are not devoting to it careful aesthetic attention. However, when many listeners pay close aesthetic attention to some music they will frequently have emotion aroused in them.

A 'Special' Emotion

Kivy believes that music does not arouse garden-variety emotions in listeners, but he maintains that it moves us to feel another sort of emotion. He calls it a 'special' emotion. Kivy can, with perfect consistency, hold this position. He has an account of how this emotion is produced in listeners that is compatible with the cognitive theory of emotion. Nevertheless, the postulation of this special musical emotion gives rise to a problem of which Kivy is aware. Kivy's position resembles that of another writer who posited a special emotion. This writer is Clive Bell, who famously maintained that all works of art evoke 'aesthetic emotion' in audience members.[92] Kivy recognizes that Bell's position is untenable: aestheticians generally believe that we do not have the same aesthetic response to all works of art. Kivy's challenge is to distinguish his position from Bell's. Kivy is unable to meet this challenge.

Let us begin by investigating the nature of the special musical emotion. In one essay, Kivy indicates that 'it is a nameless emotion'.[93] In the same essay he has a stab at giving the emotion a name, calling it 'an enthusiasm, an intense musical excitement'.[94] Elsewhere, Kivy characterizes the special emotion aroused by music in various ways. Again it is described, *faute de mieux*, as 'musical excitement'.[95] Elsewhere Kivy simply speaks of

---

[92] Clive Bell, *Art* (London: Chatto and Windus, 1914).
[93] Kivy, 'Experiencing the Musical Emotions', p. 103.
[94] Kivy, 'Experiencing the Musical Emotions', p. 105.
[95] Kivy, *Sound Sentiment*, p. 231.

the emotional response of '"being moved by" music'.[96] Most recently he has talked of the special emotion as 'a kind of enthusiasm, or excitement, or ecstasy'.[97] What the emotion is called or how it is characterized is not really important. In introducing the special emotion, Kivy notes that not every emotion has a name. What is important is how the special musical emotion is caused and how it is to be individuated and distinguished from other emotions.

Let us begin with Kivy's account of how musical emotion is caused. Kivy uses the cognitive theory of emotions to give an account of the origin of musical emotion. According to the cognitive theory, an emotion requires both an intentional object and some beliefs about this object. When listeners experience the special emotion aroused by music, their intentional object is a work of music (or a performance of the work). The listeners believe that the performance is beautiful. They are moved to feel the special emotion by the beauty of the performance. Kivy holds that the 'music moves us by various aspects of its musical beauty or perfection'.[98] Kivy allows that sometimes the beauty of the work involves its expressive properties. So, for example, one can be moved because a performance of a work is beautifully expressive of sadness or of joy. In such a case, however, the emotion aroused is not sadness or joy. Rather, the special musical emotion has been aroused and it has been aroused by the beauty of music.

Kivy is aware that this account of the origins of the special emotion may remind people of the sort of aesthetic emotion posited by Clive Bell. Kivy is also aware that, if music arouses aesthetic emotion, he faces a serious objection. He has noted that the 'theory that art arouses unique "aesthetic emotions"... is... an untenable view, long since given up by most philosophers of art'. The problem is that the claim that 'the same emotion or feeling is always felt in hearing music' is simply not in accord with most listeners' experience of music.[99] Virtually all listeners, including Kivy, agree that they have a variety of emotions aroused in them by music. The emotion aroused by, say, Beethoven's *Eroica Symphony* will differ radically from the emotion evoked by Bach's Second Brandenburg Concerto. Many listeners say that they have a variety of garden-variety emotions aroused: sadness

---

[96] Kivy, *Music Alone*, p. 160.
[97] Kivy, 'Mood and Music', p. 280.
[98] Kivy, *Music Alone*, p. 161.
[99] Kivy, *Sound Sentiment*, p. 98.

by sad music, joy by joyful music, and so on. This is the sort of story told by those who think that music arouses garden-variety emotions. This sort of story is not an option available to Kivy. He must tell some other story about how music gives rise to a variety of affects.

At times Kivy's special musical emotion certainly sounds a good deal like Bell's aesthetic emotion. In an early discussion of this emotion he writes that,

...of course I am saying there is a 'special' musical emotion, but only in the most benign, nominalistic sense. When I am moved by the beauty of music, I am experiencing 'a' or 'the' musical emotion, simply in virtue of my having been moved by the beauty of *music*, rather than by the beauty of something else. I am saying nothing more 'metaphysical' than I would be if I said there is a special botanical emotion, namely the emotion I get when I am moved by the beauty of a plant or flower.[100]

Apart from the point where Kivy hesitates between committing himself to a single musical emotion or a variety of musical emotions, this passage is highly reminiscent of Bell.

Kivy seems to posit a special musical emotion that we are moved to feel by 'the beauty of music', just as Bell believes in an aesthetic emotion that we are moved to feel by 'significant form'. Bell famously asked,

What quality is shared by all objects that provoke our aesthetic emotions? What quality is common to Sta. Sophia and the windows at Chartres, Mexican sculpture, a Persian bowl, Chinese carpets, Giotto's frescoes at Padua, and the masterpieces of Poussin, Piero della Francesca, and Cézanne?

His answer was simple:

Only one answer seems possible—significant form. In each, lines and colours combined in a particular way, certain forms and relations of forms, stir our aesthetic emotions.[101]

Similarly, Kivy might well ask what quality is shared by all musical performances that provoke musical emotion. What quality is common to the Brandenburg Concerti, Mozart's Rondo in A minor, K. 511, Tchaikovsky's *Francesca da Rimini*, Op. 32, Josquin's *Ave Maria*, and a simple melody such as 'Greensleeves'? In each, musical lines and tone colours combined in a particular way, certain forms and relations of forms, stir our musical

---

[100] Kivy, *Sound Sentiment*, p. 231.
[101] Bell, *Art*, p. 8.

emotions. Bell has a name for the 'relations and combinations of lines and colours': significant form. Kivy has a name for the relations and combinations of musical lines and tone colours: musical beauty.

Nevertheless, Kivy believes that he is not committed to the untenable view that all music arouses the same emotion and he has an argument that is designed to distinguish his position from Bell's. The key claim is that we distinguish emotions, not by how they feel, but by their objects. Having said this Kivy may seem to be in trouble. The special emotion always takes musical beauty as its object. While he grants that this is true, 'under different descriptions' musical emotion has 'many different intentional objects'.[102] Since there are many different intentional objects, we have many different musical emotions. Kivy writes that he does not

...feel the 'same' emotion when...moved by the beauty of Bach's *English Suites* as when...[moved] by the beauty of Schubert's Improptus, Op. 90. Because they are such different works...it is no more the 'same' emotion than is the love one feels for one's golden retriever the 'same' emotion as the love one feels for one's child, except in the sense that the latter two are both 'love', and the former two both 'the emotion aroused by beautiful music'.[103]

In short, Kivy's view is that someone listening to Bach's *English Suites* is in the state of being aroused to musical emotion by the *English Suites*. People who hear Schubert's Op. 90 are in the state of being aroused to musical emotion by Op. 90. The emotions are distinct because they have distinct intentional objects.

Let us assess this argument. Contrary to what Kivy believes, the emotions may not be distinct. At one point he asks whether we feel the same emotion when listening to Mozart's K. 511 and when hearing a Strauss waltz. He answers: 'yes and no... One emotion, two emotions: of course.'[104] This is not good enough. For his argument to work, the emotions listeners experience when they listen to different works of music have to be different in kind. No two affective states are ever identical. They differ in a variety ways: they occur on different occasions, they have different objects, and they have somewhat different phenomenological characteristics. We need to know whether two affective states can be of the same kind or, as we may say, tokens of the same emotion type even if they differ

---

[102] Kivy, 'Experiencing the Musical Emotions', p. 103.
[103] Kivy, 'Auditor's Emotions: Contention, Concession, and Compromise', pp. 73–4.
[104] Kivy, *Sound Sentiment*, p. 232.

in these ways. In particular, we need to know whether two affective states can be tokens of the same emotion type if they have different objects. In some respects, the emotion listeners experience when they hear the Blue Danube Waltz differs from the emotion they have when they hear K. 511. They could still, however, be tokens of the same emotion type. If so, then Kivy's argument fails.

When we are dealing with garden-variety emotions, two affective states can be tokens of the same type even when they are directed towards different objects. For example, my love of my daughter and my love of my son are tokens of the same emotion, even though my daughter and my son are completely different people with quite distinct personalities and characteristics. They differ from each other at least as much as K. 511 differs from the Blue Danube Waltz. By Kivy's principle of individuating emotions, my love for my daughter and my love for my son are distinct emotions. I have to assure you that this is false. I have very much the same feelings and dispositions to act towards each of them. The emotions I feel for my children are emotions of the same type or kind. Similarly, it is possible that one feels other emotions (such as sadness, joy, or yearning) about a variety of objects. For example, the sadness I feel about the death of my hamster is of a kind with the sadness I feel when my parakeet dies.

Kivy could dig in his heels here and simply insist that, since the objects of my emotions differ, the emotions are of different types. Any time the object differs, the emotion is of a different type. If he adheres rigidly to this position, then his argument proves too much as it is subject to the following reductio. Consider again musical emotion. Consider in particular the emotion aroused by a performance of Beethoven's Fifth Symphony, Op. 67 by the Berlin Philharmonic Orchestra, conducted by Herbert von Karajan, and the emotion aroused by a performance of the same symphony performed by the Philadelphia Orchestra, conducted by Eugene Ormandy. These two emotions have different intentional objects and, by Kivy's account, they ought to count as tokens of different emotions. Indeed, it seems that Kivy's argument, carried to its logical extent, has the consequence that the emotion aroused by listening to a recording of the Berlin Philharmonic's performance of Beethoven's Fifth at T_1 and listening to the Berlin Philharmonic's performance of the same symphony at T_2 count as different emotions. After all, the Berlin Philharmonic's performance of Beethoven's Fifth as heard (under good listening conditions) at T_1 is a different intentional object than the Berlin Philharmonic's performance of

Beethoven's Fifth as heard (under good listening conditions) at T_2. (I add the reference to good listening conditions to ensure that emotion can be aroused. The listener is not distracted in any way from experience of the music.) The emotions aroused at T_1 and T_2 will be somewhat different yet it is absurd to suggest that they are not of the same kind.

That there is something wrong with Kivy's argument becomes even more apparent when we apply it to Bell's theory of aesthetic emotion. If Kivy's argument were sufficient to save him from the view that listeners feel a single emotion while listening to music, it would show that Bell ought not to hold that viewers experience different emotions when viewing different works of art. Viewers experience, for example, aesthetic emotion as aroused by the windows at Chartres when viewing the windows at Chartres, aesthetic emotion as evoked by Giotto's frescos when viewing Giotto's frescos, aesthetic emotion as aroused by a Cézanne still life when looking at the Cézanne still life, and so on. So Bell does not subscribe to the view that the experience of visual art arouses a single sort of emotion. Bell would not be persuaded by this argument. The whole point of his theory of art is that all artworks evoke the same emotion. Of course, he would say, aesthetic emotion is aroused by a variety of works of art. Nevertheless, Bell would maintain that we experience the same aesthetic emotion on different occasions. That one emotional state is aroused by a given composition and a second emotional state is aroused by another musical work is not sufficient to establish that the emotions are not tokens of the same type.

Just the opposite is true as well. Two emotional states can be directed towards the same object and yet they are instances of completely distinct emotions. For example, on one occasion, a recording of a work irritates me. Subsequently, I come to understand the work, I listen to the recording again, and now it inspires 'enthusiasm' in me. Here we have one object and two emotions. Kivy has the wrong way of individuating emotions. We need a way, besides difference of intentional object, to distinguish emotions.

The conclusion of these reflections is that Kivy has not proved that music arouses only special musical emotion and that listeners can have a variety of emotions aroused in them by music. The mere fact that one affective state is aroused by a given work of music and a second affective state is aroused by a different piece of music does not demonstrate that the two emotions are tokens of different types. On the contrary, if musical beauty arouses an emotion, there is every reason to believe that it would be the same emotion on each occasion. Kivy indicates that phenomenologically the emotion is the same on each occasion: it is a feeling of ecstasy or excitement. He provides no reason to suppose that the disposition to behave associated with the excitement associated with one musical performance differs from the dispositions to behave associated with any other performance. On the contrary, we will have in both cases a disposition to listen.

Bell understood how to individuate emotions better than Kivy does. On Bell's view, we do not feel aesthetic emotion because the object of our emotion is significant form. We feel aesthetic emotion because of how we feel and act with regard to significant form. Bell believed that we feel the same aesthetic emotion when viewing every work of art because he believed that our phenomenological experience, depth of feeling, and our dispositions to behave (in particular, our tendency to contemplate and admire) were similar when experiencing each work. He was wrong in believing that we feel the same emotion each time we experience works of art because he is wrong in believing that we feel and act the same each time we experience works of art. Kivy is wrong for a completely different reason. He believes that our emotions vary with the music we hear, but (unlike the arousalist) he is unable to find a way of distinguishing these emotions.

Kivy's account of musical emotion faces other difficulties. Having told us that special musical emotion is aroused by musical beauty, Kivy owes us an account of musical beauty. It is hard to see, however, how he is going to be able to find a characteristic that is common to all works of music that supposedly inspire musical emotion. A complex fugue by Bach, a simple song such as 'Greensleeves', one of Hildegard of Bingen's antiphons, a Tchaikovsky symphony, a mass by Byrd, and a concerto by Mozart all inspire emotion yet they are astoundingly various. Kivy is, however, committed to saying that there is some characteristic (musical beauty) that they all have in common. Kivy provides no general account of musical beauty. Indeed, he makes this a virtue of his theory of music. (I will return to a discussion of the formalist account of musical beauty in Chapter 5.) The best he does is to identify one feature shared by works with musical beauty: they inspire musical emotion.

This leaves Kivy facing another problem associated with Bell's theory of aesthetic emotion. Philosophers soon recognized that Bell's account of aesthetic emotion was viciously circular. Aesthetic emotion, he holds, is that emotion evoked by significant form. The only characterization of significant form that he provides states that it is the characteristic of artworks that arouses aesthetic emotion. A tighter or more vicious circle would be difficult to imagine. Kivy faces the same problem. Musical emotion is aroused by musical beauty. Musical beauty is that which arouses musical emotion.

The biggest problem with Kivy's account of how music arouses emotion has not yet been mentioned. He does not want to be saddled with the view that there is a single musical emotion because he wants a position that is compatible with the reports listeners give of their experience of music. There is a much simpler explanation, as we have already seen, of the fact that listeners report that music arouses a wide variety of emotions. According to this explanation, music arouses a wide range of garden-variety emotions. As we have already seen, there is good reason to believe that music arouses such emotions.

Nothing I have said here should be taken as a denial of the hypothesis that music arouses some sort of special musical emotion. On the contrary, I believe that we often feel wonder, awe, and excitement when experiencing great music. These emotions are aroused by appreciation of the sheer aesthetic value of the music. Empirical evidence supports this view. There is, however, every reason to believe that part of what gives music this value is its capacity to arouse garden-variety emotions.

This chapter has established that music arouses a wide variety of garden-variety emotions by means of its expressive properties. To have established this conclusion, however, is not yet to have driven a stake through the heart of formalism. Still, the stake is sharpened and the hammer is poised. Only a short step separates the conclusion that music arouses emotion (and that it is expressive of emotion) from the conclusion that music is not pure contentless form.

3
The Content of Music

The Concept of Representation

Hume long ago observed that when a 'controversy has been long kept on foot, and remains still undecided, we may presume that there is some ambiguity in the expression, and that the disputants affix different ideas to the terms employed in the controversy'.[1] The controversy about whether a good deal of music is representational is just such a dispute. Once we understand what the statement that music represents emotion means, it is obvious that it often does. Having established that music is often expressive of emotion and that it often arouses emotion, all that remains for the anti-formalist is to give a satisfactory analysis of the concept of representation and it is easy to demonstrate that representation in music is commonplace.

The argument that music represents emotions is designed to explain how people could be right when they report that music provides psychological insight. If music represents emotions, it has the potential to provide insight into them; that is, it has the potential for psychological depth. The keys to establishing that music represents emotion have already been established in the previous chapters. Music represents emotion by being expressive of emotion and by arousing it. Indeed, having established that music is expressive of and arouses emotion it is obvious that it represents emotion. Only the sort of confusion of which Hume speaks stops more people from recognizing that music represents emotion.

Formalists deny that music provides psychological insights because, as we have seen, they believe that instrumental music is empty form, devoid of any content. It is not about anything. Even music with lyrics

---

[1] David Hume, *Enquiries Concerning Human Understanding and Concerning the Principles of Morals*, ed. L.A. Selby-Bigg, third edn (Oxford: Clarendon Press, 1975), p. 62.

is, from a formalist perspective, best appreciated as pure musical form. Consequently, music does not provide us with any knowledge about the extra-musical world. At least, the formalist believes, music cannot provide us with any non-trivial knowledge about the extra-musical world. The formalist can allow that music is a source of knowledge about music. Bach's *Well-Tempered Clavier* is about how to write music in all twenty-four keys for a well-tempered keyboard. Some of Bach's other didactic compositions are about how to write counterpoint. The formalist denies only that music has any interesting extra-musical content or cognitive significance. (I use the terms 'content' and 'cognitive significance' interchangeably.)

Anti-formalists, in contrast, believe that music is an important source of knowledge about the extra-musical world. They typically believe that listeners can, by listening to music, obtain deep insight into human emotion. Music is also, according to the anti-formalist, a source of knowledge about character and other matters. Anti-formalists often believe that the knowledge obtainable from music can be so important that music is properly characterized as profound. (Chapter 5 will provide an extended defence of the claim that music can be profound.) The crucial question that anti-formalists must answer concerns how music provides knowledge about extra-musical matters.

I suggest that it does so by representing something extra-musical. Anti-formalists could employ several different concepts in an effort to capture the view that music has extra-musical cognitive significance. The primary reason for choosing representation is that a concept is needed that is not necessarily linked to the concept of truth. The concept of representation is not. Some representations (pictures, for example) have cognitive significance without being true. (Here I am using the concept of representation in a broad sense and not restricting the concept of representation to items that are truth-apt.) Similarly, although musical works have cognitive significance, they do not provide knowledge by making true statements. Another reason for choosing to talk of representation is that 'representation' is the most general term for those items having cognitive significance.[2]

The concept of representation with which we are concerned may be called external representation, as opposed to mental representation. That

---

[2] For a similar point, see Laird Addis, *Of Mind and Music* (Ithaca, N.Y.: Cornell University Press, 1999), p. 33.

is, we are concerned with representations created by humans and it is to these that I refer when I use the term 'representation'. With this in mind, I propose that the following three conditions must be met if something is to be a representation. There is nothing controversial about these conditions. Formalists have stated very similar conditions for something's being a representation. The formalist, however, does not believe that works of music satisfy these conditions except in trivial ways.

The first is the content condition. To say that a representation has content is to say that it is a source of knowledge about the object represented. (This knowledge need not be propositional knowledge.) The second is the intentionality condition. If R is a representation, then someone intends that it have cognitive significance. The third condition may be called the accessibility condition. Audience members, who are distinct from the person who intended that R be a representation, must be able to recognize the cognitive significance of R. Not everyone must be able to recognize R's cognitive significance, but qualified audience members must be able to do so. I will say a little about each of these conditions in turn.

The content condition requires that, if R is a representation, then one can acquire knowledge from R about the object it represents. The concept of representation is closely tied to the concept of aboutness: any representation is about some object. A representation conveys (to a qualified audience member) knowledge about the object that it represents. A painting is a representation of Mozart, for example, only if a qualified audience member can acquire knowledge about Mozart from it. From a painting that represents Mozart one can acquire the knowledge that he had blue eyes. The sentence 'Mozart had blue eyes' is also a representation since it has cognitive significance (in this case, meaning) and conveys the information that Mozart had blue eyes. (I do not regard false sentences as representations. They are misrepresentations.)

The fact that one can acquire knowledge from something is not enough to make it a representation. If R is a representation, then an audience can acquire from R information about something other than R. That is, if something is a representation, it provides knowledge about something that it represents. By listening to a composition (or studying it in score) one can acquire information about the composition: one can acquire the information that some work is in F major, that its middle movement is seventeen bars long, and so on. This does not make the composition a representation since the knowledge is about the composition. If the composition conveys knowledge about something extra-musical (say, about emotion), then it can be a representation. As already noted, formalists can accept that musical works are the source of knowledge about music, but they deny that music conveys much, if any, information about anything extra-musical.

The intentionality condition excludes some sources of knowledge from the class of representations. The spoor left by an animal as it flees through a wood is a source of knowledge. From the spoor one can learn that an animal has passed through the wood. It is not, however, a representation of the animal or its flight because the spoor is not intended to convey knowledge. The intentionality condition also rules out the possibility that representation can occur accidentally. Suppose, for example, some ants, walking around on a beach, make a pattern that looks like a drawing of Mozart. The pattern on the beach is not a representation of Mozart because the ants had no intention of representing him. In contrast, an artist who makes a drawing of Mozart can succeed in representing him, in part because he has the intention to do so. Formalists are sceptical about the suggestion that musical works often satisfy the intentionality condition. According to formalists, composers usually do not intend their works as representations, so their works are typically not representations. Composers may occasionally represent the sound of a bird or a bell, the formalist believes, but they do not intend to represent emotion or character.

The accessibility condition requires that qualified audience members be able to extract knowledge from a representation. Suppose that I make a squiggle on a piece of paper with the intention of representing Handel. I will not have succeeded in representing him because someone other than myself cannot, by examining the squiggle, extract from it some information about Handel. On the other hand, someone who looks at a well-executed drawing of the composer will be able to acquire the information that he was rather corpulent. Similarly, someone who reads the sentence 'Handel was corpulent' can acquire the information that he was corpulent. One can do so because of semantic conventions.

Not everyone must be able to acquire information from R for R to be a representation. A blind person cannot acquire the knowledge that Mozart's eyes are blue from the composer's portrait. A person who does not understand English cannot acquire this information from the sentence, 'Mozart's eyes were blue.' Nevertheless, both the portrait and the sentence are representations of Mozart. They are representations since qualified audience members are able to acquire information from the portrait and the sentence. It is probably not possible to give a general account of who counts as a qualified audience member. The best that can be done is to indicate some necessary conditions for being part of the qualified audience for certain types of representations. For example, being sighted is a necessary (but not sufficient) condition of being part of the qualified audience for representational paintings.

Representations come in two varieties. The first sort of representation is *semantic representation*. True sentences are the most familiar examples of semantic representation. For example, 'Mozart had blue eyes' is a semantic representation. Speakers can intend to use it to convey the knowledge that Mozart had blue eyes. Such a representation depends on semantic conventions that assign referents to a finite set of words and which specify rules for generating semantic representations. For example, conventions specify that 'Kivy' refers to Kivy, 'moustache' refers to moustaches and 'has' denotes the relation in which Kivy stands to a moustache. Consequently, 'Kivy has a moustache' represents the state of affairs above Kivy's upper lip. Semantic representation need not concern us here. Such representation is not found, or is found only rarely, in music. (An example of a rare exception might be a musical work that incorporated a trumpet call with a conventional meaning. A trumpet call can mean 'Charge', 'Get out of bed now', or something of that sort.)

The cognitive significance of a semantic representation, of a sentence, is its meaning. The meaning of a sentence is given, many philosophers of language agree, by its truth-conditions. Some philosophers of music speak of the 'meaning of music', but this is to use the word 'meaning' imprecisely. I prefer to use the word 'meaning' in its Fregean sense. Works of music are not sentences and they are not composed of sentences. Works of music do not have truth-conditions and they do not have meanings in Frege's sense. Meaning is, however, only one sort of cognitive significance. Works of music have a different sort of cognitive significance.

The second sort of representation may be called *illustrative representation* or, more simply, *illustration*. Illustrations convey information since experiences of them are relevantly similar to experiences of the object they represent. A swatch of fabric is an illustrative representation. (This is a special sort of illustration, namely exemplification, of which I will say a little more below.) It represents the rest of the cloth in the bolt because experience of the swatch is similar to experience of the rest of the cloth. Pictures are also examples of illustrations. A painting illustrates Mozart only if experience of the painting is relevantly similar to experience of the composer. Crucially, the sort of representation found in music is illustration. One way of characterizing illustrations is to say that a qualified audience member can perceive the represented object in the representation. Richard Wollheim, in his discussion of representation in pictures, argues that if we see X in a painting, the painting is a representation of X.[3] He is speaking of what I have called illustrative representation. Speakers of English do not perceive a cat in the statement that, 'The cat is on the mat.' In contrast, qualified audience members (those familiar with the conventions of drawing, and so on) can see a cat in a drawing of a cat. Sight is not the only sensory modality that makes possible illustrative representation. Illustration in sound is also possible. The statement that 'The call of a cuckoo falls a minor third' and the illustration of the cuckoo's call in Louis-Claude Daquin's *Le Coucou* represent the bird's call in quite distinct ways. Again, the representation by the statement is completely conventional. In contrast, Daquin illustrates the bird's call since listeners can hear the call in his *pièce de clavecin*. When qualified audience members can perceive the represented object in an illustration, then the accessibility condition is satisfied.

This account of illustrative representation gives rise to a number of questions. One might wonder, for example, about how experience of illustrative representations must be similar to experience of the objects. One problem is that experience of an illustration can be similar to experience of many things that it does not represent. After all, everything is similar to everything else in some respect. Indeed, everything is similar to everything else in an infinite number of respects. As well, experience of an illustration will differ in important ways from experience of the object that it represents. A swatch of cloth, for example, is similar to the bolt of cloth in that they share the same colour, but are dissimilar in size and shape. At the same time, the swatch is experienced as having the colour of objects that it does not represent. Nevertheless, illustration is possible since audience members are able to identify the relevant respects in which an illustrative representation is similar to the object represented and acquire information about that object. For present purposes, we do not need to investigate illustrative representation in detail, but a few words are in order.

[3] Richard Wollheim, *Painting as an Art* (Cambridge, M.A.: Harvard University Press, 1987).

THE CONTENT OF MUSIC   93

Certain features mark out the similarities between experience of an illustrative representation and experience of the object that it represents. For a start, the similarity is intended by the person (or persons) who creates the representation. As well, the similarity between experience of the illustration and experience of the represented object can be detected by an audience and the represented object is brought to the mind of audience members. Illustrative representation is facilitated by conventions. These conventions are not the sorts of semantic conventions that make semantic representation possible. The conventions of illustrative representation do not establish a finite set of building blocks from which representations are constructed. Rather, these conventions are general principles that govern how illustrations are made and information extracted from them. So, for example, a convention of drawing specifies that lines mark the edges of objects. Illustrative representation is not, however, completely conventional. Biological fact goes a measure of the way towards explaining how illustrative representation is possible. As we have seen, in Chapter 1, humans are hardwired to hear certain patterns of sound as expressive of emotion. We are also made in such a way that certain sounds will arouse emotion in us and bring these emotions to mind.

Illustrations show rather than tell. That is, illustrations do not make statements. A portrait does not state the proposition that Mozart had blue eyes. Rather, it shows us that he did. The portrait puts audiences in a position to see that his eyes were blue. Illustrations give audience members experiences that make it possible for them to acquire knowledge. Illustrations do not provide arguments. They cannot, since an argument is a series of statements designed to establish a conclusion, and illustrations do not make statements.

That some music illustrates sounds is uncontroversial and can be accepted by the formalist. (Kivy calls this 'picturing' in music.) It illustrates birdsong, church bells, and a few other sounds. For example, Vivaldi's Flute Concerto in D major, Op. 10, No. 3 (*Il Gardellino*) represents the song of a goldfinch because experience of the flute part resembles experience of a goldfinch's song. That is, a listener can hear a goldfinch in the concerto. Music can also, perhaps in conjunction with a libretto or a programme, represent various sorts of motion. It can, for example, represent the ascent of Mary into heaven (as in Biber's *Mystery Sonata* No. 14, 'The Assumption of the Virgin') or represent the sun standing still (as in 'Oh! Thou bright orb, great ruler of the day!' from Handel's *Joshua*) by a sort of isomorphism. In Biber's sonata the music moves upward. In Handel's aria, the violas hold a single note to represent the sun standing still.

Even a formalist can accept that music sometimes represents by picturing and isomorphism. Kivy, whose formalist credentials are impeccable, has written a superb study (*Sound and Semblance*) of how music can represent in these ways. If these were the only sorts of representation in music, however, music would have very little extra-musical cognitive significance. The knowledge to be gained from musical picturing and isomorphism is trivial. This is why a formalist can grant that music provides listeners with a little mundane knowledge about the sound of the cuckoo's call or Mary's (heavenward) trajectory. None of this is controversial. What is controversial is the claim that music could illustrate something other than sounds and trajectories. In particular, the claim that music represents emotion, and can provide insight into it, is controversial and will be rejected by any formalist. Still, other works of art represent emotion. The claim that paintings or poems can represent emotions is commonplace. Understanding how these works of art represent emotion will help us understand how music might also represent emotion.

Let us consider an example. A still life may represent, say, some books and a lute, as does Jan Davidszoon de Heem's *Still Life of Books* (1628). This painting is not only a representation of some books, some papers, a violin, and so on. It has cognitive significance, but it is not merely a source of knowledge about how books and violins look. A viewer who saw that the painting represents some books and a violin but was unaware of any other significance would have missed most of the painting's content. It is a source of knowledge about how books and violins look, but that knowledge is trivial. Only someone who recognizes that the painting is also about melancholy can grasp its full cognitive significance. (One source goes so far as to say that a de Heem still life can address 'the meaning of life'.[4] I do not think that I want to go that far.)

One might wonder how a painting of some books and a violin can be an illustration of melancholy. Part of what makes it about melancholy is that it is expressive of melancholy. It is expressive of melancholy by illustrating items that are expressive of melancholy. The colours are expressive of melancholy: the palette is restricted to washed-out sepia, greys, straw, and

---

[4] National Gallery of Art, Washington, *Painting in the Dutch Golden Age: A Profile of the Seventeenth Century* (Washington: National Gallery of Art, 2007), p. 94.

similar dull hues. The books are tattered and piled messily on a table. The wall behind the table is bare and unadorned. The violin is obscured. The overall effect is highly expressive of melancholy. (Other things are going on in the painting, of course. It is also a reminder of the futility of worldly study.)

Paintings can also arouse emotions. Psychological experiments indicate that subject manner and the style in which the subject matter is represented have an effect on the emotions aroused by paintings.[5] For example, by representing a melancholy scene in a melancholy manner *Still Life of Books* is expressive of melancholy, but it also arouses melancholy. Likely the mechanisms by which paintings arouse emotions are related to those by which music arouses emotion. For example, emotional contagion probably explains, in part, how paintings arouse emotion.

The capacity of paintings to arouse emotion contributes to their cognitive significance. Viewers of a painting know what it is about, what it represents, by paying attention to how they feel as they view it. The painting can, by evoking melancholy in viewers, bring them to recognize that some scene or subject matter is melancholy. That is, viewers can be brought to see a scene as melancholy by feeling melancholy about it. Paintings are, however, often said to be about melancholy (or another emotion) itself. Paintings are about (or represent) an emotion in large part because they arouse that emotion by being expressive of it. The cognitive significance of the painting lies, in large part, in knowledge of the precise shades of emotion that it arouses. Viewers come to know what experience of some emotion is like by feeling the emotion.

Painting is not the only sort of art in which emotions can be represented. They are also frequently illustrated in novels, poems, and other works of literature. Although language is the medium of literature, works of literature do not make statements about emotion (or anything else). Works of literature are not, in other words, semantic representations. Nevertheless, it is a commonplace that emotions are represented in literature. One critic speaks, for example, of 'Tennyson's representation of melancholy inwardness in "Mariana"'.[6] Just as one might wonder about how a

---

[5] Stephen W.P. Kemp and Gerald C. Cupchik, 'The Emotionally Evocative Effects of Paintings', *Visual Arts Research*, 33 (2007), 72–82.

[6] David G. Riede, *Allegories of One's Own Mind: Melancholy in Victorian Poetry* (Columbus, O.H.: Ohio State University Press, 2005), p. 56.

still life can illustrate melancholy when it cannot look like an emotion, one might wonder about how a poem can represent emotion when it cannot sound like an emotion. The answer is that a poem illustrates emotion in very much the same way that a painting does. It begins by being expressive of an emotion, as 'Mariana' is expressive of melancholy. When a poem is expressive of an emotion it can also arouse that emotion. The processes by which poems arouse emotion are complex but, again, emotional contagion is part of the story. (In the next chapter I will have more to say about how poems and other literary forms arouse emotion.)

By arousing an emotion in us a poem becomes a representation of that emotion. A picture of an object, say a book, illustrates the book because experience of the picture is like experience of the book. Similarly, a poem illustrates an emotion because experience of the poem is like experience of the emotion. For example, 'Mariana' is about melancholy because it arouses melancholy in readers. Anyone who (under standard conditions of perception and while properly attentive) reads the poem but fails to feel melancholy would have failed to grasp what it is about; that is, what it represents. Qualified audience members can acquire from the poem knowledge about how melancholy feels. They can acquire this knowledge by the only possible means: by feeling melancholy.

Before I turn to an examination of how music represents emotion, an alternative to my account needs to be dismissed. Some writers suggest that music represents by exemplifying.[7] There is a simple reason why this cannot be how music represents emotion. An exemplar can only exemplify those properties that it possesses. A fabric swatch can, for example, exemplify a pattern, texture, and weight of fabric. A work of music can, similarly, exemplify only properties works of music can possess. A work might, for example, exemplify sonata form, or the minor mode, or music of the Italian baroque. Works of music do not have emotions, so they cannot exemplify them. Works of music can be expressive of emotions and can arouse them but it does not follow from this that they can exemplify

---

[7] Charles O. Nussbaum, *The Musical Representation: Meaning, Ontology, and Emotion* (Cambridge, M.A.: MIT Press, 2007), p. 94. Nussbaum does not suggest that works of music can exemplify emotion. This is a view associated with Nelson Goodman. See his *Languages of Art* (Indianapolis, I.N.: Hackett, 1976) and Nelson Goodman and Catherine Z. Elgin, *Reconceptions in Philosophy and Other Arts and Sciences* (Indianapolis, I.N.: Hackett, 1988). My remarks on exemplification are based on those in my *Art and Knowledge* (London: Routledge, 2001), pp. 72ff.

emotions. The only way that something can exemplify say, sadness, is by being sad. To be expressive of sadness, or to arouse sadness, is not to be sad. A work of music can be an exemplar of works that are expressive of emotion (or of works that arouse emotion).

This argument seems quite decisive, but some writers have still tried to argue that music can exemplify emotion. In order to make this argument, they have introduced the concept of metaphorical exemplification. An exemplar is supposed to be able to metaphorically exemplify those properties that it metaphorically possesses. Consider this example. A work of music may be described as a rollercoaster ride. If so, then it may be said metaphorically to possess the property of being a rollercoaster ride. One could then argue that it exemplifies the property of being a rollercoaster ride. Similarly, a work of music may be described as joyful. It is then supposed metaphorically to possess the property of being joyful and be able to exemplify joy. This argument depends entirely on there being metaphorical properties. Unfortunately, no such properties exist.

The use of metaphors to describe objects does not give them new properties. When, for example, a work of music is described as a rollercoaster ride, it does not acquire any new properties. (At least, it does not acquire any properties besides the property of being described as a rollercoaster ride.) In particular, calling it a rollercoaster ride does not give it the property of being an amusement park attraction featuring railway cars climbing and descending steep inclines and negotiating tight turns. It just has the properties it always had; namely, a quick tempo, a wide dynamic range, and so on. These are the properties that it can exemplify. Similarly, suppose that a work of music is described as sad. This description gives the work no additional (metaphorical) properties that it can now exemplify. It only has the properties that it previously had. It has a slow tempo, minor tonality, and so on. These are the properties that it can exemplify. It cannot exemplify sadness because it does not have the property of being sad.

Representation in Music

When a work of music represents emotion it does so in much the same way that other works of art do. Just as a painting can illustrate an emotion by being expressive of that emotion and arousing it, so does a work of music illustrate emotion. My account of representation in music builds on the previous two chapters. Once it is recognized that music is expressive of emotions and arouses emotions, it is a short step to the conclusion that music represents emotions. I will begin with a discussion of how music, when it is expressive of some emotion, is also a representation of the expression of that emotion. I will then go on to discuss how music's capacity to arouse emotion contributes to its cognitive significance. The second way in which music can represent is the more interesting. Representation by means of arousal makes possible the psychological insight to which writers on music frequently refer.

It is easy to state the argument for the conclusion that music expressive of emotion also represents.

(1) Some works of music are intended by their composers to be heard as expressive of emotion.
(2) Some works of music are heard by qualified listeners as expressive of emotion.
(3) A work of music heard as expressive of emotion has cognitive significance.
(4) If some works of music are intended by their composers to be heard as expressive of emotion, these works of music are heard by qualified listeners as expressive of emotion and these works of music heard as expressive of emotion have cognitive significance, then works of music represent the expression of emotion.
∴ (C) Works of music represent the expression of emotion.

The first premise of this argument is simply a consequence of the resemblance theory of musical expression. Chapter 1 has shown that the resemblance theory enjoys strong empirical support. Premise (2) is an empirical claim about the intentions of composers. Premise (3) states that when music is heard as expressive of emotion, the accessibility condition is satisfied. Each of the first three premises states that one of the conditions of something being a representation is satisfied. Premise (4) simply states that if a piece of music satisfies the three conditions for being a representation, then it is a representation. As I noted above, we just need to be clear about what a representation is to see that a good deal of music does represent since, I will argue, there is little doubt that these three conditions are satisfied. Even some of those who deny that music represents accept that the conditions are satisfied.

Let us begin by considering the satisfaction of the accessibility condition. An illustration satisfies the accessibility condition when a qualified

THE CONTENT OF MUSIC 99

audience member (who is not the creator of the representation) can perceive in the illustration the object that is represented. When qualified listeners can hear the expression of emotion in music, this condition is satisfied. The empirical evidence unambiguously indicates that listeners hear music as expressive of emotion. As noted in Chapter 1, they can determine the emotion of which some musical performance is expressive about as reliably as they can determine the emotion of which facial features are expressive.

Support for this conclusion comes from an unlikely source. At least before he abandoned the resemblance theory, Kivy believed that works of music are 'heard as' expressive of emotion.[8] Above, talk about the satisfaction of the accessibility condition was formulated in terms of the capacity of qualified listeners to hear emotion in music, but this is simply a different way of putting the same point. The distinction between saying that music is 'heard as' the expression of emotion and saying that emotion is 'heard in' music is a distinction without a difference.[9]

Kivy has made other statements that support the argument advanced here. At one time, at least, Kivy held the view 'that music represents things by being expressive... of the emotions that... things might arouse in us'.[10] Kivy's stated view is not quite the one advocated here. He takes it that music represents the things that arouse emotions, not expressions of emotion. The conclusion he states is, however, not the one to which his argument led. Music can, he notes, be expressive of an emotion, perhaps the emotion one feels when contemplating an imposing mountain. Music is expressive of an emotion in precisely the way described by the resemblance theory (which Kivy still held at the time he articulated his argument). That is, emotion is heard in the music, the way we see sadness in a Saint Bernard's face. In the same passage of *Sound Sentiment*, Kivy also spends several pages arguing that some composers have intended that their music represent emotions. (The composers Kivy quotes often speak about the 'imitation' or 'depiction' of emotion.) One would expect him to conclude that emotions are represented. Instead, and unaccountably, he

---

[8] Peter Kivy, *Sound Sentiment: An Essay on the Musical Emotions Including the Complete Text of The Corded Shell* (Philadelphia, P.A.: Temple University Press, 1989), p. 83.

[9] Jerrold Levinson, 'Musical Expressiveness', in his *The Pleasures of Aesthetics: Philosophical Essays* (Ithaca, N.Y.: Cornell University Press, 1996), 90–125.

[10] Peter Kivy, *Sound and Semblance: Reflections on Musical Representation* (Ithaca, N.Y.: Cornell University Press, 1991), p. 133.

shifts to talking about the representation in music of mountains and other things that might arouse or be expressive of emotion. Still, Kivy's argument lends support to the view that by being expressive of emotion, music represents behaviour that is expressive of emotion.

In at least one other place, Kivy has made statements that explicitly indicate that by being expressive of emotion, music represents that emotion. Kivy notes that many of Handel's operas are a sort of 'emotive soliloquy'. They are so by being expressive of emotion, in the manner recommended by Johann Mattheson in *Der vollkommene Capellmeister* (1739). From this Kivy concludes that 'the principal thematic material of the Handelian da capo arias...is pretty much always a recognizable representation of the leading emotion: that is to say, a representation of its phenomenology and behavioral manifestations'.[11] Someone who believes that music represents behaviour expressive of emotion could not have put it better. (Kivy believes, rather whimsically, that Handel's arias represent only emotions of obsessed individuals, but this feature of his view can safely be ignored.) How music could represent the phenomenology of emotion as well as behaviour expressive of emotion is not yet clear. Below I will suggest that the only way that music could represent the phenomenology of emotion would be by arousing emotion.

While Kivy (unwittingly) provides support for the claim that music expressive of emotion satisfies the accessibility condition for being a representation, he is adamant that the intentionality condition is not satisfied. Kivy is explicit on this point: 'representation implies conscious intent on the part of the composer; and that, it seems to me, is lacking, more often than not'.[12] I would argue that an intention to produce music expressive of emotion is to have an intention to produce music that represents emotion. Kivy would deny this, but he also denies that composers have, or often have, an intention to write music expressive of emotion. He writes that, 'The composer more than likely had no intention of representing expressive behaviour, nor, for that matter, need he even have intended his music to be expressive at all.'[13] On Kivy's view, the resemblance between music

---

[11] Peter Kivy, *Osmin's Rage: Philosophical Reflections on Opera, Drama, and Text, with a New Final Chapter* (Ithaca, N.Y.: Cornell University Press, 1999), p. 168. Kivy repeats this assertion a few pages later: 'the da capo aria...is...a perfect representation of human emotion, in thought and in expression' (p. 176).

[12] Kivy, *Sound Sentiment*, p. 64.

[13] Kivy, *Sound Sentiment*, p. 64.

and expressive behaviour is, very often at least, accidental. On his view, much of the time composers no more intend that their music be expressive of some emotion than a Saint Bernard intends that its face be expressive of sadness.[14]

The question about whether the intentionality condition is satisfied is empirical. In order to answer the question, we need to examine the musicological record and interview contemporary musicians. We should not expect to find that all composers intend to represent emotion in their music. Some composers do not. Neither should we expect that musicians who intend that some of their music be representational intend all of their music to be about emotion. Sometimes composers produce serious studies or amusing ephemera that are not intended to be about anything. Fortunately, anti-formalists are not committed to saying that all works of music satisfy the intentionality condition. They are only committed to the view that substantial numbers of musical works do. The musicological evidence pretty decisively indicates that many important works of music satisfy the intentionality condition.

Many musicians intend that many of their works represent the expression of emotion. In the seventeenth century, composers such as Caccini, Cavalieri, Monteverdi, and Barbara Strozzi, masters of the *stile rappresentativo*, explicitly took themselves to be representing the expression of emotion. Charles Avison, writing in the eighteenth century, noted that 'there are certain Sounds natural to Joy, others to Grief, or Despondency, others to Tenderness and Love'. The composer aims at 'imitating these various sounds'.[15] Composers carried this view into the nineteenth century. Wagner repeatedly makes clear, in *Opera and Drama*, that the true artist (such as himself) represents emotional speech. Presumably he intended that his music imitate this sort of speech. Classical musicians are not the only ones who aim to imitate the expression of emotion. African musicians and their descendants in North America and elsewhere imitate speech and other sounds in their music.[16] Blues legend B.B. King wrote that he experimented 'with sounds that expressed [his] emotions, whether

---

[14] Kivy, *Sound Sentiment*, p. 66.

[15] Pierre Dubois (ed.), *Charles Avison's Essay on Musical Expression With Related Writings by William Hayes and Charles Avison* (Aldershot: Ashgate, 2004), p. 6.

[16] Learthen Dorsey, '"And All that Jazz" Has African Roots!' in James L. Conyers (ed.), *African American Jazz and Rap: Social and Philosophical Examinations of Black Expressive Behavior* (Jefferson, N.C.: McFarland, 2001), p. 50.

happy or sad, bouncy or bluesy'.[17] (King speaks here of the expression of emotion, but it is hard to see how music could be an expression of emotion without being expressive of emotion.)

The testimony of composers is not the only source of evidence for the view that the intentionality condition is satisfied. Some composers do not explicitly speak of their music as depicting, imitating, or otherwise representing the expression of emotion. Nevertheless, the intentionality condition can be satisfied. The best guide to the intentions of composers is found, not in their writings, but in their music. It is highly unlikely that so much music, in so many styles and from so many periods, would so effectively resemble expressive behaviour unless musicians frequently intended to represent expressive behaviour. It seems that a good deal of music satisfies both the success and intentionality conditions by being expressive of emotion.

One might still doubt that music that is expressive of emotion represents emotion. Davies draws a sharp line between music being expressive of emotion and music representing emotion: 'There is all the world of difference between a work's being expressive and its being representational.' Davies identifies two reasons for drawing the distinction between music being expressive of emotion and music representing emotion. The first is that the intentionality condition is not satisfied. Davies recognizes that Kivy is wrong when he states that composers usually do not intend that their music be expressive of emotion. Nevertheless, Davies believes that music does not represent. His argument is that composers intend to write music expressive of emotion but do not intend to represent emotion. On his view, a necessary condition of representation (the intentionality condition) is not met. He concludes that music does not represent. Davies's second reason for thinking that music does not represent is that a work of music can represent only if it is a 'depiction'. According to Davies, music does not depict emotion.[18]

While Davies denies that music represents, he allows that music 'refers to' emotion or is 'about' emotion. (He apparently uses the concepts of reference and aboutness interchangeably.) Music is about emotion when a composer intentionally employs 'sounds with an expressive character'.[19]

---

[17] B.B. King, *Blues All Around Me* (London: Hodder and Stoughton, 1996), p. 123.
[18] Stephen Davies, *Musical Meaning and Expression* (Ithaca, N.Y.: Cornell University Press, 1994), p. 266.
[19] Davies, *Musical Meaning and Expression*, p. 266.

This is not enough, Davies believes, to make works of music representations of emotions.

Although Davies wants to draw a hard and fast line between music that is expressive and music that is representational, he fails to do so. As I have already argued, if composers intend to produce music in which audiences can hear human expressive behaviour, and audiences can hear human expressive behaviour in the resulting music, then music represents. Given that Davies accepts the resemblance theory (and has never reneged on it) the line between music expressive of behaviour and music that represents behaviour cannot be drawn. Davies tries to resist this conclusion. He holds that music that is expressive of emotion is merely about emotion or refers to it. The concept of aboutness is, however, very closely related to the concepts of representation and cognitive significance. Something cannot be about a second object without conveying some knowledge about the second object and representing it. This is as true of music as it is of anything else. Music cannot be about something without having cognitive significance and representing an object.

Davies makes a comment that makes even more remarkable his refusal to allow that music represents emotions. He allows that music can 'convey knowledge of the natures of emotions' of which it is expressive.[20] As the concept of representation has been analysed here, to say that something intentionally and successfully conveys knowledge is to say that it is a representation. Composers intentionally make their music expressive of emotion and listeners successfully recognize that music is expressive of emotion. If this, as Davies suggests, conveys knowledge of emotion, he has no grounds for saying that music does not represent.

This leaves to be considered Davies's belief that music does not depict emotion. Pictures depict by looking like the objects that they depict. Presumably a work of music would depict by sounding like the object that it depicts. In other words, the object is heard in the music. Davies holds that music cannot sound like the expression of emotion. He concludes that music cannot depict the expression of emotion. In fact, as we saw in Chapter 1, music often sounds like the expression of emotion. It is heard as a wail of anguish, as a threatening growl, joyful dancing, and a variety of other expressions of emotion. So long as music is heard as an expression of

---

[20] Davies, *Musical Meaning and Expression*, p. 271.

emotion, is intended to be heard as an expression of emotion, and has cognitive significance, then it is a representation of the expression of emotion. We have seen that the first two conditions are satisfied. All that remains is to show that music has (extra-musical) cognitive significance.

This follows readily from what has already been said. By listening to music, we will be able to obtain knowledge about human expressive behaviour. We can learn that sadness is expressed by slow, plodding motion, and that joy is expressed by quick, bouncing motion. We can learn that a high, piercing note expresses fear and anguish. In short, listeners can learn about the expression of emotion.

It must be admitted, however, that this knowledge is fairly trivial. Certainly anti-formalists might have hoped for more when they hypothesized that music has extra-musical cognitive significance. If music represents only by being expressive of emotion, it is hard to see how listening to music provides profound insight into the interior lives of humans. Aristotle talks of works of art that are not representations of 'states of character' but merely representations of 'indications' of a character. If musical works represent only behaviour expressive of emotion, they seem to represent only the indications of our interior states, not the interior states themselves. Another argument is needed to show that music represents in a manner that makes it possible for music to have important cognitive significance. (The representation of behaviour expressive of emotion is, by itself, not the source of profound knowledge, but the representation of such behaviour in conjunction with the representation of emotions can enhance the cognitive significance of music. This is a point to which I will return in Chapter 5.)

An argument for the conclusion that music represents and has important cognitive significance already exists and has been around since Aristotle. Earlier I discussed de Heem's representation of a desk with books, a violin, and so on. This picture is expressive of melancholy and, I would argue, is a representation of the expression of melancholy. Even if it is a representation of the expression of melancholy, it may not be a representation of melancholy. As Aristotle would say, a messy desk is an indication of a person's interior state, not a representation of it. Nevertheless, as I argued earlier, a still life can also represent an emotion. The key to this argument is the claim that a painting can do more than represent objects expressive of an emotion. It can also arouse an emotion in viewers and by doing so it represents the emotions themselves. This argument can be extended to music. Music as we have seen can arouse ordinary emotions. This fact can be used in an argument for the conclusion that music also represents emotion. An argument of this sort is not new. It is found in Aristotle's *Politics*. There Aristotle writes that paintings cannot represent 'states of character' (I do not agree with him on this point) but

> With musical compositions, however, the case is different. They are, in their very nature, representations of states of character... In the first place, the nature of the modes varies; and listeners will be differently affected according as they listen to different modes. The effect of some will be to produce a sadder and graver temper—this is the case, for example, with the mode called the Mixolydian. The effect of others (such as the soft modes) is to relax the tone of the mind.[21]

This passage is more cryptic than one could hope, but it seems clear that Aristotle is suggesting that music represents states of character (including emotions) by arousing emotions in listeners.

This is certainly how Aristotle was interpreted by Thomas Twining. According to Twining, Aristotle believes that music represents because 'the *general emotions, tempers,* or *feelings* produced in us by certain sounds, are *like* those that accompany actual grief, joy, anger, &c.'[22] The view that music represented emotion by arousing it was quite common in the eighteenth century. Rousseau was another author who held this view. In his *Dictionary of Music*, in the article on 'Imitation', Rousseau (himself a composer of sorts) writes that 'the art of the musician consists' in arousing in listeners 'movements' of the soul; that is, emotions. The musician 'will not directly represent things, but excite in the soul the same movement which we feel in seeing them'.[23]

Neither Aristotle nor any eighteenth-century author stated clearly the argument that music represents emotion by arousing emotion. The argument must be, however, that by arousing emotion, works of music satisfy the conditions for being a representation. Recall that these conditions are the content condition, the intentionality condition, and the accessibility

---

[21] Aristotle, *The Politics of Aristotle*, trans. Ernest Barker (Oxford: Clarendon Press, 1946), p. 344.

[22] Thomas Twining, *Two Dissertations on Poetical and Musical Imitation in Musical Aesthetics: A Historical Reader*, ed. Edward A. Lippman (New York: Pendragon Press, 1986), vol. 1, p. 245.

[23] Jean-Jacques Rousseau, *A Dictionary of Music*, trans. William Waring (London: J. French, 1775), pp. 198–99.

condition. If works of music represent, then composers must intend that their works arouse emotion. The accessibility condition will be satisfied if works of music actually arouse the intended emotion in listeners. Finally, by arousing emotion, works of music must have content (or cognitive significance).

The argument may be summed up as follows:

(1) Some works of music are intended by composers to arouse emotion.
(2) These works of music arouse in qualified listeners the emotions that composers intend to arouse.
(3) By arousing emotion, these works of music have cognitive significance.
(4) If composers intend their works to arouse emotion in listeners, the works arouse in listeners the emotions that composers intend, and by arousing emotions the works of music have cognitive significance, then some works of music represent emotion.

∴ (C) Some works of music represent emotion.

This argument is valid, but formalists will deny that it is sound. Likely they will hold that (1), (2), and (3) are all false. Anti-formalists will hold that all of the premises are true and that the argument is sound.

Before examining each of the premises in the argument, I should note that the use of an audience member's internal states in representation is not as singular as it might at first seem. Consider this example of similar representation. One of my friends lived for a couple of summers in Seville, Spain, where she experienced temperatures in excess of 50°C, a temperature to which I have never been exposed. I once asked my friend what it was like to experience such extreme heat. Rather than attempting to tell me what it was like (words would have failed to capture the experience), she gripped my wrist and squeezed. Feeling the pressure on my wrist, I immediately had a sense of what it was like to live through a summer in Seville. I think that we would say that my friend was representing to me what it is like to experience extremely hot weather. The three conditions of being a representation are satisfied. My friend intended to represent what it was like to experience 50°C. (In contrast, one does not represent pain merely by punching someone in the nose.) I could recognize that she was representing the experience of extreme heat and I gained knowledge of what the experience was like. The question now is whether these three conditions are satisfied in the case of music.

THE CONTENT OF MUSIC 107

Let us begin to assess this argument by considering premise (1) and the claim that composers intend to arouse emotion. Composers who intend to arouse emotion are easy to find. Several of these composers link the representation of emotion with the arousal of emotion. Leopold Mozart, for example, writes that, 'For the purposes of imitation or for the expression and excitation of this or that emotion [musical] figures... are devised' by composers.[24] Presumably he had himself in mind when he wrote this passage, so it is evidence that a composer intends to imitate (or represent) emotion by exciting it. Quantz had a very similar position: 'instrumental music, without words and human voices, ought to express certain emotions, and should transport the listener from one emotion to another just as well as vocal music does'.[25] This passage is noteworthy in that, like the passage from Leopold Mozart, it links the expression or imitation (or, as I would prefer to say, representation) of emotion with its arousal. While this passage is found in a flute method, since Quantz wrote music, the passage provides evidence about the intentions of a composer. Johann Mattheson, best known today as a music theorist, was also a composer. He wrote, in *Der vollkommene Capellmeister*, that emotions 'are things which can very naturally be presented with sound'.[26]

The eighteenth century was full of other composers who intended to arouse emotion. Gluck wrote that music is 'not only the art of entertaining the ear but also one of the greatest means of moving and exciting the senses'. He added that he 'sought great expression'; that is, he sought to move the passions.[27] C.P.E. Bach wrote, 'A musician cannot move others unless he too is moved. He must of necessity feel all of the affects that he hopes to arouse in his audience, for the revealing of his own humour will stimulate a like humour in the listener.'[28] Set aside Bach's view that a musician must feel the emotions he hopes to arouse in others. For present

---

[24] Leopold Mozart, *A Treatise on the Fundamental Principles of Violin Playing*, trans. Editha Knocker (Oxford: Oxford University Press, 1985), p. 111.
[25] Johann Joachim Quantz, *On Playing the Flute*, trans. Edward R. Reilly (London: Faber and Faber, 2001), p. 310.
[26] Quoted in Kivy, *Osmin's Rage*, p. 115.
[27] Wedwig and E.H. Mueller von Asow, *The Collected Correspondence and Papers of Christoph Willibald Gluck*, trans. Stewart Thomson (New York: St. Martin's Press, 1962) p. 109.
[28] Carl Philipp Emanuel Bach, *Essay on the True Art of Playing Keyboard Instruments*, second edn, trans. William J. Mitchell (London: Cassell and Company, 1951), p. 152.

purposes, the crucial feature of this passage is that Bach is yet another composer who intends to arouse emotions in listeners. Looking at the nineteenth century and beyond, one can find more composers who intend to represent emotion in their music. Beethoven indicates that his Symphony No. 6, Op. 68, is representational, but denies that it is a depiction of country sounds. Rather, 'it is [a record of] sentiments'. It is 'an expression of those sentiments evoked in men by their enjoyment of the country, a work in which some emotions of country life are described'.[29] Berlioz writes of 'depict[ing] a sentiment' in his music.[30] Elsewhere he says that the *Symphonie fantastique* represents not natural objects but expresses 'the *emotion* aroused in the soul' by these objects.[31] Shostakovich speaks unabashedly of what his symphonies are 'about'[32] and he clearly intended that his music be about inner lives. Not all composers agree, but enough composers have intended that their music arouse emotion and be representational for it to be clear that the intentionality condition has been satisfied by many pieces of music, among them musical masterpieces.

Not all of the composers just mentioned explicitly state that emotions are represented in music when it is aroused by music. However, it is difficult to see how else music could represent emotion. After all, music does not sound like emotion. At best, a work of music could sound like behaviour expressive of emotion. We would then be back to music representing behaviour expressive of emotion. As we have seen, it is difficult to see how music will have valuable cognitive content if it represents only behaviour expressive of emotions and not emotions themselves. Music can, however, have valuable cognitive content because of the way that it makes us feel. Paraphrasing Carroll Pratt, we could say that music feels the way emotions feel.

Let us next consider premise (2). Formalists, of course, reject this premise but it is an empirical claim that has already been partly established. The empirical evidence marshalled in Chapter 2 strongly indicates that music arouses a wide range of ordinary emotions. Listeners do not need

---

[29] Ludwig van Beethoven, *Letters, Journals and Conversations*, trans. Michael Hamburger (London: Jonathan Cape, 1951), p. 68.
[30] Hector Berlioz, *Life of Hector Berlioz as Written by Himself in His Letters & Memoirs*, trans. Katherine F. Boult (London: J.M. Dent & Sons, n.d.), p. 52.
[31] Quoted in Edward T. Cone, *The Composer's Voice* (Berkeley, C.A.: University of California Press, 1974), p. 84.
[32] Dmitri Shostakovich, *Testimony: The Memoirs of Dmitri Shostakovich*, trans. Antonina W. Bouis (New York: Harper & Row, 1979). See, for example, pp. 136 and 141.

THE CONTENT OF MUSIC 109

to imagine that they are feeling emotions, as some writers have suggested. The emotions are real. The fact that music arouses emotion is, however, not enough to establish the truth of premise (2). The emotions aroused by music cannot be just any garden-variety emotions. Works of music must arouse the emotions that composers intend that their works arouse, otherwise the accessibility condition is not satisfied.

The empirical evidence indicates not merely that music arouses ordinary emotions. It also indicates that the emotions aroused by music in qualified listeners are those that composers intend to arouse. As we saw in the first two chapters of this essay, listeners do not have just any emotion aroused by music. The same emotions are aroused in many listeners and these emotions are aroused by the properties that make the music expressive of emotion. The musicological record suggests that composers often intentionally endow their works with these properties. We can conclude, therefore, that premise (2) of the argument is correct. That is, the accessibility condition is satisfied.

This leaves us to consider whether, by arousing emotion, music has content. Having established that music arouses emotion (and that the emotions it arouses composers intend their works to arouse) it is a very short step to showing that music has content. Not for nothing do formalists so resolutely, and in the face of the compelling empirical evidence, resist the conclusion that music arouses emotion. Once this point is granted, it is clear that music has content. The content or cognitive significance of a work of music lies, in large part, in knowledge of the precise shades of emotion that it arouses. Hearing a piece of music, listeners come to know what experience of certain emotions are like by feeling those emotions. Listeners can also come to have knowledge about what it is like to experience certain patterns of emotion. By representing patterns of emotions, music can also represent character. These are points to which I will return in Chapter 5, where I will examine the value of music, including its capacity to provide insight into emotion and character.

While music has content, it has no meaning; that is, it has no semantic content. Such content depends on the existence of semantic conventions and these do not exist in the case of music. In the absence of semantic conventions in music, the representation in music cannot be semantic representation. Works of music cannot make statements whose meanings can be understood. Semantic content is not, however, the only sort of content. Above, a second form of representation, illustrative representation, was identified. Recall that *R* is an illustrative representation of an object when experience of *R* is relevantly similar to experience of the object represented. This is the sort of representation found in music. By arousing emotions in listeners, music illustrates those emotions. When listeners hear music they often have some ordinary emotion aroused in them. Consequently, experience of music is similar to experience of emotion in non-musical contexts. This similarity makes possible the illustrative representation of emotion by music. The similarity is (as we have seen) intended and it is detected by listeners in a way that brings the represented objects (emotions) to mind.

Formalists may try to find fault with the anti-formalist for saying that the content of music is ineffable. Kivy, for example, has criticized some opponents of formalism for having 'resort[ed] to the well-worn claim of ineffability'.[33] (One might pause to note that formalists are committed to the ineffability of musical beauty, as we will note in Chapter 5, but this would be to offer a *tu quoque* argument.) Kivy's animadversions are directed against the view that works of music have ineffable programmes. That is, he rejects the view that a work of music can have semantic content that is inexpressible. The view that music has semantic content, but that this content is ineffable, is, of course, untenable. Semantic content is, in its very nature, effable. Nothing is untenable about the view that we cannot capture in words what it is like to see red or feel fear. Of course, one can broadly characterize an experience. An experience of red may be described as vivid or warm. Such a description comes nowhere near capturing the full experience of red. Similarly, one could describe the experience of fear (either aroused by a present danger or by music) as tingling or harrowing. This description cannot convey all of what it is like to experience fear. The same point can be made with respect to experience of the emotions aroused by music. No description can fully capture what it is like to experience them.[34]

Some writers have suggested that we hear music as presenting (or representing) the emotional experiences of some particular person or

---

[33] Peter Kivy, *Music Alone: Philosophical Reflections on the Purely Musical Experience* (Ithaca, N.Y.: Cornell University Press, 1990), p. 54. See Nick Zangwill, 'Music, Essential Metaphor, and Private Language', *American Philosophical Quarterly*, 48 (2011), p. 3 for a different view of ineffability.

[34] For this point, see Diana Raffman, *Language, Music, and Mind* (Cambridge, M.A.: MIT Press, 1993).

THE CONTENT OF MUSIC   111

persona.³⁵ At least in the case of music without lyrics or a programme, I know of no empirical evidence that this suggestion is true. The empirical evidence strongly suggests that listeners feel joy, melancholy, and a variety of other emotions as they listen to music. This evidence does not also indicate that listeners experience the joy or melancholy as the melancholy or joy of anyone in particular. Long ago Ferdinand Hand observed that, 'Truly it is impossible to perceive in Beethoven's Funeral March [from the *Eroica Symphony*] whether a father mourns his children, or a lover his mistress, still, unmistakably is expressed therein the grief of life, in which such differences of outer relations vanish, but the heart is quite certain of its grief.'³⁶ I can only endorse this conclusion. Music seems to represent an emotion without representing the person who has the emotion. It represents a type of emotional experience, not the emotion of anyone in particular.

Without a persona, music cannot be a narrative art. Even when music is representational (and not all music is) it is not telling a story any more than still-life paintings or lyric poems tell a story. Insofar as music is representational it is simply a series of representations of expressive behaviour and the emotions that are aroused by the representation of expressive behaviour. Sometimes the representations last a few seconds. In other cases, they can go on for several minutes. Often, in extended works of music, representations succeed each other but I am not arguing that the successive representations amount to a story. I am sceptical about the claim that music can tell a story without the addition of a programme (such as that employed in Berlioz's *Symphonie fantastique*) or lyrics.

Instrumental music usually represents a type of emotion, not the emotion of some particular individual. With the addition of a programme or title, however, music can represent the emotion of an individual. C.P.E. Bach's Fantasia in F# minor (Wq 67) provides a good illustration of how music can represent the emotion of an individual person, in this case the composer himself. Bach headed the piece 'C.P.E. Bach's Feelings' (*C.P.E. Bachs Empfindungen*). Bach, writing years before any psychologist had studied the effect of music, knew precisely how to arouse affects by means of music. As we saw in the previous chapter, plodding musical

---

   ³⁵ Jerrold Levinson, 'Musical Expressiveness', p. 107.
   ³⁶ Ferdinand Hand, *Aesthetics of Musical Art; or, The Beautiful in Music*, second edn, trans. Walter E. Lawson (London: William Reeves, 1880), pp. 115–6.

lines are expressive of sadness and the work begins with a slow passage. Irregularities in rhythm and pitch are expressive of and arouse negative emotions in listeners. The slow passages are interrupted by extreme variation in rhythm and pitch. Listening to the piece, one feels alternately melancholy and frenzied. One is presented with a representation of the emotional states of Bach.

Emanuel Bach was not the only composer to represent his own emotions. During the Romantic period, composers frequently took themselves to be representing their own emotions. As we have seen, Robert Schumann believed that Schubert's music was a record of his emotions. If this is not evidence that Schubert intended to represent his emotional states, at least it is evidence that Schumann, who took Schubert as his model, did. Mahler stated that a composition originates in 'something the composer has experienced'.[37] The view that composers often represent their own emotions was not universally held in the Romantic period. Hanslick is the best known of the writers who doubted that music had much to do with emotion. Nevertheless, the view was widely held among composers of the period. Even when Romantic composers do not explicitly state that they are representing their own emotional states, the general attitudes of the period make reasonable the supposition that these are the particular states represented in their music. In general, however, we cannot say that the emotions represented in instrumental music are those of a particular individual.

The case of vocal music is completely different. When music is combined with lyrics, music can become a dramatic art. The emotions represented in vocal music are often those of a dramatic persona. They can also be the emotions of a particular individual or type of individual. This is a matter to which I will return in the next chapter.

Anti-formalist Objections

Many people—including many eminent composers—who believe that music has cognitive significance have spoken of music as expressing, rather than representing, emotion. Some distinguished philosophers who are opposed to formalism, among them Jenefer Robinson and Roger

---

[37] Knud Martner (ed.), *Selected Letters of Gustav Mahler*, trans. Eithne Wilkins, Ernst Kaiser, and Bill Hopkins (London: Faber and Faber, 1979), p. 179.

Scruton, have been explicitly sceptical about the view that music represents. They too have talked of music expressing emotion or otherwise having cognitive significance without representing. In this section I will show why their doubts about the capacity of music to represent music are misplaced. Talk of music expressing emotion can be replaced by talk of the representation of emotion.

Scruton, while no formalist, believes that music does not represent. Scruton identifies what he thinks is a crucial difference between representational arts such as literature and painting, on the one hand, and music on the other. When looking at a painting we can immediately see in the painting the object that it represents. Consequently, Scruton believes, paintings and works of literature convey thoughts (in Frege's sense of the term 'thought'). In other words, they have propositional content. In contrast, on Scruton's view, listeners normally cannot listen to, say, 'a symphonic poem' and 'know immediately what it represents'.[38] From this he concludes that music does not have propositional content. A work of music, Scruton believes, has meaning, but it does not mean 'anything specific'.[39] (As I have indicated, I think that to attribute 'meaning' to music is a mistake. Talk of content or cognitive significance is correct.) Scruton believes that representations have propositional content. They have truth-conditions while works of music do not. He concludes that music does not represent. Instead of stating specific propositions and representing, music is said to be expressive.

Scruton's argument is confused. He is certainly right when he says that works of music do not have propositional content, but mistaken in thinking that poems and paintings do. Scruton is right to note that Messiaen is not saying, in the *Catalogue des oiseaux*, 'Here is a blackbird, and it sounds like *this*.'[40] At the same time, however, Cézanne is not saying, in *Still Life with Plaster Cupid*, 'Here is what a plaster cupid looks like.' The painting makes no statements at all. It has no propositional content. That is, it has no meaning in the Fregean sense of the word. A similar point can be made about works of literature. For example, Jane Austen's *Pride and Prejudice* does not state the proposition that first impressions are a poor guide to a person's character. The content of paintings and works of literature that

---

[38] Roger Scruton, *The Aesthetics of Music* (Oxford: Clarendon Press, 1997), p. 130.
[39] Scruton, *The Aesthetics of Music*, p. 129.
[40] Scruton, *The Aesthetics of Music*, p. 129.

is interesting, from an aesthetic point of view, can no more be captured in propositional terms than can the content of musical works. Paintings and novels are no more used to make statements than works of music are so used.

Paintings, it is true, provide a basis for making statements. One can look at a painting, see a plaster cupid, and truly say of the painting that a plaster cupid is represented in the painting. This is, however, a red herring and we cannot conclude from it that paintings have propositional content. The statement that a plaster cupid is represented in a painting is a proposition about the painting and not a proposition made by means of the painting. The proposition that a cupid is represented in the painting does not capture the cognitive significance of the painting. The painting may be, for example, about melancholy and no account of the painting's cognitive significance that ignores this can be satisfactory. Scruton seems to have confused propositions made by means of paintings and propositions made about paintings.

According to Scruton, music has 'real but ineffable' content.[41] Since the content of music cannot be captured in propositional terms, Scruton says that the content (again, he uses the word 'meaning') is expressed, not represented. By parity of reasoning, he should conclude that paintings and works of literature do not represent either, for their content cannot be captured in propositional terms. He should either allow that neither paintings and novels nor music represent, or allow that all do. Scruton is free to use the word 'represent' any way that he likes, but a usage that excludes paintings and novels from the class of representations is an eccentric usage. I prefer a usage that allows that paintings, novels, and musical works all represent. Partly this is because I think that this is ordinary usage. This usage also acknowledges that music, literature, and paintings all have content in the same way.

It is true that one can immediately recognize that, say, a painting is a representation of a plaster cupid. Similarly a poem may easily be seen to represent shepherds. Once one has grasped this, however, one has not grasped all that the painting or poem represents. It may also represent melancholy or loneliness. The same double layer of representation is found in some works of music. Listeners may know immediately that a

[41] Scruton, *The Aesthetics of Music*, p. 143.

concerto or a symphony represents birdsong or church bells. (Scruton's view is that this is an 'imitation' of birdsong or bells, not a representation. Most philosophers accept the commonsense view that music can represent the sounds of birdsong and bells.) The same work of music may also be a representation of gaiety or gloom. It may not be so readily apparent that the musical work represents gaiety as that it represents birdsong. But in this respect concerti do not differ from paintings or poems.

It must be admitted that there is a distinction between representation in paintings and poems, on the one hand, and representation in musical works on the other. Paintings and poems typically represent ordinary objects such as plaster cupids and shepherds as well as, say, melancholy or pastoral contentment. A viewer will not grasp the full cognitive significance of a painting who does not first recognize that it represents ordinary objects. In contrast, symphonies and sonatas (unlike paintings and poems) typically represent melancholy and gaiety without first representing church bells and birdsong. This distinction between representation in music and representation in other arts does nothing, however, to support Scruton's position. None of the representation in paintings and poems is the sort that involves propositions. And the representation in paintings, poems, and symphonies that is of aesthetic value (the deeper cognitive significance, such as the representation of melancholy in a still life) is not propositional.

Robinson is another anti-formalist who believes that music 'only rarely *represents* the world'.[42] (Like Scruton, she believes that music can be expressive.) Robinson takes pictures as paradigm representations. A picture represents only when viewers can see in a painting what is represented. So, for example, a Gainsborough portrait represents Mrs Siddons only when viewers can see Mrs Siddons in the painting. In other words, Robinson believes that a necessary condition of something being a pictorial representation is that viewers be able to see in the painting what is represented. Robinson believes that if musical works are to represent, then a similar condition must be met. That is, she holds that a necessary condition of something being a musical representation is that listeners be able to hear in the music what is represented.

---

[42] Jenefer Robinson, 'Music as a Representational Art', in Philip Alperson (ed.), *What is Music? An Introduction to the Philosophy of Music* (University Park, P.A.: Pennsylvania State University Press, 1987), p. 184.

If music is to represent, Robinson holds, it 'must be subject to the "seeing-in" requirement'.[43] Just as a picture represents only if a qualified audience member can see what is represented in the picture, she holds, so a piece of music can represent only if one can hear in the music what is represented there. Robinson doubts that many works of music satisfy the hearing-in requirement. A few works of music do satisfy the hearing-in condition. In addition to the usual works that represent birdsong, Robinson mentions Mendelssohn's *Overture to a Midsummer Night's Dream*, in which one can hear the braying of an ass, and Honegger's *Pacific 231*, in which one can hear the chugging of a steam locomotive. Robinson regards these as exceptions to the rule. One cannot hear the sea in Debussy's *La Mer* or a spinning wheel in Schubert's setting of *Gretchen am Spinnrad*. At least, one cannot hear the sea or the spinning wheel without the assistance of a programme. A fortiori, Robinson would conclude, works such as Bach's Brandenburg Concerti or Mozart's symphonies are not representational. Even more obviously than *La Mer*, she thinks, they fail the hearing-in condition.

The trouble with Robinson's argument is that it is mistaken about what works of music represent. Beethoven in the *Pastoral Symphony* did not take himself to be representing physical objects. On the contrary, Beethoven makes clear that his Symphony No. 6 is about emotions. As we have already noted, he stated that the *Pastoral Symphony* is a depiction of 'sentiments' rather than merely a representation of rural sounds. A similar point could be made about other representational works of music.

When musical works are regarded as representing affective states (usually emotions), it is obvious that many works, including symphonies and concerti without a programme, easily satisfy the hearing-in condition. The empirical research on this point is quite clear. As we saw in Chapter 1, listeners readily hear emotions in music. Listeners hear joy in the Second Brandenburg Concerto and sadness in Mozart's G minor symphony, even though these works are without a programme. Often listeners will say something like 'This music is sad' or 'This movement is joyful', but this is just an elliptical way of saying that the music is heard as expressive of sadness or heard as expressive of joy. To say that the music is heard as expressive of sadness or joy is just another way of saying that we hear the expression of sadness or joy in the music.

---

[43] Robinson, 'Music as a Representational Art', p. 183.

While Robinson doubts that music often represents, she is an opponent of formalism and believes that music has extra-musical cognitive significance. She writes that, 'music, like painting, can and does characterize the world in new, inventive, and insightful ways, and in this way performs an important cognitive function'.[44] Music 'characterizes' or 'describes' the world, in Robinson's terminology, but it does not represent it, as pictures do. This suggests that Robinson believes that music has cognitive content that is 'expressed'.

Partly my disagreement with Robinson is terminological. A work of music that characterizes or describes will have cognitive content. (The choice of the word 'description' is unfortunate. Description involves the use of propositional content and music is not propositional.) I take it that a work of music that is expressive in Robinson's sense also has cognitive content. In any case, Robinson agrees that music has cognitive content and, by my lights, that makes it representational. At least, cognitive content is enough to make music representational so long as the other necessary conditions of being a representation are satisfied. There are, I believe, other advantages to eschewing talk of music expressing emotion. To express emotion literally means to display or manifest emotion. In Chapter 1 we saw that there is good reason to doubt that composers use their music to manifest their current emotional states. On the other hand, many composers intend their works to convey insights about emotion and this is best understood as an intention to represent emotion.

Formalist Arguments Against Representation in Music

Formalists have an array of arguments against the conclusion that music represents. Some of these arguments have been anticipated and undermined but others remain to be considered. It is to a consideration of these remaining arguments that we now turn.

I have maintained that there is a short step from saying that music is expressive of emotion to the conclusion that music represents expressive behaviour. Formalists, notably Kivy, deny that this is so. Even if music is expressive of emotion, Kivy is adamant that this view should not 'be

---

[44] Robinson, 'Music as a Representational Art', p. 182.

construed as the theory that music "represents" the voice and gesture of human expression, the way paint on canvas represents the visible features of the world'. He adds that the concept of representation 'does not capture the way we experience the emotion qualities of music'. He gives the following argument for his conclusion:

> We do not…hear sounds as representations of melancholy and cheerful behavior, the way that we see paint on canvas as a representation of melancholy and cheerful men and women, and *then* hear the music, in virtue of these representations as melancholy and cheerful. We hear the melancholy and cheerfulness of music immediately, in the music, and can be quite unaware of the features of the music in virtue of which it is melancholy. And even if we are consciously aware of the expressive-making features of the music, which we may frequently be, we do not perceive them as representations of anything.[45]

This passage is not as clear as it might be so I will attempt to restate the argument in more perspicuous terms. Kivy begins by indicating that our experience of emotions in paintings and in music is quite different. When we look at a painting, we see representations of, for example, people. Presumably, when we see a painting as melancholy these people are represented as expressing melancholy by their demeanour, attire, or in some other way. In contrast, we do not hear music as melancholy because we have perceived a representation of something that is melancholy. In the case of music, Kivy believes, listeners are directly aware of melancholy. Listeners may even be unaware of why they regard the music as melancholy. Even if we are aware of the properties that make a work expressive of an emotion, Kivy believes, we do not hear them as representations of anything. In short, in his view, music is not melancholy because it represents melancholy or anything expressive of melancholy.

This argument has several problems. The first is that the distinction between experiencing melancholy in paintings and in music is less sharply defined than Kivy would have us believe. Kivy says that we can perceive music as, say, melancholy while being unaware of what makes it melancholy. This seems to be false if the resemblance theory is correct. Recall that according to this theory, we hear music as expressive of emotion when we perceive that it resembles expressive behaviour. Moreover, both paintings and works of music seem to be expressive of emotion because experience of them resembles experience of behaviour expressive of emotion.

---

[45] Peter Kivy, *Introduction to a Philosophy of Music* (Oxford: Clarendon Press, 2002), p. 40.

Consequently, the difference between perceiving that a painting is melancholy and perceiving that some music is melancholy is rather elusive. On Kivy's view, a painting is melancholy because it represents the expression of melancholy. Some music is melancholy because it resembles the expression of melancholy. The only difference is that paintings are melancholy when they represent the expression of melancholy while music is melancholy when it resembles the expression of melancholy. If music is intended to resemble the expression of some emotion, then it represents the expression of that emotion, and the difference disappears completely. The music is melancholy because it represents behaviour expressive of melancholy.

The second problem with Kivy's argument is that it provides us with no reason to believe that music is not perceived as a representation. He allows that we may sometimes be aware of the properties that make music expressive of some emotion and then asserts that, 'we do not perceive [these properties] as representations of anything'. According to the resemblance theory, we perceive certain properties of music as resembling human expressive behaviour. It is unclear why this is not to perceive the music as representing human expressive behaviour.

We are, as Kivy grants, 'hardwired by evolution to read ambiguous patterns as animate whenever possible'. This explains why we '"read" music emotively where it gives us the opportunity to "read" it as animate'.[46] In this passage, Kivy mentions the 'seeing-faces-in-clouds phenomenon'. But when we see a face in the clouds, we are seeing the cloud *as* a face. And so the cloud is seen as resembling a face. Of course, the cloud does not represent a face because it is not intended as a representation. The case of music is different. Suppose that composers intend that emotions be heard in their compositions. It seems that we ought then to conclude that music represents emotion.

Finally, the argument under consideration is question begging, or very close to question begging. Ultimately, the argument comes down to saying that music does not represent because we do not perceive music as representing. This is one of the issues under dispute. The anti-formalist believes that we hear music as representational. It is no argument at all against anti-formalism simply to assert that we do not perceive music as representational. Reasons for believing that music does not represent need to be provided.

[46] Kivy, *Music Alone*, p. 176.

Another of Kivy's arguments against anti-formalism remains to be considered. This argument is very simple. I will call it the *argument from repetition*. The argument from repetition starts with the claim that 'musical repetition makes sense where linguistic repetition does not'. In everyday conversation, people do not 'repeat verbatim what they have just said a minute after they have said it'.[47] Just as repetition makes no sense in the course of ordinary conversation, the formalist will suggest, it makes no sense in the context of literature. On the other hand, repetition in music is commonplace. Sometimes we find note for note repetition, as when a whole section of an aria or symphony is repeated. Sometimes the repetition involves development, as in the case of works in sonata form. In either case, the argument from repetition suggests, repetition in music is inexplicable if works of music have content. We are invited to conclude that repetition would add nothing to the content of a musical work. This conclusion is not justified. The argument from repetition is unable to refute a well-formulated anti-formalism.

While there is a question about whether anti-formalism is able to explain the prevalence of repetition in music, formalism appears to have a simple explanation of this prevalence. Music, according to the formalist, presents listeners with sonic patterns which they find intellectually intriguing. Frequently, repetition is an integral part of a pattern, and the pattern is less interesting if the repetition is omitted. Kivy draws an analogy between musical patterns and an iterated design on an oriental carpet. The second or third repetition of the pattern on a carpet is not dispensable. A carpet would not be just as good without it. Its proportions would be less pleasing. Without the repeats, the carpet would provide less scope for the eye to delight in the twists and turns of the pattern. The formalist holds that musical repeats play a role analogous to the repetitions of a carpet. According to Kivy, a 'sonata movement is a sonic carpet, its repeats the burgeoning forth of its pattern'.[48] This may be part of the explanation of the appeal of repetition in music. Anti-formalists need not deny that listeners enjoy musical patterns. Anti-formalists will, however, argue that this cannot be the complete explanation of why repetition is common in music.

---

[47] Peter Kivy, *The Fine Art of Repetition: Essays in the Philosophy of Music* (Cambridge: Cambridge University Press, 1993), pp. 334–5.
[48] Kivy, *The Fine Art of Repetition*, p. 350.

The fact that repetition in literature is far more common than the argument from repetition suggests is a clue that something is wrong with the argument. Sometimes repetition in literature is verbatim. Sometimes only a few words are repeated, as in Donne's use of anadiplosis in 'The Expiration'. Repeated refrains at the end of verses, as in Tennyson's 'Mariana', and Homer's use of stock epithets (for example, 'Hector, tamer of horses' and 'gray-eyed Athena') are other examples. Sometimes longer passages are repeated. Consider, for example, the beginning of Book V of the *Odyssey*, where the council of the gods is a word for word repetition of a passage from Book I. Another example of verbatim repetition is found in these two passages from *Bleak House* (Chapter 18). In the first, Dickens writes:

'How d'ye do, Miss Dombey?' said Mr Toots. 'I'm very well, I thank you; how are you?'

Half a page later we find this passage:

'How d'ye do, Miss Dombey?' said Mr Toots. 'I'm very well, I thank you; how are you?'

Further examples could easily be provided.

Examples of repetition that involves development are equally easy to find. Dickens's novels abound with this sort of repetition. Early in *Bleak House* we find a poignant instance of this type of repetition. In Chapter 1, Louisa exhorts Fanny Dombey, lying on her deathbed, in these terms:

It's necessary for you to make an effort, and perhaps a very great and painful effort which you are not disposed to make; but this is a world of effort.

A little later, Louisa addresses the nursemaid, Richards, saying,

...you have only to make an effort—this is a world of effort, you know, Richards.

Perhaps even more poignant are the frequently repeated descriptions of the dying Paul Dombey as 'old fashioned'.

Repetition is common in ordinary conversation. Imagine that you are talking with a friend about which job offer to accept or about whether she should dump her unsatisfactory boyfriend. You are likely to find yourself saying the same thing over and over again or making the same point in slightly different words as you go over the pros and cons. In such a case, the meaning of your words is of secondary importance. Your tone of voice, your willingness to continue talking about the matter at length, and other considerations are much more important. Repetition does not add to the semantic content of literature or ordinary conversation, but it does contribute to literature's cognitive significance. One of its important functions is to arouse emotion. When, in the final line of the *Iliad*, Hector is, again and for the last time, described as a tamer of horses, any sensitive reader is moved:

hōs hoi g' amphiepon taphon Hektoros hippodamoio.

At the end of the day and after all, Hector was a tamer of horses. The point is not to inform us that Hector tamed horses. We feel Toots's awkwardness as he repeats his carefully prepared speech. When Louisa addresses Richards, we cannot help but be reminded of Fanny's death. With each iteration of the adjective 'old fashioned', readers more keenly anticipate young Paul's end. Talking to your friend about her career choices or boyfriend, your words are meant to encourage and calm. Your tone of voice and repeated reassurances are more important than any semantic content your words have.

The argument for repetition fails because it is based on a misunderstanding of how music has content. This misunderstanding is based on a misunderstanding of how language works. Sentences have meaning (semantic content) but that is not the only content that they have. In both the case where one is counselling a friend, and in the case of literature, language can also affect emotions. This effect on emotions adds another dimension to the content of the sentences. Kivy apparently ignores this dimension of language. In particular, he seems to believe that the only content of literature is semantic content. Kivy explicitly adopts a propositional theory of literature.[49] In the next chapter I will explain what is wrong with this theory of literature. Here I will only observe that the examples of repetition in literature just provided indicate that the content of literature depends in large part on its capacity to arouse emotion. Anti-formalists need not accept the view that musical works have content by making statements. Music, like literature, has content in virtue of its capacity to arouse emotion, not in virtue of a capacity to make statements.

---

[49] Peter Kivy, *Philosophies of Arts* (Cambridge: Cambridge University Press, 1997), p. 122.

The use of repetition in music can contribute to music's capacity to arouse emotion and, consequently, contribute to its content. An example from Bizet's *Carmen* illustrates how repetition can contribute to the arousal of emotion, just as it does in literature. Carmen's introductory aria ('L'amour est un oiseau rebelle') is vaguely dangerous, but at the same time sultry and alluring. At this point in the opera, Don José has not yet fallen in love with Carmen and the threat is not specific. After Don José has fallen in love with her, Carmen sings a reprise of her aria. Now her warning is much more sinister and menacing. When Carmen first sings, no one in particular is threatened. On hearing the reprise, however, the audience immediately realizes that her warning is meant seriously. More importantly, the intervening sections of the opera can lull the audience into a false sense of security. When an audience hears the return of the theme, they can recognize with a start and a feeling of horror that Don José is doomed. The capacity of the repeated music to evoke this response in an audience contributes to the content of music. The words Carmen sings do not add anything to what has already been asserted. Nevertheless, the repetition adds to the content of the opera. Someone who complained that people do not just repeat themselves would have missed the point of the use of repetition.

I have just given an example of the use of repetition in music with lyrics. The use of repetition in purely instrumental music can, however, contribute to the arousal of emotion. Music, as we have seen, arouses emotion by means of emotional contagion and by means of its somatic effects. The use of repetition provides enhanced opportunities for emotional contagion and for music to have a somatic effect.

The use of repetition in music contributes to the arousal of emotion in at least one more way. It establishes expectations and, as noted in the previous chapter, the violation of expectations can arouse emotions in listeners. This is true both of the use of repetition in literature and its use in music. Consider a literary example of this phenomenon. Each of the first six verses of Tennyson's 'Mariana' ends with a repeated refrain, with repetition within repetition:

> She only said, 'My life is dreary,
> He cometh not,' she said;
> She said, 'I am aweary, aweary,
> I would that I were dead!'

The seventh and final verse ends with a variation on the refrain:

> Then said she, 'I am very dreary,
> He will not come,' she said;
> She wept, 'I am aweary, aweary,
> O God, that I were dead.'

The variation of the refrain evokes an affective response in many readers which contributes to the content of the poem.

A similar effect can be achieved in music. A good example is found in Handel's cantata *Apollo e Dafne*, HWV 122. Most of the arias in this cantata are in da capo form, as were most arias of the period, but one aria is a notable exception. In the climactic aria of the piece ('Mie piante correte'), Apollo chases Daphne through the A and B sections of what gives every appearance of being an aria of the standard form. However, just at the moment when listeners expect the repetition of the A section, Daphne is suddenly transformed into a laurel bush. The expected A section never materializes. Just as Apollo is startled by Daphne's metamorphosis and the frustration of his expectations, the audience is startled by the frustration of their musical expectations.

The argument from repetition is based on the false belief that the only content is semantic content. In fact, the content of music and literature is partly the result of the effects that they have on the emotional states of audience members. Repetition, both in music and literature, can affect the emotional states of audience members.

The arguments of formalists are unable to undermine the conclusion that music represents, and has extra-musical cognitive significance. The experience of music is aesthetically rewarding and anti-formalists believe that the content of music contributes to the aesthetic value of many musical works. We need to examine the ways in which the content of music contributes to its value. We have already been provided with a clue about how music's capacity to represent contributes to its value. This clue is found in the widespread view that music provides psychological insight. However, before examining how the content of music contributes to its aesthetic value, I will briefly examine music with lyrics.

4
Music and Lyrics

Music and Lyrics: Allies or Antagonists?

Formalists typically believe that music and literature are fundamentally different arts. This view can be traced at least as far back as Hanslick. Formalists can admit that literature has content while denying that music does. Literature can be, even according to formalists, a representational art. They can even allow that literature arouses emotion. Consequently, when music is combined with lyrics, formalists can allow that the works that result from the combination represent extra-musical objects and arouse emotion. Of course, formalists believe that all of the arousal of garden-variety emotion and all of the representation will be done by the lyrics. From an anti-formalist perspective, in contrast, there is no fundamental difference between vocal music and purely instrumental music. Music and literature both arouse and represent emotion. (Literature, of course, can represent other things as well.) When combined, they can be particularly successful in providing psychological insight.

The debate about vocal music has focused on opera. Musical formalists, notably Kivy, believe that there is a 'problem of opera'. The problem stems, they believe, from a fundamental difference between the literary and musical elements of opera. On their view, literature is a narrative genre with semantic content and works of literature unfold in a manner determined by semantic considerations. In contrast, formalists believe, music is contentless form and makes sense only in purely musical terms. Formalists believe that composers face a stark choice when they set a libretto to music: they can compose music that is subservient to the text and enhances its semantic content, or they can write music that is successful in purely musical terms. They cannot, formalists believe, do both. This is the 'problem of opera'. Formalists only think that this problem exists because they are mistaken about both literature and music. There is no 'problem of opera'. The problem does not need to be solved. It needs to be dissolved.

Although the debate has focused on opera, the problem that formalists have identified applies to any vocal music. According to Kivy, a problem supposedly exists any time words are set to music: an 'inevitable conflict between the purely musical and music in the service of textual "representation" shapes, for all time, the aesthetics of opera, and, indeed, of all vocal music'.[1] The 'problem of opera' 'is only the extreme case of the problem'.[2] This problem is a remarkable discovery. People have been listening to vocal music for as long as music has existed and yet no one had noticed the problem until philosophers revealed its existence late in the day. Opera has been around for over 400 years, and yet people have quite happily been composing, performing, and listening to it, oblivious to the problem that haunts it. Four centuries of composers and critics have thought that words and music could be successfully combined as *dramma per musica*.[3] This is a clue that the 'problem of opera' is not a real problem. It is a philosopher's problem, a problem caused by a philosophical theory run wild. (That said, some philosophers, notably Aaron Ridley, have been critical of philosophers' suspicions about vocal music.[4]) Unfortunately, as Wittgenstein recognized in the *Philosophical Investigations*, the only cure for philosophical problems is more philosophy. Philosophy is the therapy that cures the problems it creates; hence the need for this chapter.

Not everyone who has spoken about problems with opera is speaking about the same problem. Sometimes, people speak of a problem of opera and mean nothing more than that composers of opera face a problem of getting words and music to work together. When Alban Berg used the phrase 'the problem of opera' in a 1928 essay, this was the problem to which he referred.[5]

---

[1] Peter Kivy, *Osmin's Rage: Philosophical Reflections on Opera, Drama, and Text with a New Final Chapter* (Ithaca, N.Y.: Cornell University Press, 1999), p. 15.

[2] Peter Kivy, *Introduction to a Philosophy of Music* (Oxford: Clarendon Press, 2002), p. 164. More recently, Kivy has suggested that the problem is restricted to opera. See *Sounding Off: Eleven Essays in the Philosophy of Music* (Oxford: Oxford University Press, 2012), p. 94.

[3] For this point, see Joseph Kerman, *Opera as Drama*, new and revised edn (Berkeley, C.A.: University of California Press, 1988), p. 10.

[4] Aaron Ridley, *The Philosophy of Music: Theme and Variations* (Edinburgh: Edinburgh University Press, 2004), ch. 3.

[5] Alban Berg, 'The Problem of Opera', in Richard Kostelanetz and Joseph Darby, *Classic Essays on Twentieth-Century Music* (New York: Schirmer Books, 1996).

Winton Dean speaks of the 'problems of opera'.[6] An opera production is more than a combination of words and music. It also involves acting, scenery, and (often) dance. A variety of problems must be overcome if these are to be effectively combined. For example, Dean notes that there is a problem of finding a pace that works both for music and for lyrics. For example, as is shown by Verdi's *Macbeth*, a work of literature must be highly compressed (in comparison to spoken drama) if it is to be successfully combined with lyrics. This is a genuine practical artistic problem, not one of the problems that philosophers concoct a priori. The 'problem of opera' of which Kivy speaks is, in contrast, an unsolvable problem. On his view, music and lyrics cannot work together towards a common end and any opera will necessarily have either musical or dramatic shortcomings.

The 'problem of opera' begins with formalism about music. (I will use quotation marks when talking of the philosophical problem or pseudo-problem as opposed to the practical problems.) Formalists believe that music is 'pure, empty decoration', comparable to a design on wallpaper, a pattern of colours viewed through a kaleidoscope, or the decoration on a Persian carpet.[7] Music is set apart from the other decorative arts, on this view, only by the intellectual challenge involved in grasping the structure of the music. The problem gets worse when literature is misunderstood. If a work of literature is seen as a series of statements whose only cognitive content is its semantic meaning, it will be difficult to see how (except very fortuitously) an opera can be both musically and dramatically successful.

According to Kivy, as composers grapple with the 'problem of opera', two outcomes are possible. In the first outcome, composers put music at the service of the libretto. The music is used to assist a libretto in conveying meaning; that is, semantic content. This outcome is found in the works composed in the *stile rappresentativo*. Kivy regards these works as 'music drama' rather than opera. Music drama is held to be unsatisfactory because the musical component of a work in this style will fail as pure music: it will lack musical interest. According to Kivy, 'After a while the *stile rappresentativo* begins to pall, whether it is by Peri, Caccini, or even Monteverdi.'[8] This is another clue that something has gone wrong

---

[6] Winton Dean, *Essays on Opera* (Oxford: Clarendon Press, 1990), p. 228.
[7] Peter Kivy, 'The fine art of repetition', in his *The Fine Art of Repetition: Essays in the Philosophy of Music* (Cambridge: Cambridge University Press, 1993), p. 348.
[8] Kivy, *Osmin's Rage*, p. 65.

for the formalist. The judgement that *Orfeo* is a masterpiece is a data point that cannot be disregarded. When someone finds himself writing that Monteverdi palls, the only thing to do is to go back and find out where the argument has gone wrong.

A second response to the 'problem of opera' is to err on the side of music. This is, in Kivy's view, opera proper, which he calls 'drama-made-music'.[9] One example of this solution is found in the operas of Handel. Here the drama is shunted off into the recitative. In the recitatives, particularly of the *secco* variety, music is the handmaiden of the lyrics and lacks interest qua music. Kivy suggests that the musical function of the recitatives is to make listeners impatient and whet their appetites for the ensuing arias.[10] In the arias, however, music is allowed free rein and the lyrics take a backseat. Kivy regards Mozart as a composer who goes even further towards making drama into pure music. We see this most clearly, Kivy believes, in Mozart's great dramatic ensembles: 'no better description of the Mozartian dramatic ensemble can be given, from the musical point of view, than a *sinfonia concertante* for voices and orchestra'.[11] According to Kivy, an entire opera (*Così fan tutte*) is a *sinfonia concertante* for four voices. Kivy believes that in the case of drama-made-music we are primarily interested in the opera qua musical form. This reading of the opera has, needless to say, not found many adherents, even among philosophers who are not anti-formalists.[12]

Not very many composers have been persuaded that there is a 'problem of opera'. Kivy tries to make the case that Mozart was aware of the problem. Kivy points to two well-known passages from a letter to Mozart's father. The first is the passage in which the composer describes his musical treatment of Osmin's rage:

...just as a man in such a towering rage oversteps all the bounds of order, moderation and propriety and completely forgets himself, so must the music too forget itself. But as passions, whether violent or not, must never be expressed in such a way as to excite disgust, and as music, even in the most terrible situations must never offend the ear, but must please the hearer, or in other words must never cease to be *music*, I have gone from F (the key in which the aria is written), not into a

---

[9] Kivy, *Osmin's Rage*, p. 232.
[10] Kivy, *Osmin's Rage*, p. 156.
[11] Kivy, *Osmin's Rage*, p. 235.
[12] See, for example, Stephen Davies, 'Così's Canon Quartet', in his *Musical Understandings and Other Essays on the Philosophy of Music* (Oxford: Oxford University Press, 2011), 141–50.

remote key, but into a related one, not, however, into its nearest relative D minor, but into the more remote A minor.

The second passage concerns Constanze's first act aria in *Die Entführung aus dem Serail*:

I have sacrificed Constanze's aria a little to the flexible throat of Mlle Cavalieri, 'Trennung war mein banges Los und nun schwimmt mein Aug' in Tränen.' I have tried to express her feelings, as far as an Italian bravura aria will allow.[13]

Together these passages are almost the entirety of the evidence Kivy provides for the claim that composers are aware of the 'problem of opera'. Kivy takes from these passages that Mozart accepted that the demands of musical 'syntax' placed constraints on his setting of a drama and that musical considerations dominated his thinking at the cost of dramatic concerns. In the first passage, the constraints are those established by key relationships. In the second, Mozart explicitly accepts the restrictions imposed by the conventions of the Italian bravura aria. Kivy takes Mozart to have given a clear statement of 'the problem of opera', but he has done nothing of the sort. Mozart has simply identified the musical resources that he will draw upon to capture the emotions associated with each passage. In order for there to be a 'problem of opera', Mozart's compositional choices must be in some way in tension with the text. Nothing in the passages indicates that Mozart believed that his compositional choices are in any way in tension with the texts he is setting. Kivy is not right simply because Mozart has a musical style and is aware of his compositional choices. Below I will return to this point and indicate that the choice of musical forms is not necessarily in conflict with dramatic ends.

Other composers have made statements that suggest the existence of a 'problem of opera'. For example, sometimes composers say that music must serve the lyrics. This way of speaking simply reflects the fact that, in most cases, a libretto exists before music is composed. In a successful opera, music and drama serve each other. Berg wrote that, in composing *Wozzeck*, he intended 'to make a music that serves the drama, and is in every instant conscious of this obligation'. This passage can easily be misunderstood. It might be thought to support the view that there is a 'problem of opera'. In fact, for Berg the problem of opera is the problem of

---

[13] Emily Anderson (ed.), *The Letters of Mozart and His Family* (London: MacMillan, 1938), pp. 1144–45.

finding a way for music and libretto to work together. There is no suggestion that by making a work dramatically successful, it will have musical shortcomings. On the contrary, a little earlier in the essay, Berg wrote that he 'wished nothing else apart from the desire to make good music, to fulfill musically the spiritual content of Büchner's immortal drama'.[14] This earlier statement cannot be ignored. Berg wants the music and drama to be complementary. If Berg saw himself as serving the text this was, in large part, because he was setting to music an already existing work that he regarded as an 'immortal drama'.

While there is little evidence that composers have thought that there is a 'problem of opera', formalists have been remarkably successful in persuading some philosophers that there is. Even people not sympathetic to formalism have become troubled by the problem. Jerrold Levinson, for example, believes that Kivy has discovered a genuine problem. Levinson identifies properties that are characteristic of a successful musical composition: 'continuity, balance, symmetry, repetition, motivic economy, harmonic coherence, rhythmic drive', and similar properties. In contrast, a successful opera will closely model 'the psychological character and progression of the behaviors and actions transpiring in the course of the drama'. The trouble is that 'Human reality is jerky, hidden, convoluted, unmeasured, rambling, and inconclusive; musical reality is flowing, perspicuous, punctual, directed, and definitive.' Consequently, 'the more music gives itself over to the slavish task of mimicking dramatic event, the less likely, except by accident, that it will achieve purely musical conviction'.[15]

Unlike Kivy, Levinson believes that the 'problem of opera' can be resolved without completely sacrificing literary ends to musical ones or vice versa. He believes that a tension exists between musical and dramatic desiderata but that compromises can be reached. The composer of opera must make musical compromises and the audience for opera must make allowances. He writes that when listening to an opera audiences need to adopt 'a different set of expectations or tolerances'.[16]

[14] Alban Berg, 'The Problem of Opera', p. 278.
[15] Jerrold Levinson, 'Song and Music Drama', in his *The Pleasures of Aesthetics: Philosophical Essays* (Ithaca, N.Y.: Cornell University Press, 1996), p. 54.
[16] Levinson, 'Song and Music Drama', p. 56.

One might wonder about whether the tension is as serious as Levinson suggests. He makes a mistake when he writes of the incongruity between music and human life. Human life has, indeed, many of the characteristics which Levinson attributes to it. This point is scarcely apropos. Composers of opera do not set human lives to music. They set a libretto to music. A libretto is a model of human reality that is frequently conclusive, directed, economical, open, and so on. Consider, for example, Nahum Tate's libretto for *Dido and Aeneas*. It could hardly be more conclusive, economical, directed, or open (for example, it is full of dramatic irony). Purcell's setting of the libretto certainly has all of these characteristics. Music can have the formal properties that Levinson identifies and yet still perfectly match a work of literature. That said, a work of literature sometimes models the unpredictability of life by being unpredictable. The problem of opera cannot be resolved if the formalist's presuppositions are not questioned.

Levinson makes a more fundamental error. He concedes too much to the formalist when he conceives of musical success in purely formal terms. Continuity, balance, symmetry, repetition, economy of motif, harmonic coherence, and rhythmic drive are neither necessary nor sufficient conditions of a successful work of music. One can easily name musical compositions with all of these characteristics that are musically unsuccessful and works of music that have none of them but are musical masterpieces. For example, C.P.E. Bach's Fantasia in F# minor, Wq 67, is discontinuous, unbalanced, asymmetrical, has a variety of motifs, and is (in parts, at least) lacking in rhythmic drive. It is not flowing, perspicuous, punctual, directed, or definitive. Yet it is a minor masterpiece of keyboard writing. Plenty of trivial music has any formal characteristics a formalist may wish to identify.

A successful anti-formalist strategy requires an anti-formalist criterion of musical success. One way in which music can be aesthetically valuable from an anti-formalist perspective, is to provide insight into emotion by arousing emotion. Of course, formalists believe that music cannot do this, but whether they are right is at issue. The 'problem of opera' can only be dissolved if the formalist's starting point is not assumed. The adoption of an anti-formalist account of musical success is only the first step towards the dissolution of the 'problem of opera'. We also need to understand what makes a work of literature, particularly a work of drama, successful.

Contrary to what formalists believe, literature and music can both be successful in the same way. They are not, in Kivy's phrase, 'antithetical arts'.[17] Both can successfully engage our emotions, and provide insight into the interior lives of humans. (This is not to say that literature and music cannot serve other purposes.) Moreover, both literature and music provide this insight into our affective lives in much the same way. Often music and lyrics are said to provide insight by being 'expressive', but this is a misleading way of describing these arts. It is better, as I have suggested, to say that works of art arouse emotion. As we have seen, this claim enjoys considerable experimental support. By arousing emotion music and literature can engage our emotions and provide the sort of insight that perceptive listeners have long reported finding in music and literature. In opera, music and words can work together to arouse emotion in complementary ways. Once it is recognized that music and literature both arouse emotion, and thereby provide insight, the 'problem of opera' dissolves. Music and lyrics (together with staging) can be partners in arousing emotion and conveying insights into human emotion. In an effort to demonstrate this point, I will examine how literature functions. Crucially, works of literature arouse emotion. I will then return to an examination of music and the ways in which it works (together with lyrics) to arouse emotion.

How Literature Works

The 'problem of opera' emerges in part out of a misunderstanding of works of literature, including dramatic works. The perception that there is a 'problem of opera' is partly the result of adopting a propositional theory of literature. According to this theory, (some) works of literature explicitly or implicitly make statements about the world. By making statements, on this theory, works of literature can provide insight into emotion, character, and other matters. Kivy explicitly adopts this theory of literature.[18] Music cannot make statements, he believes, but literature can. The propositional theory of literature is fundamentally mistaken. Works of literature do not

---

[17] Peter Kivy, *Antithetical Arts: On the Ancient Quarrel between Literature and Music* (Oxford: Clarendon Press, 2009).

[18] Peter Kivy, *Philosophies of Arts: An Essay in Differences* (Cambridge: Cambridge University Press, 1997), p. 122.

make statements. Literary works provide insight by changing how people see the world. One way of doing this is to evoke emotions. Kivy does not merely adopt a propositional theory of literature. He also extends this theory to opera libretti. Kivy uses some of Handel's operas to illustrate his view that libretti can be used to make statements. Kivy rejects Winton Dean's suggestion that, considered as works of music, 'Dall'ondoso periglio' from Handel's *Giulio Cesare* and the prison scene in *Arminio* can express 'with piercing intensity the brevity of life and the futility of mortal hopes'. Music can, Kivy believes, have no such semantic content. The libretto of such a work, however, 'expresses the proposition: life is short and hope is futile'.[19]

The propositional theory of literature is an answer to the question about how works of literature can provide insight into important matters (such as the brevity of life and the futility of mortal hopes). This answer is unsatisfactory for at least two reasons. The first is that it is hard to see how literature could provide insights into profound matters simply by making statements. The bare statement that life is short and mortal hopes are futile is not a deep insight. It is a bumper sticker. Perhaps if works of literature provide a series of statements that form an argument one could make the claim that literature could provide deep insights. It is very difficult, however, to extract an argument from works of literature. Certainly, I cannot think of any opera libretti that provide anything like the sort of argument found in a philosophy essay.

There is a more fundamental reason why the propositional theory of literature is unsatisfactory. A work of literature is not a series of statements. Most of the sentences found in works of literature are simply not the right sort of illocutionary act. In particular, they are not assertions. A sentence in a work of literature is not a statement of fact. Rather, sentences in works of literature are invitations to make-believe. If this problem could somehow be overcome, there is another reason why works of literature do not make statements. Nowhere will you find the libretto of *Giulio Cesare* say 'Life is short and mortal hope futile.' Instead, it says things like

> Ah, you breezes, for pity's sake
> Fill my breast
> And bring comfort, O gods!
> To my woe.

---

[19] Kivy, *Osmin's Rage*, p. 263. The passage Kivy cites is from Winton Dean, *Handel and the Opera Seria* (Berkeley, C.A.: University of California Press, 1969), p. 61.

> Tell me, tell me where
> The idol of my heart,
> The beloved and sweet treasure
> Of my life is now and what she is doing.

This does not literally say that life is short and mortal hopes vain. In order to claim that a work of literature is a series of statements one needs to argue that statements in literary works have secondary meanings. For example, the advocate of the propositional theory of literature needs to argue that the sentences quoted from *Giulio Cesare* somehow mean that, 'Life is short and mortal hope is futile.' I have argued elsewhere[20] that this is an untenable position. Meanings exist only in virtue of semantic conventions. There is no convention according to which 'Ah, you breezes, pray fill my breast and bring comfort, O gods, to my woe' means anything other than 'Ah, you breezes, pray fill my breast and bring comfort, O gods, to my woe'.

Yet literature can provide insights into matters such as the brevity of life and the futility of human hopes. This is possible because literature can shape audience members' perception of the world. One way it can do this is by arousing emotions in its audience, a point well established by psychology[21] and one not disputed by a formalist such as Kivy.[22] Jenefer Robinson makes this point using the example of *Anna Karenina*.[23] The statement that betraying one's spouse can lead to misery is not a substitute for reading Tolstoy's novel. The insight that the novel provides cannot be summed up in a statement. Rather, the insights that readers gain come from having their ways of looking at the world shaped in new ways. This shaping of perception is often accomplished by feeling emotions in response to the novel. I suggest that music can have content in very much the same way that literature does.

Music and literature arouse emotion in different ways. In particular, literature seems to arouse emotion in three ways that music alone cannot (unless some version of the persona theory is correct). The first of these

---

[20] James O. Young, *Art and Knowledge* (London: Routledge, 2001), pp. 44ff.
[21] P.N. Johnson-Laird and Keith Oatley, 'Emotions, Music, and Literature', in Michael Lewis (ed.), *Handbook of Emotions* (New York: Guilford Press, 2008), 102–13.
[22] Kivy, *Antithetical Arts*, p. 106.
[23] Jenefer Robinson, *Deeper than Reason: Emotion and its Role in Literature, Music, and Art* (Oxford: Clarendon Press, 2005), p. 156.

mechanisms is identification. Even though the characters in literature are generally imaginary, readers identify with them. By identifying with characters, readers are moved to feel the emotions experienced by the characters in the situations in which they find themselves. For example, readers feel fear when a character is in a dangerous situation. The second mechanism is sympathy. Readers feel emotions as a result of a sympathetic response. For example, readers feel pity for Anna Karenina. The third mechanism is association. Readers may find similarities between characters, or the situations in which characters find themselves, and the readers or their situations. The awareness of these similarities arouses emotions in readers.

The ways in which music arouses emotion differ from the ways in which literature arouses emotion. As we saw in Chapter 2, four mechanisms by which music arouses emotion are reasonably well established: automatic brain reflexes, emotional contagion, somatic effects, and the frustration and realization of musical expectations. While music and literature arouse emotions in different ways, there appears to be some overlap. We do not have a full picture of how literature arouses emotion until we are aware that some literature is designed to be read (or sung) aloud. When literature is delivered orally, some of the mechanisms by which literature arouses emotion resemble mechanisms by which music arouses emotion. Words can, when uttered, have properties akin to those of music and the sounds of words can have an emotional impact. A large majority (83%) of English phonemes appear more frequently in words with a specific emotional association. For example, the vowel sound in 'alone' is found more frequently in words regarded as sad (such as 'lonely' and 'low') than in words regarded as cheerful.[24] Poets take advantage of this fact to enhance the emotional impact of their work. For example, statistical analysis has shown that the poems of Milton, Pope, and Tennyson have more phonemes with a negative valence in sad passages of their verse than in cheerful passages. It seems likely that word sounds in libretti and other lyrics similarly contribute to an opera's emotional impact. This is, however, a matter for further empirical research. Another area that requires further research is the extent to which literature moves by means of other properties that it shares with music. Literature, particularly spoken drama and

---

[24] Cynthia Whissell, 'Sound and Emotion in Milton's *Paradise Lost*', *Perceptual and Motor Skills*, 113 (2011), 257–67.

recited poetry, has a series of properties in common with music. These include rhythm and assonance.

While further research is needed, even the available evidence indicates that the audible properties of literature contribute to the arousal of emotion. Just as music heard as expressive of some emotion arouses that emotion by contagion so does literature heard as expressive of emotion lead to emotional contagion. Experimental evidence shows that the tone of voice in which an emotionally neutral text is spoken will have an impact on the affective states of listeners.[25] The articulation of a given phoneme has an impact on the facial expression of the person who utters it. The word 'alone', for example, causes the face to droop in a manner expressive of sadness.[26] The letter 'e' (as in 'cheese') brings a smile to faces, as every photographer knows. These facial expressions elicit sympathetic emotional responses in interlocutors.[27] Likely the expressive delivery of words in song enhances the words' emotional impact.

There is one crucial difference between the emotions aroused by literature and the emotions aroused by music. The semantic properties of literature make it possible for the emotions aroused by literature to have properties lacked by the emotions aroused by music alone (that is, music without lyrics or a programme). In particular, the emotions aroused by literature can be directed at some specific object. For example, in reading *Bleak House* one can be angry about the Court of Chancery or feel sad about the lot of orphans whose fate is determined by the court. Sometimes literature can arouse objectless emotions. A lyric poem may, for example, arouse melancholy without arousing melancholy about anything in particular. As noted in Chapter 3, music alone, without lyrics or a programme, seems able only to arouse objectless emotions. For example, a sonata or a symphony arouses joy *tout court* rather than joy about something in particular. This suggests that music and literature combined can do more than music alone, a point to which I will return below.

---

[25] Roland Neuman and Fritz Strack, '"Mood Contagion": The Automatic Transfer of Mood Between Persons', *Journal of Personality and Social Psychology*, 79 (2000), 211–23.

[26] Cynthia Whissell, 'Emotion Conveyed by Sound in the Poetry of Alfred, Lord Tennyson', *Empirical Studies of the Arts*, 20 (2002), p. 140.

[27] Riitta Hari and Miiamaaria V. Kujala, 'Brain Basis of Human Social Interaction: From Concepts to Brain Imaging', *Physiological Reviews*, 89 (2009), 453–79.

The net result of these reflections is that music and literature can both act by a series of mechanisms to arouse emotions in audiences. Sometimes the mechanisms are different and sometimes they are the same. Even when the two art forms employ different mechanisms, in the hands of a skilful composer they can work in concert to affect the emotional states of audience members. This is the key to realizing that the 'problem of opera' is a pseudo-problem. Both music and literature owe at least some of their content to the capacity to arouse emotion. More needs to be said, however, about music's capacity to arouse emotion, about which the formalist is so sceptical.

Music and the Arousal of Emotion, Again

The most fervently held tenet of the formalist's credo states that music alone does not arouse common- or garden-variety emotions. They can allow that music in combination with lyrics arouses emotion, but all of the arousal is done by the words (and, perhaps, other extra-musical factors). As we have seen, the experimental and anecdotal evidence for the claim that music (without lyrics) arouses emotion is now overwhelming. Rather than rehash this evidence, I will discuss a few experiments that specifically examine the effect of music and lyrics on emotion. These experiments include components that examine the capacity of music to arouse emotion independently of lyrics. These components of the experiments confirm the results obtained in the large body of experiments that have focused exclusively on instrumental music.

One series of experiments by S. Omar Ali and Zehra F. Peynircioğlu indicates that music contributes more towards the arousal of emotion than lyrics do. In their first experiment, thirty-two melodies (from classical music, jazz, and movie soundtracks) were selected, divided into quarters, each expressive of one of four emotions: happiness, sadness, calmness, and anger. (Prior testing ensured that the melodies were unfamiliar to the test subjects so that any emotional arousal could not be attributed to prior associations.) Half of each of the eight melodies associated with each emotion included lyrics expressive of that emotion. Test subjects randomly listened to the melodies with and without the lyrics and then reported the extent to which the music had aroused each of the four emotions. An interesting result was found: the test subjects 'rated the emotion conveyed only by melodies as more intense than that conveyed by the same melodies coupled with lyrics'.[28] This suggests that, when music and lyrics are combined in a composition, the music contributes more to the arousal of emotion than the lyrics do.

This conclusion was reinforced by additional experiments conducted by the same psychologists. In the next experiment, melodies expressive of a given emotion were matched with lyrics expressive of that emotion and with lyrics expressive of another emotion. Test participants heard melodies paired with four different lyrics, each expressive of a different emotion. For example, one group of subjects heard sad melodies that were combined with sad lyrics and with lyrics expressive of the other three emotions (happiness, calmness, and anger). As would be expected, the highest arousal ratings were received when the music and lyrics were expressive of the same emotion. Both music and lyrics contributed to the arousal of emotion. Again, however, the experiment showed that the music makes a more important contribution to the arousal of emotion than the lyrics do.

This was shown by the results from the cases in which the melodies and lyrics were mismatched. When melodies expressive of happiness were combined with lyrics expressive of sadness, test subjects still reported that happiness was aroused. Less happiness was aroused than when lyrics and music were both expressive of this emotion, but the subjects still reported the arousal of happiness. In contrast, when the lyrics were expressive of happiness, and the music expressive of another emotion, the subjects reported a markedly lower arousal of happiness. The authors of the study conclude that 'melodies were indeed the dominant element' when it comes to arousing emotion.[29]

The outcome of these experiments confirms results found in an earlier experiment, which concluded that 'music, not lyrics, had a more powerful influence in changing mood'.[30] The experimental evidence strongly suggests that music and lyrics have a cumulative emotional impact on listeners. The best available evidence suggests that the impact of music is greater than that of lyrics.

Some final experiments in the most recent series are particularly interesting for the study of opera. The experiments show that music is able to

---

[28] S. Omar Ali and Zehra F. Peynircioğlu, 'Songs and emotions: are lyrics and melodies equal partners?' *Psychology of Music*, 34 (2006), p. 517.

[29] Ali and Peynircioğlu, 'Songs and emotions', p. 521.

[30] Shaden Demise Sousou, 'Effects of Melody and Lyrics on Mood and Memory', *Perceptual and Motor Skills*, 85 (1997), 31–40.

have an impact on emotional responses to pictures. This is relevant since operas are visible as well as audible. In the first of the experiments involving pictures, participants heard melodies with lyrics while viewing pictures of common objects. Each melody was paired with four different lyrics. So, for example, a melody expressive of happiness was paired with lyrics expressive of happiness and with lyrics expressive of sadness, calmness, and anger. One group of subjects heard the melody paired with the happy lyrics, a second the melody paired with sad lyrics, and so on. The participants were asked to rate how happy the pictures made them feel. The outcome of this experiment was in keeping with the previous results. The melody was the most important factor in determining the emotion aroused by the pictures.

The highest arousal of a given emotion was reported when both music and lyrics were expressive of that emotion. So, for example, the pictures aroused the most happiness when viewed while listening to music and lyrics expressive of happiness. The second highest arousal of emotion was reported when the music was expressive of the aroused emotion, but the lyrics were not. When the lyrics were expressive of an emotion (say, happiness) but the music was expressive of another emotion (say, sadness), the pictures were found to arouse low rates of the emotion of which the lyrics were expressive and higher rates of the emotion of which the music was expressive. Again, music had more impact on emotional states than did lyrics. Pictures by themselves (that is, viewed without any music or lyrics) had a lower tendency to arouse some emotion than pictures viewed with music and lyrics expressive of that emotion.

The relationship between music and moving pictures may be helpful in shedding light on the role of music in opera. Many studies have examined the relationship between music and motion pictures.[31] These studies have consistently indicated that music has an impact on how moving images are perceived. Music expressive of happiness will lead audience members to perceive a scene as happy while music expressive of sadness will have the opposite effect. A recent study has confirmed that music and images work together to arouse emotions in audiences.

---

[31] For a review of the experimental literature, see Annabel J. Cohen, 'How Music Influences the Interpretation of Film and Video: Approaches from Experimental Psychology', in Roger A. Kendall and Roger W.H. Savage (eds.), *Perspectives in Systematic Musicology* (Los Angeles, C.A.: Department of Ethnomusicology, University of California, Los Angeles, 2005), 15–36.

This study combined video clips with musical tracks expressive of an opposite emotion.[32] So, for example, test participants viewed a video clip while listening to music expressive of negative emotion and music expressive of positive emotion. The participants were asked to report the emotion aroused by the combination of the music and the images. A variety of physiological changes were also measured. Since the video clips were the same on each occasion, differences in response could be attributed to the differences between the music tracks. The results indicate that music and video worked together to arouse emotion in test subjects. For example, when positive music and positive images were combined, subjects reported higher arousal of emotion. Perhaps most interestingly, music could arouse one emotion even when the video was expressive of an opposite emotion. For example, positive music led test subjects to report higher arousal of positive emotions, both when viewing positive and negative video clips.

The physiological data collected in this experiment were less clear-cut. As previous studies have shown, music affects heart rate and skin conductance. These changes indicate that emotional responses have been aroused. (I will discuss these further below.) However, music affected heart rate and skin conductance only when music was combined with positive films. This shows that emotional responses to films are somewhat unpredictable. Nevertheless, the experiment indicates that, just as words and music can work together to arouse emotion, so can music and images similarly work together.

These results suggest that a considerable part of the emotional responses that opera audiences experience, when viewing an opera, will be attributable to the music they are hearing. Likely acting is experienced as arousing a given emotion in part because opera audiences have that emotion aroused by the music. This is contrary to the prediction of formalists who believe that any ordinary emotions opera goers experience will be a response to the acting that they see (and the lyrics that they understand).

Psychological experiments have shed some light on the question of why music tends to contribute more than lyrics to the arousal of emotion. In a series of experiments subjects were presented with unpleasant musical stimuli (including dissonant chords and notes with harsh timbres) and

---

[32] Robert J. Ellis and Robert F. Simons, 'The Impact of Music on Subjective and Physiological Indices of Emotion While Viewing Films', *Psychomusicology*, 19 (2005), 15–40.

pleasant musical stimuli (including consonant chords and notes with pleasing timbres). After hearing the stimuli, the subjects were shown a word with a positive or negative valence. The words with a positive valence included 'charm', 'harmony', 'peace', 'love', and so on. The words with a negative valence included 'fear', 'anger', 'hatred', 'suffering', and so on. Test subjects were asked to decide as quickly as they could whether the meaning of the word was pleasant or unpleasant. When the subjects heard a word with a valence that did not match the valence of the sound stimuli, the subjects took longer to determine the valence of the word than when the valences of the stimuli and words matched. For example, having heard a dissonant chord, the subjects took longer to determine that a word such as 'love' has a pleasant meaning than they did when they viewed the word after hearing a pleasant sound stimuli. These results hold for both trained musicians and non-musicians. The experimenters concluded that the perception of word meaning and expressiveness is shaped by musical stimuli.[33]

Another experiment, which focuses on opera, provides results that show that both music and lyrics contribute to the arousal of emotion. In this experiment, the classic performance of *Tosca*, featuring Maria Callas and Renato Cioni, filmed at Covent Garden in 1964, was at the heart of the experiment.[34] The test subjects were Romanian students who had no knowledge of Italian and who were unfamiliar with Puccini's opera. One group of participants in the experiment heard excerpts from Act II of the performance of the opera three times. The first time they heard a sound recording of the performance (without knowing the meaning of the libretto). The second time they heard the sound recording after having been told the plot of *Tosca*. Finally this group of test subjects watched the video of the performance. After each listening, the test subjects reported the extent to which emotions were aroused. The experimenters also monitored a wide range of physiological responses in the subjects each time they heard the opera excerpts. A control group heard the sound recording of the performance three times without being told the plot or seeing the video.

---

[33] Nikolaus Steinbeis and Stefan Koelsch, 'Affective Priming Effective of Musical Sounds on the Processing of Word Meaning', *Journal of Cognitive Neuroscience*, 23 (2010), 604–21.

[34] Felicia Rodica Balteş, Julia Avram, Mircea Miclea, and Andrei C. Miu, 'Emotions induced by operatic music: Psychophysiological effects of music, plot and acting', *Brain and Cognition*, 76 (2011), 146–57.

The results of the study reinforce the view that music and lyrics (and the visual aspects of opera performances) work together to arouse emotion in listeners. I will focus on the results that are most relevant to present purposes. When the listeners were aware of the plot, they reported the arousal of higher levels of sadness. When the video was added, the arousal of sadness went up again. But prior to knowing the plot or seeing the video, subjects still reported the arousal of sadness. A similar pattern was found with the arousal of tension. The group that listened to the sound recording by itself three times did not report any significant differences in emotional arousal from hearing to hearing.

When we look at the physiological measures we also find some interesting results. In some cases, the physiological changes were more marked when the test subjects listened to the music without knowing the plot or seeing the video. For example, inter-beat intervals (that is, the intervals between heartbeats) were highest when listening to the music for the first time (in ignorance of the plot and without video). Changes to inter-beat intervals are indications of emotional arousal. Skin conductance levels, which have been found by some experimenters[35] to be particularly good measures of emotional response, varied most from the baseline measures the first time the test subjects heard the music, that is when they heard the music in ignorance of the plot and without video. (Some physiological measures showed greater variation from the baseline measures as knowledge of the plot and video were added to the experiment.)

Experimental evidence supports the view that music and lyrics work together to the same end, namely arousing emotion in listeners. The empirical evidence thus supports Levinson's proposal that opera is an 'integrative' hybrid.[36] That is, the lyrics and the musical elements of opera (together with the visual elements) work together towards a common end. Having established that both literature and music arouse emotion, we can proceed to dissolve the 'problem of opera'.

---

[35] Nikki S. Rickard, 'Intense emotional responses to music: a test of the physiological arousal hypothesis', *Psychology of Music*, 32 (2004), 371–88.

[36] Jerrold Levinson, *Music, Art, and Metaphysics* (Ithaca, N.Y.: Cornell University Press, 1990), p. 35.

Music Plus Lyrics Equals Music Drama

The view that opera has psychological depth or is a source of psychological insight is a commonplace of opera criticism. For example, at the outset of this book, I noted that Abert praises Mozart for his 'true psychological insight' in his treatment of Donna Elvira.[37] Formalists are adamantly opposed to this view. The psychological depth of opera is, Kivy believes, 'an illusion'.[38] (Strangely, however, he also writes that 'the most favored and most successful subject of musical representation in opera...is human emotion'.[39]) The most recent empirical evidence indicates that formalists are wrong and the insightfulness of opera is not an illusion. The available evidence suggests that both literature and music arouse emotion. Opera (and other forms of vocal music) involves the coordination of two arts that both arouse emotion. Combined, as they are in opera, music and literature can work together to arouse emotion. This combination makes it possible for opera to be a source of psychological insight into emotion.

Not everyone who believes that opera has content has talked about the emotions. Often opera is said to provide insight into character or human nature, but this is to say much the same thing. Character is largely to be understood in terms of emotional responses. For example, a person who feels a given range of emotions may be said to have a passionate character. A person with a resolute and courageous character feels another range of emotions. A person of bad character is subject to anger and jealousy. There is more to character than emotional dispositions. Character is also to be partly understood in terms of principles: a person of upright character consistently adheres to certain moral principles. Nevertheless, if we know what emotions people feel, and what they feel these emotions about, we know a good deal about their characters. Similarly, the suggestion that music provides insight into human nature is closely allied to the claim that it provides insight into emotion. There is more to human nature than emotion, but emotion is a large part of human nature.

Opera provides insight into emotion by arousing emotion. As I have argued in Chapter 3, by arousing emotion music also represents emotion. Oddly, this position receives support from the leading advocate

---

[37] Hermann Abert, *W.A. Mozart*, trans. Stewart Spencer (New Haven, C.T.: Yale University Press, 2007), p. 1101.
[38] Kivy, *Osmin's Rage*, p. 269.
[39] Kivy, *Osmin's Rage*, p. 254.

of formalism. Speaking of Handel's da capo arias, which he describes as 'emotive soliloquies', Kivy says that these works can be 'a recognizable representation of the leading emotion: that is to say, a representation of its phenomenology and behaviour manifestations'.[40] (Kivy adopts the peculiar view that Handel adopted a Cartesian theory of the emotions and that his arias reflect his Cartesianism. This aspect of his views can be safely ignored for present purposes.[41]) It is hard to see how opera can represent the phenomenology of emotion save by arousing emotion. Formalists have only ever had one argument against the proposal that music represents emotions by arousing them. The key premise in this argument is that music does not arouse garden-variety emotions.

Formalists also doubt that there is enough drama in opera to arouse emotion. Sometimes the text of a libretto may be the source of insight into our interior lives. Kivy gives the example of Berg's *Wozzeck* which preserves much of the plot of Büchner's play. (The example is an odd one, given Berg's view that his opera is a drama.) In order to gain access to this insight, however, a listener would need to concentrate on the words and 'treat Berg's score as so much background noise, to be filtered out as much as possible'.[42] This can scarcely be the right way to listen to an opera, which Kivy regards as an essentially musical genre.

The empirical evidence strongly suggests that formalists are wrong. Opera does arouse emotion. The emotion is aroused by the text, how the text is expressed and by musical form. The use of musical form does not lead to the conclusion that there is a tension between music and lyrics. On the contrary, musical form works together with the lyrics to arouse emotion and to form a coherent musical drama.

The da capo aria is an instructive case in point. Kivy takes it that the repetition found in such an aria puts music and lyrics in conflict and provides us with a striking illustration of the 'problem of opera'. The problem is that Kivy is wrong about both literature and music. The libretto of an opera makes statements no more than any other literature does. The libretto is in the business of arousing emotion. Repetition does not add

---

[40] Kivy, *Osmin's Rage*, p. 168.
[41] Michael Tanner is sceptical about the suggestion that Handel's operas display the influence of Cartesian psychology. See his 'Review of Joseph Kerman, *Opera as Drama*, new and revised edn, and Peter Kivy, *Osmin's Rage: Philosophical Reflections on Opera, Drama, and Text*', *Cambridge Opera Journal*, 1 (1989), 299–306.
[42] Kivy, *Osmin's Rage*, p. 270.

semantic content to a text, but it may contribute to the text's capacity to arouse emotion. As the empirical evidence indicates, increased use of phonemes with a particular emotional association will contribute to the emotional impact of a text. As phonemes are repeated in the course of an aria, the emotional impact will be intensified. Research has shown that the repeated reading of a statement intended to elate subjects (such as 'This is great—I really do feel good—I *am* elated about things') has a positive effect on mood. Repeatedly reading a depressing statement has a negative effect on mood.[43] Repetition of words also increases the opportunity for emotional contagion. This indicates that the repetition found in a da capo aria is not simply empty form.

The use of the da capo form can also enhance the emotional impact of a work in another way. Eighteenth-century theorists maintained that the contrasting B section enabled the A section, on its return, to arouse the passion represented in the first section with renewed vigour.[44] Empirical evidence now suggests that these theorists were right and that we feel an emotion more intensely when it is juxtaposed with a contrasting affect.[45]

A departure from an expected musical form can, in the manner Meyer suggests, arouse emotions. We have already considered the example of Handel's *Apollo e Dafne*, where Apollo chases Daphne through what appears to be a standard da capo aria. We hear what appears to be a standard A section, then what appears to be a standard B section, but the A section never reappears. At the moment when Daphne is transformed into a laurel tree, a brief, confused accompagnato ensues. The conventions of musical form are violated in Handel's cantata, but the passage is emotionally engaging. Many similar examples can be given of the violations of expectations established by operatic conventions being used to induce emotional responses. Act I, Scene 5 of Handel's *Orlando* (in particular, 'Ritornava al suo be viso') provides another instance where the conventions of the da capo aria are violated for dramatic effect. The anti-formalist will argue that, if the music is emotionally engaging, then it is musically successful.

---

[43] Emmett Velten, Jr, 'A Laboratory Task for Induction of Mood States', *Behavior Research and Therapy*, 6 (1968), 473–82.
[44] Dean, *Handel and the Opera Seria*, p. 10.
[45] Charles O. Nussbaum, *The Musical Representation: Meaning, Ontology, and Emotion* (Cambridge, M.A.: MIT Press, 2007), p. 198.

Berg's *Wozzeck* provides another illustration of how the use of musical forms is not incompatible with enhancing dramatic ends. As noted above, Berg wished in his opera to compose music that 'serves the drama'. His method of serving the drama involves the employment of a variety of musical forms including the passacaglia, rondo, sonata, fugue, and several others. Similarly, 'Dido's Lament', from Purcell's *Dido and Aeneas*, is dramatically compelling and also takes the form of a passacaglia.

Sometimes when music is coordinated with lyrics musical forms may be employed that would not be employed in instrumental music. We should not conclude from this that vocal music is, from a strictly musical perspective, less than satisfactory. For a start, there is no strictly musical perspective, if this means that musical form is all that is relevant to determining the aesthetic value of a composition. Musical success is (at least sometimes and in part) measured by the degree to which a work is emotionally engaging. At any rate, the success of a piece of music, contrary to what formalists believe, is in large part a function of its capacity to arouse and provide insight into emotion.

We do not need (as Levinson suggests) to adapt the standards of musical excellence when judging operas so long as we have adopted accurate measures of musical excellence in the first instance. *Orfeo* may 'pall' by some arbitrarily chosen formalist standards, but it successfully engages listeners' emotions and is a great work of music.

As noted previously, the empirical evidence suggests that when music and lyrics are combined, music does more than the lyrics to arouse emotion. This supports the widely held view that, in the hands of a great composer, the music of an opera contributes more to emotional insight than does the libretto. Winton Dean, for example, writes that a Handel opera 'tells us far more about human nature than we could ever guess from the libretto'.[46] It is fair to say (as Kivy does)[47] that Da Ponte's libretti are not profound, and yet Mozart's settings of them frequently are. While the words, by themselves, are not emotionally engaging (in part because they must be so terse), the music certainly is. Ultimately, I agree with Kivy that opera is essentially a musical genre if by this it is meant that most of the emotional impact of an opera is produced by the music.

---

[46] Dean, *Handel and the Opera Seria*, p. 122.
[47] Kivy, *Osmin's Rage*, p. 269.

Working together, music and drama can do more than music can do alone. Kivy states the motto, '*What music can't do, opera can't do.*'[48] This seems to be false. The combination of words and music can give specificity to emotional responses. Listening to instrumental music, an emotion such as despair or joy is aroused. When words and music are combined, the emotion aroused can be despair at the thought of romantic betrayal or the joy of triumph over an enemy. This seems to be what Thomas Twining had in mind when he wrote that

...the *expressions* of Music considered in itself, and *without words*, are, (within certain limits), vague, general, and equivocal. What is usually called its power over the *passions*, is, in fact, no more than a power of raising a *general emotion, temper*, or *disposition*, common to several different though *related*, passions; as pity, love—anger, courage, &c. The effect of *words*, is, to strengthen the expression of Music, by confining it—by giving it a precise direction, supplying it with ideas, circumstances, and an *object*, and, by this means raising it from a calm and *general* disposition, or emotion, into something approaching, at least, to the strong feeling of a particular and determinate *passion*.[49]

I doubt that Twining is right when he writes that the emotions aroused by instrumental music are vague. I agree, however, with his proposal that lyrics give the emotions aroused by music an object towards which they are directed.

Wagner seems to have adopted a similar view: 'the expression of an altogether definite, a clearly-understandable individual Content, was in truth impossible in this language [absolute music] that had only fitted itself for conveying the general character of an emotion'.[50] Push through the thickets of Wagner's nearly impenetrable prose, and it turns out that the addition of poetry to music solves the problem. In the works of Gluck, Mozart, and Wagner, poetry is added to music to add specificity to the emotions aroused by music. (Wagner often speaks of the emotions expressed by music, but he also talks of arousal.)

The combination of words and music gives vocal music another sort of specificity. Above I noted that evidence is lacking for the claim that we hear a persona in instrumental music. Instrumental music represents general

[48] Kivy, *Osmin's Rage*, p. 274.
[49] Thomas Twining, *Two Dissertations on Poetical and Musical Imitation in Musical Aesthetics: A Historical Reader*, ed. Edward A. Lippman (New York: Pendragon Press, 1986), vol. 1, p. 246.
[50] Richard Wagner, *Richard Wagner's Prose Works*, trans. William Ashton Ellis (London: K. Paul, Trench, Trübner, 1893), vol. 2, p. 70.

types of emotions, emotions that belong to no one in particular. Music with lyrics can, in contrast, represent the emotions of specific individuals or types of individuals. Pergolesi's *Stabat Mater* represents the suffering of Mary. In the music that Handel composed for Cleopatra (in *Giulio Cesare*) is represented the emotions (as Dean notes) of 'an immortal sex-kitten'.[51] Monteverdi's *Il lamento d'Arianna* specifically represents the despair of the unjustly abandoned woman.

Being a hybrid; that is, combining literature and music, far from being the source of a problem, gives opera (and other forms of vocal music) an enhanced capacity to arouse emotions and to provide insights into our interior lives. The experimental evidence indicates that this capacity is greater than that of either the words or the music alone. This capacity of words and music to act in concert goes a long way towards explaining the power of opera to move audiences and to provide insight into emotion.

Kivy holds that instrumental music has come to 'surpass in importance' opera and other vocal music.[52] He provides no evidence for this conclusion. He does not even indicate what it means to say that instrumental music has surpassed vocal music in importance. Certainly instrumental music is not more popular. Most of the music that most people hear (on the radio, in church, and on their iPhones) is vocal music. No one doubts that, since the eighteenth century, leading composers have devoted more of their attention to instrumental music than they had previously. It is far from obvious, however, that the aesthetic value of instrumental music has, in any era, surpassed that of vocal music. I am surprised that there has been so little pushback against Kivy's claim about the relative value of instrumental music.

The 'problem of opera' only exists if the formalist's starting point for reflection on opera is accepted. The formalist assumes that music does not arouse emotion and that literature is an exclusively semantic art. The empirical evidence strongly suggests that the formalist's starting point is comprehensively mistaken. Music and lyrics can work together to arouse emotion. The empirical evidence also indicates that the dominant partner in opera is the music. By engaging our emotions, the composer becomes the dramatist.[53] Opera is not empty form and the composer, even more

---

[51] Dean, *Handel and the Opera Seria*, p. 68.
[52] Kivy, *Osmin's Rage*, p. 58.
[53] Here I am paraphrasing Kerman: 'in opera the dramatist is the *composer*'. *Opera as Drama*, p. xiii.

than the librettist, contributes to the music's content. While a composer must overcome many practical problems to produce a successful opera, the 'problem of opera' is a pseudo-problem.

This examination of vocal music and, in particular, opera, has lent support to the widespread view that music is able to provide psychological insight and to have psychological depth. We are now in a position to answer some fundamental questions about the aesthetic value of music.

5

The Value of Music

The Value of Musical Form

The question of why listeners find the experience of music so aesthetically valuable lies at the heart of the philosophy of music. The answer to this question is complex. A variety of factors make the experience of music aesthetically rewarding (or aesthetically valuable). Formalists are unable to take all of these factors into account and inevitably fail to give a complete explanation of why listening to music is aesthetically valuable. Formalists are not, however, completely mistaken about the experience of music. They have identified a way in which at least some listeners find the experience of music aesthetically valuable. That said, a full and satisfactory account of why the experience of music is valuable depends on the recognition that music has content. Anti-formalism can recognize the contributions formalists have made to the understanding of why the experience of music is aesthetically rewarding and add additional insights based on the capacity of music to be expressive of emotion and to arouse and represent it. Only anti-formalists can explain how music can be profound.

Formalists have an account of what makes music aesthetically valuable. They believe that listeners delight in pure musical form. Hanslick held that a listener 'delights in the sounding forms and musical structures'.[1] According to Kivy, contemplation of musical form is 'one of the most satisfying and engrossing experiences the arts have to offer'.[2] This may well be true, but having said that music is pure form, formalists need to provide an explanation of why experience of pure, contentless form is aesthetically rewarding. Formalists have provided several explanations. While these

---

[1] Eduard Hanslick, *The Beautiful in Music*, trans. Gustav Cohen (Indianapolis, I.N.: Bobbs-Merrill, 1957), p. 49.

[2] Peter Kivy, *Music Alone: Philosophical Reflections on the Purely Musical Experience* (Ithaca, N.Y.: Cornell University Press, 1990), p. 200.

explanations are satisfactory up to a point, none of them amounts to a full account of the aesthetic value of music.

Formalists begin by trying to explain our delight in pure form by saying that it can be beautiful. That is all very well, but then we are owed an account of musical beauty. Here formalists are often uninformative. Some formalists have sought to identify formal characteristics (such as 'uniformity amidst variety') shared by all aesthetically rewarding works of music. Most recent formalists have realized that this search is a mug's game and have abandoned the attempt to find a characteristic shared by Tchaikovsky's *Francesca di Rimini*, Op. 32, 'Greensleeves' as played on a lute and a Mozart string quartet that makes them all beautiful. (Formalists cannot, as we saw in Chapter 2, define musical beauty in terms of the capacity to arouse aesthetic emotion. That way lies vicious circularity.) Instead, they fall back on the claim that musical beauty cannot be described. That is, musical beauty is ineffable.

Leading musical formalists seem to be unanimous on this point. Hanslick tells us that, 'It is extremely difficult to define this self-subsistent and specifically musical beauty.'[3] Following in Hanslick's footsteps, Kivy makes no attempt to give an account of musical beauty: 'if someone should ask me to define musical beauty, I would, of course, decline the invitation, as any sensible person ought.'[4] According to Kivy, 'the beauty of...music...is a brute aesthetic fact.'[5] Zangwill joins the formalist chorus, holding that the aesthetic properties of music are ineffable.[6] If musical beauty is ineffable, the formalist explanation of why music is aesthetically rewarding is doomed to be incomplete.

Formalists have, however, made some attempts to explain the aesthetic value of music. One suggestion is that listeners, while listening to music, play a game that Kivy calls musical hide and seek or *cherchez le thème*.[7] Listeners play *cherchez le thème* when, while listening to a composition, they search for the principal themes of the piece. Perhaps the composer has inverted a theme or perhaps it has been re-introduced backwards.

---

[3] Hanslick, *The Beautiful in Music*, p. 50.
[4] Kivy, *Music Alone*, p. 77.
[5] Peter Kivy, *Osmin's Rage: Philosophical Reflections on Opera, Drama, and Text, with a New Final Chapter* (Ithaca, N.Y.: Cornell University Press, 1999), p. 269.
[6] Nick Zangwill, 'Music, Essential Metaphor, and Private Language', *American Philosophical Quarterly*, 48 (2011), p. 2.
[7] Peter Kivy, *Introduction to a Philosophy of Music* (Oxford: Clarendon Press, 2002), p. 78.

The listener, on this view, enjoys the process of understanding the musical form; in this case, grasping that the second theme is the inversion of the first. Kivy suggests that, 'this special case of musical enjoyment can be generalized for *all* musical enjoyment'.[8] Notice the 'all', which Kivy emphasized. In other words, the experience of music is only rewarding since we enjoy the process of comprehending the patterns (some of them, the enhanced formalists will say, expressive of emotion) that composers (and performers) have produced.

Kivy has also suggested, albeit rather tentatively, that listeners find vocal, particularly operatic, music rewarding for a similar reason. As noted in the previous chapter, on Kivy's formalist view, listeners do not appreciate vocal music primarily for the content of the lyrics. Opera 'affords the pleasures and satisfactions of pure musical form'. As we have seen, Kivy holds that, in a best-case scenario, an opera is like a *sinfonia concertante*. Still, listeners can recognize the 'non-musical part in the musical whole'.[9] This can be a challenge, Kivy suggests, and listeners can find satisfying the successful discovery of the drama amid the music.

Kivy has suggested another explanation of the listener's appreciation of pure musical form. This he calls the hypothesis game. When playing this game, listeners form hypotheses about what will happen next as they listen to a composition. A listener may hypothesize, for example, that a work will modulate into the parallel minor, or that a theme will be repeated in the sub-dominant. Listeners can then be pleased by the realization of their musical hypotheses or agreeably surprised by an unexpected turn that a composition takes. Players of the hypothesis game, like players of musical hide and seek, are delighting in the twists and turns of pure musical form. The hypothesis game is, perhaps, just a variant of *cherchez le thème*.

The proposal that listeners' enjoyment of music is the pleasure they take in playing *cherchez le thème* and related games suggests an account of musical beauty. The formalist can say that the beauty of a musical work is proportional to the intellectual challenge that it presents to listeners. A Bach fugue is beautiful, on this account, because it presents a good deal of scope for *cherchez le thème* and other intellectual games. In contrast, 'Twinkle, twinkle little star' is not beautiful because there is 'absolutely

[8] Kivy, *Music Alone*, p. 73.
[9] Kivy, *Osmin's Rage*, p. 277.

nothing in it to think about'.[10] Musical beauty is still in large part ineffable: necessary and sufficient conditions for a work presenting an intellectual challenge to listeners will be difficult, if not impossible, to specify. For example, complexity is not a necessary condition of musical beauty. 'Greensleeves' and sequences by Hildegard of Bingen are quite simple but a formalist does not want to be forced to deny that they are beautiful.

I see no reason to doubt that formalists are telling the truth when they say that they enjoy contemplating the formal features of music. Kivy says that playing *cherchez le thème* 'is something that [he] enjoy[s]'[11] and I have no reason to doubt that he is sincere. (Other sophisticated listeners tell me that they have never played this game.) He provides no explanation of why either musical hide and seek or the hypothesis game is rewarding, but none is needed. Posing and solving puzzles is a type of activity that many people enjoy. I doubt, however, that music is appreciated only as a source of intellectual puzzles. The aesthetic value (or beauty) of music cannot, I will argue, be completely understood in terms of the pleasure that listeners take in solving intellectual puzzles.

Some works of music offer, to the exclusion of others, the sorts of rewards that listeners receive from attention to musical form. Works by Schoenberg, Webern, Babbitt, and other avant-garde composers are examples of such pieces. These works typically do not resemble human expressive behaviour and they do not have the somatic effects typical of tonal music. Consequently, they have a limited capacity to arouse and represent emotion. (These works may be able to arouse emotions via the Meyer mechanism in listeners who are familiar with the conventions of a given sort of avant-garde composition.) Precisely because many avant-garde artworks are limited in this respect, listeners who appreciate the emotional content of music do not find these compositions rewarding. On the other hand, serialist compositions can be expected to be particularly rewarding for listeners primarily interested in playing the hypothesis game. These works are composed in accordance with a theory or system and this makes them particularly apt for a purely intellectual appreciation. Interested listeners will be able to form hypotheses about how a composer will solve the compositional challenges presented by serialism. To my mind, serialist compositions, abandoning those features of music that

[10] Kivy, *Music Alone*, p. 85.
[11] Kivy, *Music Alone*, p. 73.

make the representation of emotion possible, are rather impoverished. The formalist, however, who delights in pure form, will disagree.

The Heresy of Substitutable Experience

The suggestion that our interest in music is limited to interest in abstract patterns gives rise to what may be called the *heresy of substitutable experience*. Suppose that we listen to music only to play *cherchez le thème*, the hypothesis game, and similar intellectual games. We could play the same games while reading a score. Reading a score, one can form hypotheses about how the composer is going to develop some theme and be pleased to find that one's hypothesis is correct or pleasantly surprised by an unexpected resolution of a musical passage. Similarly, reading a score one can follow the entry and re-entry of themes, notice that the second theme is the retrograde inversion of the first, and so on. So it seems that the formalist is committed to saying that music lovers can substitute experience of reading the score of a composition for experience of listening to a performance of the composition, and receive the same aesthetic reward. If all enjoyment of music is enjoyment of musical form, then any aesthetic reward available from listening to music can be had by studying a score. This is, at best, a peculiar consequence of formalism. At worst, by committing the heresy of substitutable experience, formalists reduce their position to absurdity.

Formalists may try to resist the conclusion that they are committed to the heresy of substitutable experience. They could argue that playing *cherchez le thème* presents more of an intellectual challenge when one is listening to a composition as it is being performed than it is when reading a score. It is often easier to see (while studying a score) that a theme is the retrograde inversion of another than it is to hear (while listening to a performance) that it is. Even the hypothesis game may be easier to play while studying a score. One can move through the score at one's own pace, pausing to think about what will come next. Since many formalists believe that we appreciate music because of the intellectual challenges that it presents, they could maintain that the challenges are greater while listening to music. They may conclude that the rewards to be had from listening to music are greater than the rewards to be had from studying a score.

The formalist's argument here is unconvincing. For a start, well-trained musicians are just as able to hear that a new theme is the retrograde inversion of the first as they are able to see on a score that it is. Some may even find hearing a theme's relation to another easier than seeing it in a score. At least for such musicians, the formalist seems committed to saying that the experience of reading a work's score can be substituted for the experience of hearing a performance of the work and the heresy cannot be avoided.

On the other hand, most listeners are not so easily able to hear themes and their relationships. Many listeners cannot hear that two series of notes are composed of the same notes in the same order if the notes in the two series have different rhythms (that is, the relative lengths of the notes vary). For example, many listeners cannot hear the folk song 'L'homme armé' in a Josquin mass because the note values have been changed. Similarly, the patterns in serialist compositions frequently cannot be heard, even on repeated listening. It seems that the formalist should recommend that people give up listening to such music and read the score. At least, the formalist seems committed to saying that they should do so until they become better at listening to music. By reading scores, they will be better able to enjoy intellectual challenges posed by a piece of music. Consequently, less skilled listeners should be advised to read scores rather than listen to music. Again, it seems that formalists are committed to the heresy of substitutable experience.

In some cases, even skilled listeners are unable to detect patterns in certain musical compositions. The composer Fred Lerdahl noted that, listening to *Le marteau sans maître*, by Pierre Boulez, 'competent listeners... even after many hearings, still cannot even begin to hear its serial organization. For many passages they cannot even tell if wrong pitches or rhythms have been played.'[12] This anecdotal evidence has been supplemented by psychological inquiry. Several experiments confirm that listeners, even listeners familiar with the principles of atonal composition, cannot discern the patterns in atonal composition.[13] The formalist seems committed to the view that studying the scores of serialist compositions is just as good as, if not better than, listening to performances of the works.

A second formalist response to the heresy of substitutable experience suggests itself. Formalists could argue that the formal features of musical

---

[12] Fred Lerdahl, 'Cognitive Constraints on Compositional Systems', in John Sloboda (ed.), *Generative Processes in Music* (Oxford: Oxford University Press, 1988), p. 232.

[13] For a discussion of these experiments, see Diane Raffman, 'Is Twelve-Tone Music Artistically Defective?' *Midwest Studies in Philosophy*, 27 (2003), 69-87.

performances will frequently differ from the formal features of musical scores. For example, a violinist performing a trio sonata may introduce ornaments not specified in a score. As a result, the formal structure of the performance differs from the formal structure of the score and, the formalist may conclude, a reading of the score cannot be substituted for a hearing of the performance. The formalist can claim that the form of the performance is more aesthetically valuable than the form of the score.

One rejoinder to the formalists' second argument immediately suggests itself. As the argument is set up, the score and the performance are supposed to have different formal properties. For this reason, the argument runs, the reading of the score cannot be substituted for listening to the performance. The heresy of substitutable experience says, however, that when the formal properties of the score and those of the performance are the same, then experience of one can be substituted for experience of the other. This formalist argument does not, then, address the heresy. It simply says that when two objects have different formal properties, experience of one cannot be substituted for experience of the other. And no one denies that. (Even the anti-formalist who believes that music arouses emotion believes that the capacity of a musical work to arouse emotion is supervenient on its formal properties.)

For at least two other reasons the formalists' second response to the heresy will not do. For a start, there is nothing to stop someone reading a score from imagining embellishments of precisely the sort that the musician adds. Indeed, someone familiar with the sort of work that is ornamented in performance will be likely to imagine the addition of embellishments. (The reading of a score is a sort of performance of a work of music.) It may very well turn out that the embellishments that a score reader adds are identical to those the listener hears. If so, there is no formal difference between the score and the performance and the formalist is still committed to the heresy of substitutable experience. But even if the formal properties of the score and a performance differ, the formalist is not out of the woods. The formal properties of the score may be more beautiful than those of the performance. Perhaps the performance has added ornaments, but these detract from the beauty of the work. Sometimes, after all and in some cases, simple form is preferable to a more complex one. Alternatively, the score reader may imagine the addition of more beautiful ornaments than the performer produced. In either case, it seems that experience of reading the score may be substituted for experience of the performance.

A final strategy for dealing with the heresy of substitutable experience is available to formalists. They can grasp the thistle and maintain that reading a score can provide all of the aesthetic rewards that listening to a performance can provide. The view that the experience of reading a score can be substituted for the experience of hearing a performance is not completely crazy. Some people find reading scores rewarding. Brahms, for example, is reported to have resisted attending a performance of *Don Giovanni* saying, 'I enjoy it much better from the score. I've never heard a good *Don Giovanni* yet.'[14] (The rest of the anecdote is less often remembered, however: Brahms ended up going to the performance and loving it. The conductor on this occasion was Gustav Mahler.)

The anti-formalist believes that grasping this thistle is too painful. As we have seen, listeners regularly report that listening to music arouses emotions. Many of these listeners report that they value the experience of listening to music precisely because it arouses emotion. I have not done any experiments to prove that these rewards are not available from reading a score, but I very much doubt that reading a score will provide the same rewards. I also doubt that scores are seen as expressive of human behaviour. (I suspect that the reading of scores is most rewarding for those with vivid imaginations, who can imagine how the work sounds when performed and who can receive some of the rewards of listening to music.) Again, the reading of scores is not substitutable for listening to performances without aesthetic loss. Certain experiences are available when listeners hear performances that are not available when people read scores.

Formalists have a response to this argument. They could maintain that they are concerned only with the way that canonical listeners experience music. Canonical music lovers focus purely on musical form. The experience of canonical listeners, they could hold, is purely cognitive; that is, such listeners do not have merely sensory pleasures when listening to music. Nor does music arouse emotions in them and they do not concern themselves with the expressive properties of music. Formalists could then argue that canonical musical lovers lose nothing by studying the score of a work rather than listening to a performance of it.

---

[14] Kurt Blaukopf and Zoltan Roman (eds.), *Mahler: A Documentary Study*, trans. Paul Baker, Susanne Flatauer, P.R.J. Ford, Daisy Loman, and Geoffrey Watkins (London: Thames and Hudson, 1976), p. 189.

This would be an unpromising approach for formalists to adopt. Here formalists are simply being self-denying ascetics. We are trying to answer the question of what makes the experience of music aesthetically valuable. Formalists may announce that they (and other canonical listeners) are not interested in any of music's aesthetic rewards, other than those provided by the intellectual appreciation of pure musical form. That is their decision. But it does not follow from the lack of interest that formalists have in other aesthetic rewards that music cannot provide these rewards. The current project is to uncover all of the aesthetic rewards that music can provide.

I conclude that formalists are guilty of the heresy of substitutable experience. Formalists must say that reading a score is just as good as listening to a performance. This is, however, a highly implausible view. In important respects, the experience of hearing a work of music is different from the experience of reading the work's score.

Sensory Pleasure and Valuable Emotions

The anti-formalist wants to maintain that the content of music contributes to its aesthetic value. Before considering this possibility, two other ways in which music can be valuable deserve attention. The first is the possibility that the experience of music is often rewarding, in part, simply because it affords sensory pleasures. The second is the possibility that listeners value for their own sake the emotions aroused by music. The anti-formalist can accept that music is rewarding in part because of its capacity to provide sensory pleasure and intrinsically enjoyable garden-variety emotions. In contrast, some formalists deny that music provides sensory pleasures and all of them are sceptical about the claim that it arouses intrinsically enjoyable garden-variety emotions.

Many listeners report receiving sensuous pleasure from music. St Augustine, for example, identifies some pleasures that are not pleasures of the mind and adds that, 'Neither do we usually name rational what calls our attention to colours, nor do we do so with regard to the sweetness of the ears, i.e. when a string is struck and it sounds, so to say, smooth and pure.'[15] More recently, Stephen Davies has observed that listeners 'take pleasure in

---

[15] Augustine, *De ordine* II, xi, 33, quoted in Frank Hentschel, 'The sensuous music aesthetics of the Middle Ages: the cases of Augustine, Jacques de Liége and Guido of Arezzo', *Plainsong and Medieval Music*, 20 (2011), p. 6. Hentschel argues that, in the Middle Ages, the view that music was a source of sensuous pleasure was widely held.

the rumbling throb of the organ pedal, the lush fruitiness of the low register of the alto flute, the ethereal character of string harmonics, the piquant combination of piccolo and contra-bassoon, and so on'.[16] On this view, listening to music is rewarding, in part at least, in the way that tasting a fine wine, feeling soft velvet, or seeing the dazzling blue of an alpine lake is rewarding.

Some formalists attempt to assimilate this sort of pleasure to the pleasure listeners receive from contemplating musical form. Kivy, for example, acknowledges the delight a listener receives from hearing the violinist Arthur Grumiaux draw 'his bow across the G-string'.[17] This is not, however, according to Kivy, a sensory pleasure. (In contrast, Hanslick seems to allow that the experience of music is rewarding in part because of the sensory pleasures that it affords. He talks of us appreciating beautiful forms but also of our appreciation of 'beautiful tints' or tones.[18] Hanslick is an anti-contentist more than he is a dogmatic formalist.) Kivy holds that a single note has a 'formal structure': the note swells or dies away, as its dynamics change, its pitch can be subtly varied through the use of vibrato and so on. Kivy believes that listening to the note is a pleasure because we appreciate its formal features.

In order to reject Kivy's position it must be possible to distinguish between sensuous and intellectual pleasures. The line between these types of pleasure is not completely hard and fast. Appreciating the taste of a cabernet sauvignon might initially seem to be a purely sensuous pleasure, but wine tasting can have an intellectual component. At least for sophisticated tasters, wine tasting yields intellectual pleasures. Part of the pleasure of wine tasting can come from knowledge of how a given wine compares to other wines of the same and different varietals. Tasters can enjoy discovering and describing the various nuances of taste. Nevertheless, there is a rough and ready distinction between sensuous and intellectual pleasures. There is a difference between the pleasure of solving a chess problem and the pleasure of experiencing the colour of an alpine lake. At the very least, the second pleasure has a sensory component that the former lacks.

Nevertheless, Kivy believes that all of the pleasures of music are intellectual pleasures. He tries to push all of the rewards of music into formalism's Procrustean bed and insists that we appreciate only form, even when

---

[16] Stephen Davies, *Musical Meaning and Expression* (Ithaca, N.Y.: Cornell University Press, 1994), p. 322.
[17] Kivy, *Music Alone*, p. 75.
[18] Hanslick, *The Beautiful in Music*, p. 48.

we delight in the sound of a single note. The note has a shape or form, but it does not follow from this that our appreciation of the note is not a sensory pleasure. Consider this parallel argument. The taste of a cabernet sauvignon has a structure. It has an initial attack, a middle, and a finish (or after-taste). It does not follow from the fact that the wine has this structure that tasters' appreciation of it is not (in large part, at least) a sensuous pleasure. Similarly, we cannot infer from the premise that notes have a formal structure that our enjoyment of them is not sensuous pleasure.

Kivy has said that all appreciation of music can be reduced to playing *cherchez le thème*, but it is hard to see how listeners can be playing this game when they appreciate a single note. A formalist could grant that there are no themes to find in notes, but hold that they have patterns and it is these patterns, one might think, that make possible the formalist's intellectual games. A listener could hypothesize about how a note will evolve. The listener might wonder about whether the vibrato will be quickened or whether the note will become louder or softer. I know of no evidence that listeners ever do this, but in principle it is possible that listeners do. While this must be admitted, it is hard to see how a listener can be constantly forming hypotheses about what is going to happen next in each note that comes along. There simply is not enough time. The same listener will also, on Kivy's account, be constantly forming hypotheses about the overall structure of the work. I find it hard to believe that a listener will be able to attend to a work while constantly forming hypotheses of these sorts. The proposal that listeners receive sensuous pleasure from listening to a note seems to be a more satisfactory explanation of why we find them aesthetically valuable.

Sensory pleasures are not the only non-intellectual pleasures that listeners report receiving from music. Many people report that their primary motivation for listening to music is that they value its emotional effects.[19] I see no reason to disbelieve this claim, but it is important that we understand what listeners mean when they make it. Listeners could mean that the emotions aroused by music are intrinsically valuable. That is, listeners could mean that they enjoy the emotional states that music arouses in them. Alternatively, listeners could mean that the emotions aroused in them could have some extrinsic value. That is, listeners could be saying

---

[19] Carol L. Krumhansl, 'Music: A Link Between Cognition and Emotion', *Current Directions in Psychological Science*, 11 (2002), pp. 45–50.

that they value the arousal of emotion because it leads to some end that they value. Or they could mean that the arousal of emotion is both intrinsically and extrinsically valuable. I will begin by considering the suggestion that listeners value the arousal of emotion for its own sake.

The empirical evidence certainly seems to suggest that many listeners find that a good deal of music arouses emotions that the listeners enjoy experiencing. Listeners frequently report that music arouses calmness, joy, excitement, and a variety of other emotions. These emotions are ones that people ordinarily find intrinsically valuable and there is no reason to deny that they are intrinsically valuable when they are aroused by music. There is nothing puzzling about why listeners would want to have such emotions aroused. The experience of music is rewarding, in part, because it arouses such emotions. Pleasant emotions are not, however, as we have seen, the only emotions that music arouses. Subjective reports and physiological evidence both indicate that music also arouses unpleasant emotions such as fear and sadness. One might think that the arousal of such emotions might detract from, rather than contribute to, the aesthetic value that music can provide.

Let us consider what we may call the *paradox of sad music*. As is so often the case, Kivy provides the *locus classicus* of this paradox. He writes that, 'it would be utterly inexplicable why anyone would willfully submit himself' to music that arouses unpleasant emotions.[20] There are two basic strategies for resolving the paradox: the elimination and compensation strategies. The elimination strategy is to deny the existence of any unpleasantness associated with sad music. The paradox is resolved if listeners do not experience any unpleasant emotions while listening to sad music. Either no painful music is composed (and so no painful emotions aroused) or apparently painful emotions are somehow transformed into a pleasant one. The compensation strategy begins by acknowledging that there is something painful about listening to sad or tragic music. Advocates of this strategy go on to maintain that, by listening to painful music, we receive compensation that outweighs any pain that results from the music. The paradox of sad music has been widely discussed[21] but the reflections on

---

[20] Peter Kivy, *Sound Sentiment: An Essay on the Musical Emotions Including the Complete Text of The Corded Shell* (Philadelphia, P.A.: Temple University Press, 1989), p. 23.
[21] See, for example, Jerrold Levinson, 'Music and Negative Emotion', in his *Music, Art, and Metaphysics* (Ithaca, N.Y.: Cornell University Press, 1990), and Davies, *Musical Meaning and Expression*, pp. 307ff.

music and emotion presented in this essay, based on empirical evidence, shed some additional light on the matter. I advocate a compensation strategy with a side order of the elimination strategy.

First comes the small piece of elimination strategy. As we have seen, the emotions aroused by music are distinct from the emotions aroused in the course of our quotidian lives. The emotions aroused by music are less intense and more transitory than ordinary emotions. The sadness, fear, melancholy, and so on aroused by music are instances of garden-variety emotions, but they are less painful than the corresponding emotions felt in the course of our non-musical experience. The paradox of sad music would be much more difficult to resolve if music put us into the sort of state that we are in when something truly tragic occurs. It is difficult to imagine why anyone would choose to undergo such an experience.

While this is true, one ought not to deny that the sadness and other negative emotions aroused by music are painful to a degree. Psychological studies of music and emotion lend support to this conclusion. One study asked subjects to report the emotions that were aroused by the music they heard over the course of a week. That is, the subjects reported their responses to music that they had chosen to listen to. Interestingly, only quite rarely did subjects report that sadness was aroused, despite the fact that music can arouse sadness.[22] I suggest that this is to be explained by the fact that listeners in the study often avoided listening to music that arouses sadness. Another study indicates that between 10% and about a third of listeners agree with the statement, 'I don't really enjoy listening to sad music.'[23] My own experience is that sometimes I do not enjoy sad music. I need to be in the right frame of mind before I will listen to musical works that arouse sadness. Sometimes I am just not up to coping with music that arouses sadness, melancholy, or similar emotions.

Davies does well to remind us that most people are not Sybarites.[24] We engage in many activities that we know will cause discomfort or even pain. We read about the Republican primaries in the morning newspaper. We climb mountains and run marathons. Still, if music arouses sadness, then

---

[22] Marcel Zentner, Didier Grandjean, and Klaus R. Scherer, 'Emotions Evoked by the Sound of Music: Characterization, Classification and Measurement', *Emotion*, 8 (2008), 494–521.

[23] David Huron, 'Why is sad music pleasurable? A possible role for prolactin', *Musicae Scientiae*, 15 (2011), p. 147.

[24] Davies, *Musical Meaning and Expression*, p. 317.

we need to ask what compensation we receive. We receive compensation for reading the morning newspaper or running a marathon. We come to understand the world around us, and we are willing to put up with reading about Republican candidates in order to do so. Or we develop our self-mastery and have a sense of achievement by running marathons despite the associated pain. We need to ask whether listeners stand to gain anything from having sadness aroused by sad music.

The first answer to this question starts from the fact that listeners are able to experience more than one emotion at a time. Consider this case: You hear that an old and dear friend is to marry someone that you have long admired from afar. The person in question will make your friend happy and this in turn makes you happy. At the same time, you can feel an undercurrent of melancholy as you wonder about what might have been. One can, in this way, feel more than one emotion at a time. Music may well arouse sadness, but perhaps it also arouses other emotions that compensate one for the feeling of sadness. The empirical study of listener responses to sad music is at an early stage. Recent empirical evidence suggests, however, that just as an event in the course of our lives can arouse contrasting emotions, so can listening to sad music arouse a range of emotional responses. Sadness is one response, but compensating pleasing emotions are also aroused.

A psychological study found that sadness is not the only emotion aroused by sad music. The study involved 148 Finnish university students, who were played sixteen film music excerpts. (Only music unfamiliar to the test subjects was employed.) The subjects were divided into four groups. Members of the first group were only asked whether they enjoyed each musical excerpt. The second group was asked about the arousal of garden-variety emotions: sadness, happiness, tenderness, fear, and anger. The third group was asked only about the valence (positive or negative) of their emotions and the intensity of these emotions. Members of the fourth group were asked about the emotions on the Geneva Emotional Musical Scale (GEMS): wonder, transcendence, power, tenderness, nostalgia, peacefulness, joyful activation, sadness, and tension.

The test participants were told that 'the music may not necessarily arouse any emotions' and they were asked 'carefully to separate [their] own feelings from the emotions expressed by the music'.[25] Nevertheless,

---

[25] Jonna K. Vuoskoski, William F. Thompson, Doris McIlwain and Tuomas Eerola, 'Who Enjoys Listening to Sad Music and Why?' *Music Perception*, 29 (2012), 311–18.

many of the subjects reported having sadness aroused. This was, however, not the only emotion aroused. The participants using the GEMS categories also reported the arousal of nostalgia, peacefulness, and wonder. These are emotions with a demonstrated positive valence. These additional emotions may be some sort of aesthetic emotion or they may be other garden-variety emotions. At least in some listeners, these additional emotions may be enough to outweigh any unpleasantness associated with the experience of sadness. The pleasant emotions aroused by sad music may be attributable to the fact that sad music leads to the release of prolactin.[26] It seems that positive emotions could compensate listeners for the unpleasantness of negative emotions.

This study reached additional interesting conclusions about the sort of person who enjoys sad music. The participants in the study were given a standard personality test with a view to finding out the extent to which they possessed two personality traits, namely openness to experience and empathy. Most of the participants were given an additional test to determine which aspects of empathy they possessed. (Psychologists divide empathy into four traits, which they call fantasy, perspective-taking, empathetic concern, and personal distress.) The researchers found that openness to experience and two aspects of empathy—fantasy and empathetic concern—are co-related with enjoyment of music that arouses sadness. Individuals with the fantasy trait are able imaginatively to take on the feelings and situations of fictitious people. Empathetic concern involves feelings of compassion and solicitude for people in unfortunate circumstances.

Openness to experience is associated with a capacity to appreciate aesthetic experience, so it is not surprising that people with this trait appreciate sad music to a greater extent than other people do. Likely, openness to experience makes possible an aesthetic emotion such as wonder. (I would not be surprised to learn that they also appreciate other sorts of music to a high degree.) The more interesting result, I suggest, is that aspects of empathy are associated with appreciation of music that arouses sadness. A feeling of compassion or solicitude is, I suggest, pleasant. The fantasy trait may lead to a feeling of compassion or solicitude when listening to sad music, where no actual person is in distress. As a result, an empathetic

---

[26] Huron, 'Why is sad music pleasurable?', 146–58.

person will have sadness aroused by music, but will also have pleasing feelings of compassion and concern aroused.

The empirical research on music and the paradox of sad music is currently quite limited. A little more research on other arts and the paradox of tragedy has been done. Some of this research suggests ways in which the arousal of sadness by music can be rewarding. In one study, 361 undergraduates were shown an abbreviated version of *Atonement* (2007), a sad movie about betrayal and frustrated love.[27] An interesting result was found. The film aroused sadness in listeners but after watching the movie they reported more happiness with their lives. In fact, the more sadness the movie aroused in listeners, the more satisfaction they had with their lives. The mechanism seems to be that the movie prompted viewers to reflect on their lives and, in particular, on their relations to other people. This led in turn to an increase in happiness. There is no reason that music (since it is a representational art) could not have the same effect on listeners.

In the two previous chapters, I have suggested that music has cognitive significance or content. In particular, I have said that it represents human emotions. If it does, then there is another way in which listeners can be compensated for the sadness they experience while listening to sad music: they can gain knowledge about emotions. Kivy gives just this sort of answer to questions about why we view painful dramas. What a good production of *King Lear* 'reveals to us is painful indeed in the contemplation. We cannot, however, have the knowledge without the pain.'[28] The anti-formalist can explain our willingness to listen to painful music in exactly the same way. If this is the right solution to the paradox of sad music, then listeners are compensated with knowledge for any unpleasant emotions that they experience. In other words, the arousal of emotion by music is extrinsically valuable. (If we value knowledge for its own sake, then the arousal of emotion can be both intrinsically and extrinsically valuable.)

This approach to the paradox of sad music is supported by one of the features of sad music. Sadness is intrinsically unpleasant but it has some advantages. In particular, sadness confers some cognitive advantages. Research has found that when people are sad they are able to think more effectively in

---

[27] Silvia Knobloch-Westerwick, Yuan Gong, Holly Hagner, and Laura Kerbeykian, 'Tragedy Viewers Count Their Blessings: Feeling Low on Fiction Leads to Feeling High on Life', *Communications Research*, forthcoming.
[28] Kivy, *Sound Sentiment*, p. 237.

certain respects than when they are happy. In particular, sad people can think more clearly about details, are less subject to bias, and rely to a lesser extent on stereotypes in their thinking. The sadness aroused by music has been shown to confer these cognitive advantages.[29] Perhaps the cognitive advantages of sadness contribute to the value of sad music, particularly if music has cognitive significance.

A defence of the anti-formalist's strategy depends on the claim that music provides valuable knowledge about human emotions. The anti-formalist must provide a defence of this claim, which is central to a defence of anti-formalism. Prior to an examination of this claim, I will consider the question of whether music can be profound. Nothing I have said so far in this chapter has indicated that the rewards offered by music make it profound. Music's capacity to provide sensory pleasure and to arouse emotions does not explain how music could be profound. A rollercoaster ride arouses emotions, but no one would suggest that it is profound. Similarly, music's capacity to arouse emotion would not by itself explain its profundity. Similarly, no one is likely to regard music as profound simply because it is the source of sensory pleasure.

Nevertheless, music is frequently described as profound. Schweitzer, for example, describes the trio sonata from Bach's *Musical Offering* in these terms: 'it is profound and severe, without any of the gracious charm that distinguishes the work of the youthful period.'[30] Abert speaks of the 'profound human emotions that lie concealed within' Mozart's Symphony No. 40.[31] Dvořák characterized Beethoven's *Hammerklavier* sonata as profound.[32] Beethoven's string quartets, particularly the later ones, are routinely described as profound.[33] In my view, only the anti-formalist, who believes that music has content, can explain the profundity of music. First, however, let us see what the formalist can do to account for the profundity of music.

---

[29] Huron, 'Why is sad music pleasurable?' p. 148.
[30] Albert Schweitzer, *J.S. Bach*, trans. Ernest Newman (New York: Dover, 1966), vol. 1, p. 421.
[31] Hermann Abert, *W.A. Mozart*, trans. Stewart Spencer (New Haven, C.T.: Yale University Press, 2007), p. 1124.
[32] R. A. Sharpe, 'Sounding the Depths', *British Journal of Aesthetics*, 40 (2000), p. 69.
[33] See, for example, Philip Radcliffe, *Beethoven's String Quartets*, second edn (Cambridge: Cambridge University Press, 1978), p. 182.

Profundity and Purism

Musical works may frequently be described as profound but, as Kivy notes, it is difficult to see how 'a quasi-syntactical structure of sound understandable solely in musical terms and having no semantic or representational content, no meaning... [or] reference... beyond itself' can be profound.[34] In his initial discussion of musical profundity, Kivy tried to offer an explanation of how music, as he conceives of it, can be profound. He faltered at the last fence and concluded that no rational justification can be given for thinking that any musical work is profound (though he believed that some are). A subsequent discussion of profundity ended in aporia.[35] A third ends with the bald assertion that, 'Absolute music cannot be profound.'[36] Other philosophers who doubt that music has content, among them Davies, have also had difficulties accounting for the profundity of music. The anti-formalist, in contrast, has no trouble explaining how music can be profound.

I will begin by exploring the proposal for accounting for the profundity of music that Kivy initially floated, only to reject. Much can be said in favour of Kivy's proposal. Ultimately, however, his proposal is unsatisfactory and he is left with an unappealing trilemma. He can adhere to an unsatisfactory account of musical profundity, embrace irrationality, or accept that music cannot be profound. Since I find all of these alternatives unsatisfactory, I conclude that an anti-formalist account of profundity in music is required.

Kivy's discussion of profundity in music is limited to instrumental music, or what he calls 'music alone': music without a text, programme, descriptive title, or any other clue that may provide a work of music with content. Kivy says that there is no puzzle about works of literature. Such works can be profound because they explore in an insightful manner some profound subject matter, such as redemption or responsibility. That is, Kivy allows that works of literature are profound and are so in virtue of their content. In combination with music, Kivy suggests, a libretto can retain its profundity. But the profundity depends on the text. This position

---

[34] Kivy, *Music Alone*, p. 202.
[35] Peter Kivy, *Philosophies of Arts; An Essay in Differences* (Cambridge: Cambridge University Press, 1997), ch. 6.
[36] Peter Kivy, 'Another Go at Musical Profundity: Stephen Davies and the Game of Chess', *British Journal of Aesthetics*, 43 (2003), p. 409.

is not completely consistent with what he has to say about opera. In his discussions of opera, as we have seen, Kivy suggests that operas are to be appreciated as pure musical form and are not able to provide psychological insight or otherwise be profound. In any case, Kivy is clear about music alone. It has no content and so its profundity is puzzling. I suggested in Chapter 4 that instrumental and vocal music are not as different as formalists believe, but in this section I will stick to a consideration of instrumental music.

Of course, profundity in one sense of the word is not in the least puzzling. Kivy distinguishes between adjectival and adverbial senses of the word 'profound'.[37] The adverbial sense of profound is not in the least puzzling. As an adverb, 'profoundly' can be interchanged with 'very' or 'extremely'. For example, one may say that Beethoven's *Eroica Symphony* is profoundly moving. One cannot, however, validly infer that the adjectival sense of 'profound' applies to a work from the premise that the word, in its adverbial sense, applies. This point is clear when we reflect that a work of music could be profoundly dull or profoundly trivial, in which case it is unlikely to be profound (in the adjectival sense of the word). Kivy is only concerned with the adjectival sense of the word and, from now on, that is the only sense of the word that concerns us.

In calling a work of art profound, we are doing more than saying that it is good, or skilfully executed. One of Kivy's examples is *The Importance of Being Earnest*. One can grant that Wilde's comedy is a great work of art, and perfectly realized, without being committed to the conclusion that it is profound. (It is not.) On the other hand, *Oedipus Rex* or *Hamlet* is a profound work of art. These plays treat fundamental questions about morality and what it is to be human. That is, the tragedies of Sophocles and Shakespeare are about profound matters. That these questions are skilfully addressed seems also to be essential to their profundity. Poetasters may address questions about human mortality or filial piety in a ham-fisted fashion. Their works will not, despite their subject matter, be profound. Kivy concludes that it seems that three conditions must be met for an artwork to be profound. A profound work must be about something, that something must be profound, and the profound something must be treated in an 'exemplary' manner.

---

[37] Kivy, *Philosophies of Arts*, p. 145.

The trouble, as Kivy recognizes, is that on his account of things, pure instrumental music appears not to satisfy all of these conditions. Such music is, Kivy believes, not about anything. If pure music is not about anything, it cannot address any profound matter. *Ipso facto*, it cannot address a profound matter in an exemplary fashion. Even if one grants, as Kivy does, that music has expressive properties, it is hard to see how it can be profound. One might think that music that is expressive of serious emotions is profound, but Kivy is unmoved by this suggestion: 'there seems absolutely no reason for believing that a structure with serious expressive properties is any more profound that a structure with frivolous or happy ones'.[38] Music that is expressive of serious emotions, Kivy believes, is no more about those emotions than is music that is expressive of pleasing ones. And yet, at one time Kivy believed that music can be profound.

Kivy held this view when he wrote *Music Alone*. There, he wrote that, 'for certain works, I can find no other word as appropriate' as 'profound' and 'I find myself...unable to refrain from thinking that some musical works are profound.'[39] He is clearly thinking about absolute music in this passage since he gives Bach's *Well-tempered Clavier* and Beethoven's late quartets as examples of profound works. More recently, Kivy has rewritten history a little. In a more recent essay, he states that, 'I have argued previously [in *Music Alone*] that the art of absolute music...is not capable of profundity.' Even in this essay, however, Kivy sometimes talks as if he believes that music is profound. For example, he notes the 'crucial distinction between great works of absolute music that *are* profound and great works of absolute music that are *not*'.[40] Kivy cannot keep straight whether or not he believes that music is profound. On one page he will say that Mozart's wind sextets lack profundity. He contrasts them with Beethoven's *Eroica Symphony*, implying that it is profound. On the very next page he will say of Beethoven's work that, 'I do not think it is...profound.'[41]

In other, even more recent, essays the same sort of confusion persists. Kivy's most recent pronouncements on profundity in music are found in responses to some of his critics. Kivy quotes with approval a comment made by Arthur Danto, to the effect that Rembrandt's *Polish Rider* is one of the deepest paintings. It is a painting, Danto says, 'through which a person

[38] Kivy, *Music Alone*, p. 205.
[39] Kivy, *Music Alone*, p. 218.
[40] Kivy, 'Another Go at Musical Profundity', p. 401.
[41] Kivy, 'Another Go at Musical Profundity', pp. 407–8.

might define his life'. Kivy then states that it is this experience of depth that he is 'trying to talk about and make sense of in [his] philosophy of music'.[42] Now, as far as I can tell, 'deep' and 'profound' are synonyms in this context. If music is deep, then it is profound. And yet, a few pages later in a different essay, we find Kivy saying that 'absolute music ... cannot be profound'.[43] He apparently cannot make up his mind. Perhaps his position is that, 'there is serious doubt'[44] about the claim that music is profound.

In his initial discussion of profundity, having reached a roadblock, Kivy decided to discover what sort of music the 'musically learned' regard as profound. Perhaps some reason can be given for thinking that such works are profound. Kivy takes Bach's Organ Chorale BWV 668, *Vor deinen Thron tret ich hiermit*, as an example.[45] Kivy wonders whether he has discovered something about profound music, viz., that contrapuntal music is profound. Certainly, as he notes, many people have associated counterpoint and musical profundity. The question is why this has been. Kivy suggests that contrapuntal works are regarded as profound because they are an exploration of what is sonically possible. He then suggests that all profound music reveals 'in some deep sense the very possibilities of musical sound itself'.[46] Having hit upon this suggestion, Kivy can fit works of pure music into the schema for works of profound art. Such works are about something, namely sonic possibilities. Sonic possibility is a profound subject matter. And this subject matter can be treated in an exemplary manner, as it was by Bach.

Kivy's position has some counterintuitive consequences. The first is that every single piece of music has a profound subject matter. This follows from the claim that every piece of music is equally about sonic possibility and that sonic possibility is a profound subject matter. Kivy's sole ground for saying that a composition is about sonic possibility is that it is an exploration of sonic possibility. Some composers, he believes, contribute

---

[42] Peter Kivy, 'Moodology: A Response to Laura Sizer', *Journal of Aesthetics and Art Criticism*, 65 (2007), p. 317.
[43] Peter Kivy, 'Moodophilia: A Response to Noël Carroll and Margaret Moore', *Journal of Aesthetics and Art Criticism*, 65 (2007), p. 325.
[44] Kivy, 'Another Go at Musical Profundity', p. 410.
[45] Kivy accepts uncritically the apocryphal story that Bach dictated this work on his deathbed. He did not. See Russell Stinson, *J.S. Bach's Eighteen Great Organ Chorales* (New York: Oxford University Press, 2001), p. 36.
[46] Kivy, *Music Alone*, p. 208.

more to the exploration of sonic possibility. In particular, the composer of counterpoint is 'the Columbus and the Newton of our musical universe'. Counterpoint, Kivy says, 'pursues to the outer limits the ultimate possibilities of melody, in terms of melody's possible combinations with itself'. Even if that is granted, non-contrapuntal musical works are still discoveries about what is sonically possible. Such works are simply less dramatic discoveries. To one degree or another, every composer 'discovers what sound can do'.[47]

Of course, even if all musical works are about a profound subject matter, we cannot conclude that all musical compositions are profound. Some works will not satisfy Kivy's third criterion of profound works: they will not treat their subject in an exemplary manner. Kivy is not even committed to the conclusion that all contrapuntal music is profound. Bach's counterpoint is profound while the counterpoint of lesser composers is clumsy or pedantic. Still, the conclusion that all music has a profound subject matter is a bizarre consequence of the account of musical profundity that Kivy once entertained. Worse than that, however, the conclusion that all music is equally about sonic possibility leaves Kivy with only one way to distinguish profound from non-profound music. The profound works are the ones characterized by supreme musical craftsmanship, while the poor works are not. 'Supreme musical craftsmanship is,' Kivy writes, '...the common denominator between counterpoint and other instances of musical profundity.'[48] Once craftsmanship is the sole distinguishing mark of profundity, the concept becomes useless.

As it is normally understood, the concept of a profound work of art is distinct from the concept of a well-crafted work of art. *The Importance of Being Earnest* is a supremely well-crafted work of art, but no one believes that it is profound. Gilbert and Sullivan's *Pirates of Penzance* is another example of a beautifully crafted work of music that is anything but profound. The problem now is that Kivy cannot preserve the distinction between profound and supremely well-crafted music. Even worse, he is committed to analysing the concept of musical greatness in terms of the concept of supremely well-crafted music. Consequently, the concept of musical profundity is collapsed into the concept of musical greatness. Kivy explicitly denies that this is so: he is not, he writes, 'using the word

---

[47] Kivy, *Music Alone*, p. 209.
[48] Kivy, *Music Alone*, p. 211.

"profundity" as synonymous with the word "great" or any other word like it'.[49] It is, however, one thing to claim that one is preserving this distinction and another actually to preserve it. Kivy's formalism simply does not provide the resources to preserve the distinction. It seems clear that music could be great in the way that *Pirates of Penzance* is great. That is, music can be great without being profound.

Davies has attempted to articulate an account of the profundity of pure music that is distinct from Kivy's account. Davies begins by rejecting the view that, in order to be profound, a work of music must be about something. In particular, on his view, a profound work of music need not be about some profound subject matter. He does so because he is sceptical about the view that instrumental music is able to convey anything interesting about human emotion or any other profound subject. Instead, he adopts the view that some activity or the product of an activity is profound if, and only if, it displays profundity. Something displays profundity when it is the product of great creativity, ingenuity, or insight. Davies illustrates his sense of profundity by reflecting on some games from the history of chess that manifest 'to a jaw-dropping degree the inexhaustible fecundity, flexibility, insight, vitality, subtlety, complexity, and analytical far-reachingness of which the human mind is capable'.[50] In these games, profundity is on display. Works of music, Davies believes, can be profound in the same way that 'some chess play is [profound], namely, for what it exemplifies and thereby reveals about the human mind'.[51]

Ultimately, Davies's view of musical profundity does not differ dramatically from Kivy's position in *Music Alone*. Kivy's position boils down to the view that a work of music is profound when it is the product of supreme craftsmanship. Davies's view amounts to the belief that a work of music is profound when it displays what is responsible for supreme craftsmanship, namely mental powers such as great creativity and great ingenuity.[52]

---

[49] Kivy, *Music Alone*, p. 218.
[50] Stephen Davies, 'Profundity in Instrumental Music', in his *Musical Understandings and Others Essays on the Philosophy of Music* (Oxford: Oxford University Press, 2011), p. 195.
[51] Davies, 'Profundity in Instrumental Music', p. 199.
[52] In his report on the manuscript of this essay, Davies takes issue with my characterization of his position: 'It seems to me that the examples I discuss (Bartók's *Music for Strings, Percussion and Celesta* and the first movement of the *Eroica*) and the manner in which I discuss them show that something more than craftsmanship is under consideration. The Beethoven, in particular, is interesting because his treatment is significantly in tension with the formal template that the work is supposed to be following...: there is a conventional surface structure and there is a much deeper structure created by the composer that is at odds

Given the similarities between the two views, it is not surprising that they fall victim to the same problems. Like Kivy, Davies has no way to distinguish between music that is the product of supreme craftsmanship (great music) and profound music. The difference between Davies and Kivy is that Davies does not want to preserve the distinction. Nevertheless, the distinction corresponds to a difference.

Kivy is right to maintain, in this context, that there is a distinction between the great but not profound work (*The Importance of Being Earnest* or *Pirates of Penzance*) and the great *and* profound work. Or, to use the example Kivy gives, Beethoven's *Eroica Symphony* is profound, while Mozart's wind sextets, for all that they are the product of a febrile imagination, are not. That is, according to Kivy, the distinction that we are trying to capture, and since Davies cannot capture it in his account of profundity in music Kivy believes that Davies's account fails.[53] Notice that this argument against Davies requires Kivy to adopt a position as starkly contradictory as one can reasonably hope to find in a refereed journal. In the space of a page or two, Kivy holds both (1) no absolute music is profound and (2) Davies is wrong because some supremely well-crafted music is profound and some supremely well-crafted music is not profound.

Having reached this point, we are faced with the trilemma. The first alternative is to reject the view that instrumental music can be profound. Kivy sometimes embraces this alternative. For many people, however, this option is implausible. That instrumental music is profound is a data point that many people simply cannot bring themselves to reject. Even Kivy cannot bring himself, as we have seen, to abandon completely the profundity of music. The second alternative is to embrace irrationality. This is the option that Kivy endorses in *Music Alone*, where he professes himself convinced that music can be profound, but declares that he is unable 'to provide any rational grounds' for thinking that it is. This option is also

---

with it. It is the generation of that tension and its resolution, not orthodox craftsmanship, that displays profundity.' Here Davies holds that a work of music is profound when it displays a particular sort of form (a deep structure as well as a conventional surface structure). Works with this form are remarkable, however, in that they are manifestations of the mind of a supreme craftsman or artistry. (After all, it is hard to see how pure form can be profound by itself.) Consequently, Davies does not succeed in distinguishing between profound works and works that are manifestations of supreme craftsmanship or artistry. Again, however, for his purposes, Davies does not need to make this distinction. Only an anti-formalist will insist on this distinction.

[53] Kivy, 'Another Go at Musical Profundity', p. 407.

unappealing. The final alternative is to maintain that music can, contrary to what Kivy believes, be about some profound subject matter and convey something profound about that subject. This is the option that I wish to explore.

Formalists have dismissed attempts to show that music is capable of providing profound insights. Kivy and Davies have considered the possibility that Mozart's Symphony No. 40 could, with its mournful first subject and happy second subject, express the proposition that happiness could naturally follow unhappiness. Kivy states that, 'It scarcely needs pointing out that whatever this assertion is, it is scarcely profound.'[54] Here opponents of anti-formalism are looking in the wrong place for the profundity of music and attacking a straw man. Anti-formalists do not hold that musical works can make profound statements. Levinson's considered view on the profundity of music makes no reference to truth or propositions. He writes that profound works of music could give listeners 'the impression of having been *shown or revealed* something particular about how life is, or goes, or might be, something previously undisclosed to him'.[55] This is the possibility that I will now consider.

Music and Insight

Music is expressive of emotion, arouses emotion, and, consequently, as we have seen, represents emotion. The anti-formalist holds that we cannot understand the full aesthetic value of music unless we take into account the content it has qua representational art. As a result of being a representational art, music is able to provide (as many perceptive commentators on music, including some of the greatest composers, have observed) psychological insight into emotion and character. This capacity of music to provide psychological insight is the source of its capacity for profundity.

---

[54] Kivy, *Philosophies of Arts*, p. 170. See also Kivy, *Antithetical Arts: On the Ancient Quarrel Between Literature and Music* (Oxford: Oxford University Press, 2009), pp. 222–3. In this context, Kivy attributes to Levinson the statement that Mozart's Symphony No. 40 states that happiness can follow unhappiness. In fact, he makes no such claim. Rather he says that some indeterminate work might make this suggestion. See Jerrold Levinson, 'Truth in Music', in his *Music, Art, and Metaphysics*, p. 298.

[55] Jerrold Levinson, 'Musical Profundity Misplaced', *Journal of Aesthetics and Art Criticism*, 50 (1992), pp. 59–60.

Music can be about the emotional life and character of humans, and this is a profound subject.

When anti-formalists say that music provides psychological insight, they are not saying that every work of music that arouses (and represents) emotion provides psychological insight. Some pieces of music neither arouse nor represent emotion. Other works of music arouse and represent only commonplace and familiar emotions. A good deal of dance music, including Mozart's German Dances, arouses (and represents) emotion but does so in a way that provides no new insights. The muzak version of 'She's leaving home' arouses emotion, but it is schmaltzy and sentimental. It provides no insight into complex and unusual emotions or patterns of emotion. While such works represent emotion, they do not owe much of their value to their representational content.

Some genres of music are appreciated primarily or exclusively as intellectual puzzles and neither arouse nor represent emotion. I have suggested that serialism is one such genre. Works of music in such genres cannot be profound. Works of music in other genres are valuable primarily or exclusively as sources of sensory pleasure and pleasing emotions. Some writers have suggested that rock music is valued as a source of sensory pleasure.[56] The suggestion that rock and other forms of pop music are valued for their emotional effects, and not as a source of intellectual insight, also seems plausible.[57] In my view, a musical work with the highest aesthetic value will be one that, as Nicholas Brady proposed, both 'charms the Sense and captivates the Mind'. Works that merely charm the senses are not capable of profundity.

Some works of music, including some of the greatest works of music, owe much of their aesthetic value to their representation of emotion. One may ask why humans find representations rewarding. Aristotle had an answer to this question, and no one has advanced a better one. We are, Aristotle believed, just built in such a way that we take pleasure in representations. He notes in the *Poetics* that 'We find an indication of this in experience: for we view with pleasure reproductions of objects which in real life it pains us to look upon.' In this passage Aristotle was not speaking

---

[56] Bruce Baugh, 'Prolegomena to Any Aesthetics of Rock Music', *Journal of Aesthetics and Art Criticism*, 51 (1993), 23–9.
[57] For this suggestion, see Joel Rudinow, *Soul Music: Tracking the Spiritual Roots of Pop from Plato to Motown* (Ann Arbor, M.I.: University of Michigan Press, 2010), p. 88.

about music, but his point can be extended to musical representations. Part of the attraction of music is simply that we enjoy contemplating representations of expressive behaviour and emotion. There is, however, another reason why listeners find rewarding the experience of musical representations. We value the knowledge that representations make possible. As Aristotle noted, 'mankind's pleasure in beholding likenesses of objects is due to this: as they contemplate reproductions of objects they find themselves gaining knowledge'.[58]

We need to ask about the extent and importance of the knowledge that can be gleaned from those works of music that represent and have extra-musical cognitive significance. For a start, music provides us with knowledge of what emotions are like. Music provides us with knowledge about a wide range of human emotions: all of the emotions that it can arouse. Many authors have remarked on the capacity of music to provide insight into a range of emotions. Donald Grout noted that the number and variety of Handel's arias 'is so great, and the power of capturing the most subtle nuances of feeling so astounding, that one is tempted to believe there is no emotion of which humanity is capable that has not found musical expression somewhere in Handel's operas'.[59] Listening to music, one is exposed to subtle gradations of emotion that one might not otherwise experience. This, T.S. Eliot wrote, gives music much of its cognitive interest. He wrote that, 'beyond the nameable, classifiable emotions and motives of our conscious life when directed towards action... there is a fringe of indefinite extent, of feeling which we can only detect, so to speak, out of the corner of the eye and can never completely focus'. Eliot believes dramatic poetry can explore this realm of emotion but, he indicates, so can music. These elusive emotions are the 'feelings which only music can express'.[60] When music expresses (or, as I would prefer, represents) non-mundane emotions it can be psychologically insightful.

The capacity of music to provide knowledge of what it is like to experience an emotion or emotions is part of what makes music rewarding; that is, aesthetically valuable, at least for many listeners. As Levinson says,

---

[58] Aristotle, *The Poetics of Aristotle*, trans. Preston H. Epps (Chapel Hill, N.C.: University of North Carolina Press, 1942), p. 6.

[59] Donald Jay Grout and Hermine Weigel Williams, *A Short History of Opera*, fourth edn (New York: Columbia University Press, 2003), p. 191.

[60] T.S. Eliot, *Poetry and Drama* (Cambridge, M.A.: Harvard University Press, 1951), pp. 42–3.

listening to a variety of musical works, 'We become cognoscenti of feeling, savoring the qualitative aspect of emotional life for its own sake.'[61] Music can lay out before us the panoply of human emotion and let us know what each is like.

As noted previously, the content of a work of music cannot be fully captured in propositional terms. That is, from a work of music, audiences do not acquire knowledge that some proposition about emotion is true. Rather, a work of music conveys knowledge of what experience of some emotion is like by arousing the emotion in us. Music shows us what emotion is like rather than telling us something about emotion. We acquire the knowledge about emotion that music conveys in the only possible way: by feeling emotions. The cognitive significance of music lies in the knowledge of what it is like to feel these emotions. This conclusion is one that several composers have reached. Mahler remarked that, 'as long as I can express an experience in words I should never try to put it into music.'[62] Similarly, Copland balked at trying to capture in words the 'inner depth' of Bach's music: 'We would only find ourselves groping for words, words that can never hope to encompass the intangible greatness of music, least of all the intangible in Bach's greatness.'[63]

A possible misreading of my position needs to be ruled out at this point. In endorsing the views of Mahler and Copland, I am not adopting anything like the formalists' ineffability thesis. Contrary to what formalists believe, it is possible to say what makes works of music beautiful. Beautiful works of music are ones that provide profound psychological insights. (Perhaps other works, that provide sensory pleasure or are valuable in some other way, may also be described as beautiful.) That said, it is not possible to capture fully the insights provided by music in propositional terms. Only in this sense is the content of music inexpressible. There is no mystery about why music is beautiful.

As noted in Chapter 3, instrumental music by itself represents and provides insight into types of emotions, not into the emotions of some particular individual. A title (*Semper Dowland, semper dolens*, for example), notation (such as 'C.P.E. Bach's feelings'), or other commentary by a composer can, however, specify the person whose emotions are represented in a particular

---

[61] Levinson, 'Music and Negative Emotion', p. 324.
[62] Knud Martner (ed.), *Selected Letters of Gustav Mahler*, trans. Eithne Wilkins, Ernst Kaiser, and Bill Hopkins (London: Faber and Faber, 1979), p. 179.
[63] Aaron Copland, *Copland on Music* (Garden City, N.Y.: Doubleday, 1960), p. 38.

musical work. When the emotions being represented have been specified in this manner (and a composer is skilful enough), listeners are provided with insight into the emotional life of some particular individual, frequently the composer. Similarly, as noted in Chapter 4, the addition of lyrics to music makes it possible for a composition to represent and provide representations of the emotions of individual people or types of person. Schubert's *Gretchen am Spinnrade* represents, for example, the emotional state of people like the infatuated Gretchen. Good composers are thus able to provide psychological insight into the emotional lives of certain people or types of person.

Music is able to provide a more general sort of psychological insight. It is a commonplace, almost a cliché, that music can transport listeners to 'another time and place'. Perhaps the best example of this is found in music of the Romantic era. Listening to Beethoven and his successors one gets a sense of what it was like to live in that tumultuous time, and how it differed from the politeness of Mozart's day. Or consider, for example, joyous Christmas music from eighteenth-century Latin America. (I have in mind works by composers such as Juan de Araujo and Esteban Salas.) Such music is expressive of, arouses in us, and represents the emotional states experienced by long-ago worshippers. Listening to such music, listeners (unless they are very formalist indeed) cannot help but gain insight into the joy and gaiety experienced by those participating in long-ago and far-away (relative to where I live) feast days. Contrast this music with, say, the medieval Song of the Sibyl, which was (and is) performed annually on Christmas Eve. Those who listened to this music in medieval Catalonia can only have gone about their Christmas devotions in a frame of mind dramatically different from that of later Latin Americans. When we listen to a work such as the Song of the Sibyl, we gain insight into what it was like to experience a grim sense of sin and dejection in those hardscrabble days.[64]

Music can also provide insight into the inner lives of individual composers or performers. At least, music can do so in combination with a text (again, the cases of 'C.P.E. Bach's Feelings' and *Semper Dowland, semper dolens*) or against a background of compositional practice, such as that which prevailed during the Romantic period or in certain contexts of the production of blues music.

---

[64] Stephen Davies pointed out, in his referee's report, that only comparatively recently has music been valuable in the way indicated in this paragraph. Only since the eighteenth century has it been common to listen to music from the past and other cultures.

Music does more than provide listeners with insight into the experience of individual emotions. Musical compositions with significant scale and scope are expressive of a wide range of emotions. (Even Kivy, as we have seen, grants this much.) Music can also arouse and represent patterns of emotion. So, for example, a work of music can represent what it is like to feel joy after longing, or despair after triumph. One of the functions of a da capo aria is to represent emotions in relation to each other. Concerti and sonatas often similarly compare and contrast emotions. As a result, music can do more than give listeners knowledge of what it is like to experience certain emotions. A work of music can also show listeners what it is like to experience a given series of emotions.

Music is often held to provide insight into character. Liszt's *Faust Symphony*, for example, sketches the characters of Faust, Gretchen, and Mephistopheles. We are now in a position to see how this is possible. A person's character is, as was noted in the previous chapter, in large part manifested in a person's emotions and patterns of emotional response. Consequently, by representing patterns of emotional experience, music also represents characters and, more usually, types of characters. (Notice that music represents a type of character or a particular character, not some indeterminate persona.) These representations of character can, as in the case of the *Faust Symphony*, be psychologically insightful.

These remarks leave us with an incomplete picture of the content that music can have by representing emotion. Works of music, at least some great works of music, provide listeners with a perspective on certain emotions. By a perspective on an object I mean a way of thinking about or perceiving the object. Having a perspective on something is 'thinking as'. That is, to have a perspective on something is to think of it as possessed of certain characteristics. I have, for example, a perspective on Wall Street. I think of it as a den of iniquity. Or I have a perspective on the current Leader of the Opposition. I think of her as principled and compassionate. Similarly, one can have a perspective on emotions. For example, one can think of an emotion as noble, tragic, or dignified.

Music is regularly described in these and similar terms. Jahn speaks of the 'dignity and solemnity' of Mozart's 'Jupiter' Symphony, K. 551.[65] Levinson states that it is 'straightforwardly true that the *Eroica* Symphony

---

[65] Otto Jahn, *Life of Mozart*, trans. Pauline D. Townsend (London: Novello, Ewer, and Co., 1882), vol. 3, p. 37.

is noble'.[66] Spitta uses the same adjective to describe Bach's Toccata and Fugue in D minor, BWV 565.[67] Tchaikovsky's *Pathétique Symphony*, Op. 74, is routinely described as tragic. Philosophers and musicologists are not the only ones to employ such adjectives in describing music. 'Tragic', 'solemn', and 'dignified' are among the adjectives that psychologists have long found to be applied to musical performances by ordinary listeners.[68]

The formalist has difficulty explaining how these adjectives are applicable to works of music. It is difficult to see how empty form can be noble, humane, tragic, or dignified. I dare say that no image seen through a kaleidoscope has ever been noble. I have never seen a tragic Persian carpet. Neither are carpets frivolous or shallow. In contrast, the anti-formalist has a ready explanation for the fact that music is often described as noble, solemn, and so forth. To call a work of music noble or dignified is an elliptical way of saying that it presents the perspective that some emotion is noble, dignified, or possessed of some similar characteristic. Music can do more than represent. It can 'represent as'. For example, some emotions, or series of emotions, can be represented as dignified, noble, or tragic.

Music's capacity to 'represent as' or present perspectives on emotions requires that it both arouse and be expressive of the emotions. The listener can recognize what emotions have been aroused and what expressive behaviour is represented in a piece of music. For example, the listener can feel sadness and at the same time recognize that the behaviour expressive of that emotion is dignified or noble. Listening to a different performance, the listener can feel joyful and yet recognize that the expression of the emotion is stately or playful. As a result, when listeners grasp the content of a work of music they can know more than what the emotion feels like. They can also gain insight into the moral character of an emotion. They can learn, for example, that grief can be noble, dignified, or despairing.

These reflections lead to the conclusion that a full account of the content of music must recognize that works of music do more than show listeners what certain emotions are like. Music can also show listeners that emotions are possessed of certain moral characteristics. Emotions are represented as noble, solemn, tragic, and so forth. A work of music arouses, say,

---

[66] Jerrold Levinson, 'What a Musical Work Is', *Music, Art, and Metaphysics*, p. 72.

[67] Philipp Spitta, *Johann Sebastian Bach*, trans. Clara Bell and J.A. Fuller-Maitland (London: Novello, Ewer, and Co., 1885), vol. 3, p. 208.

[68] Kate Hevner, 'Experimental Studies of the Elements of Expression in Music', *American Journal of Psychology*, 47 (1935), p. 246.

grief but it also represents the grief as noble or possessed of some other property. Schweitzer speaks, for example, of Bach's Passions and cantatas as presenting either 'distressful or noble grief'.[69] Hospers similarly characterizes the grief of the second movement of the *Eroica Symphony* as 'noble grief'.[70] Grout describes 'Lascio ch'io pianga' (from Handel's *Rinaldo*) as 'nobly mournful'.[71] Berlioz speaks of a performance of 'J'ai perdu mon Eurydice', from Gluck's *Orphée et Eurydice*, as delivered at first with 'contained grief' and then with 'distracted grief'.[72] The contained grief can have a nobility to it, while the distracted grief does not. In all of these cases, a work of music shows us what an emotion is like and characterizes the emotion in moral terms.

One might wonder about whether listeners receive genuine psychological insights from works of music. The claim that music shows us what certain emotions feel like is not controversial. Once music has aroused the emotion, one can feel what it is like. Other claims are more controversial. Consider, for example, the claim that music provides insight into character or that a work of music shows listeners that a certain sort of grief is noble. Listening to the work, someone may grasp that the composer is conveying the perspective that the particular sort of grief is noble. The question is whether the listener can know, on the basis of having listened to a composition, that grief can be noble. The composer presents this perspective on grief, but perhaps the composer is wrong and people in the grip of grief cannot comport themselves with nobility.

Even if listeners had no other reason than that a composer presents a given perspective on an emotion, they would not be without justification for believing that they have been given insight into emotion. Testimony is a source of knowledge, and composers may be assumed to be sincerely conveying insights that they have had into emotion. The usual reliability of testimony is not, however, the sole basis for saying that music can, by presenting a perspective on emotion, be a source of insight. By presenting a perspective on emotion or character, a work gives listeners a way of looking at their experience of emotion. Listeners need to look again at their experience of emotion and ask themselves whether the perspective

---

[69] Schweitzer, *J.S. Bach*, p. 51.
[70] John Hospers, *An Introduction to Philosophical Analysis*, third edn (London: Routledge, 1990), p. 341.
[71] Grout and Williams, *A Short History of Opera*, pp. 191–2.
[72] Hector Berlioz, *Gluck and His Operas* (London: W. Reeves, 1915), p. 20.

presented in a work of music is in accord with this experience. The insightful work of music is useful in making sense of our experience of emotion.[73]

Envoi

Only when we see that music is the source of insight into emotion can a complete account be given of the aesthetic value of music. Music is (at least for some people) rewarding as a source of intellectual puzzles. Many people enjoy the sensations and emotions that music arouses. Only, however, as a source of insight into the interior human emotional life can music be profound. The achievement of the great musician is more valuable than the achievement of even the greatest vintner, perfumer, or creator of chess problems. The greater value of the musician's achievement cannot be explained if music only pleases our senses and provides the opportunity to play intellectual games. Only when it is recognized that music has content can the relatively greater importance of the musician's achievement be explained.

Anti-formalism has another conspicuous advantage over formalism. Formalism, as we have seen, leads to the view that the beauty of musical works is ineffable. Formalists have no explanation for why a work of music is beautiful. Anti-formalism, in contrast, has an explanation. Musical works with the highest aesthetic value will be those that provide the deepest psychological insight. Anti-formalists even have an account of how works come to have psychological depth. The explanation begins with an account of how music is expressive of emotion. It continues with the explanation of how music arouses emotion. The explanation culminates in the account of how music represents emotion. Some of these representations will provide psychological insight. The ones that provide the deep psychological insights are the ones that we call profound or beautiful. The precise psychological insights provided by a particular work of music may not be completely capturable in propositional terms, but the anti-formalist is able to give a general account of what makes works of music aesthetically rewarding.

There is a limit to what a philosopher can say about the insights that music can provide. To a certain extent this is because the content of music

---

[73] Here I am drawing on my *Art and Knowledge* (London: Routledge, 2001), p. 106.

cannot be fully expressed in words, and words are a philosopher's stock in trade. There is, however, another reason why philosophers cannot be particularly informative about the content of music. The capacity to talk insightfully about music is a skill completely distinct from the skills possessed by philosophers (qua philosophers). The capacity to talk insightfully about music is possessed by some musicians, music critics, and musicologists. This is partly the capacity to notice and draw attention to subtle features of music. Partly this capacity is the ability to describe the experience of music. No description can, as I have indicated, capture the full phenomenological character of the experience of music. The best music critics nevertheless possess the capacity to speak (or gesture) in ways that draw attention towards the content of music. They are particularly good at indicating the perspective on emotions and on characters that are presented in works of music. Up to a point, these perspectives can be captured in propositional terms.

Once the question of whether musical works have content is turned over to musicians and music critics, it will become much more focused on individual works and even on individual performances. Ultimately, the dispute between formalists and anti-formalists will be a long, drawn-out campaign, fought one work of music or one performance at a time. Anti-formalists get a little closer to victory each time critics show that, on the most convincing reading, a work of music has content. Each time critics successfully argue that listeners miss something when they fail to see that a work of music is about human experience, particularly the emotional life of humans, anti-formalists are a step closer towards completing the critique of pure music.

Bibliography of Works Cited and Consulted

Abert, Hermann, W.A. *Mozart*, trans. Stewart Spencer, New Haven, C.T.: Yale University Press, 2007.
Addis, Laird, *Of Mind and Music*, Ithaca, N.Y.: Cornell University Press, 1999.
Ali, S. Omar and Zehra F. Peynircioğlu, 'Songs and emotions: are lyrics and melodies equal partners?' *Psychology of Music*, 34 (2006), 511–34.
Anderson, Emily (ed.), *The Letters of Mozart and His Family*, London: MacMillan, 1938.
Anderson, Sheila E., *The Quotable Musician from Bach to Tupac*, New York: Allwork Press, 2009.
Aristotle, *The Poetics of Aristotle*, trans. Preston H. Epps, Chapel Hill, N.C.: University of North Carolina Press, 1942.
—— *The Politics of Aristotle*, trans. Ernest Barker, Oxford: Clarendon Press, 1946.
Bach, Carl Philipp Emanuel, *Essay on the True Art of Playing Keyboard Instruments*, second edn, trans. William J. Mitchell, London: Cassell and Company, 1951.
Balkwill, Laura-Lee and William Forde Thompson, 'A Cross-Cultural Investigation of the Perception of Emotion in Music: Psychophysical and Cultural Cues', *Music Perception*, 17 (1999), 43–64.
—— and Rie Matsunaga, 'Recognition of emotion in Japanese, Western, and Hindustani music by Japanese listeners', *Japanese Psychological Research*, 46 (2004), 337–49.
Balteş, Felicia Rodica, Julia Avram, Mircea Miclea, and Andrei C. Miu, 'Emotions induced by operatic music: Psychophysiological effects of music, plot and acting', *Brain and Cognition*, 76 (2011), 146–57.
Bartlett, Dale L., 'Physiological Responses to Music and Sound Stimuli', in Donald A. Hodges (ed.), *Handbook of Music Psychology*, second edn, San Antonio, T.X.: IMR Press, 1996, 343–85.
Baugh, Bruce, 'Prolegomena to Any Aesthetics of Rock Music', *Journal of Aesthetics and Art Criticism*, 51 (1993), 23–9.
Baumeister, Roy F., Kathleen D. Vohs, C. Nathan DeWall, and Liqing Zhang, 'How Emotion Shapes Behavior: Feedback, Anticipation, and Reflection, Rather Than Direct Causation', *Personality and Social Psychology Review*, 11 (2007), 167–203.
Beethoven, Ludwig van, *Letters, Journals and Conversations*, trans. Michael Hamburger, London: Jonathan Cape, 1951.
Bell, Clive, *Art*, London: Chatto and Windus, 1914.

Berg, Alban, 'The Problem of Opera', in Richard Kostelanetz and Joseph Darby, *Classic Essays on Twentieth-Century Music*, New York: Schirmer Books, 1996, 277-9.

Berlioz, Hector, *Life of Hector Berlioz as Written by Himself in His Letters & Memoirs*, trans. Katherine F. Boult, London: J.M. Dent & Sons, n.d.

—— *Gluck and His Operas*, London: W. Reeves, 1915.

Bharucha, Jamshed J., Meagan Curtis, and Kaivon Paroo, 'Varieties of musical experience', *Cognition*, 100 (2006), 131-72.

Bicknell, Jeanette, *Why Music Moves Us*, Basingstoke: Palgrave Macmillan, 2009.

Blaukopf, Kurt and Zoltan Roman (eds.), *Mahler: A Documentary Study*, trans. Paul Baker, Susanne Flatauer, P.R.J. Ford, Daisy Loman, and Geoffrey Watkins, London: Thames and Hudson, 1976.

Bowling, Daniel L., Kamraan Gill, Jonathan D. Choi, Joseph Prinz, and Dale Purves, 'Major and minor music compared to excited and subdued speech', *Journal of the Acoustical Society of America*, 127 (2010), 491-503.

Brower, Candace, 'A Cognitive Theory of Musical Meaning', *Journal of Music Theory*, 44 (2000), 323-79.

Budd, Malcolm, 'Motion and Emotion in Music: How Music Sounds', *British Journal of Aesthetics*, 23 (1983), 209-21.

—— *Music and the Emotions: The Philosophical Theories*, London: Routledge and Kegan Paul, 1985.

—— 'Music and the Communication of Emotion', *Journal of Aesthetics and Art Criticism*, 47 (1989), 129-37.

—— *Aesthetic Essays*, Oxford: Oxford University Press, 2008.

Burney, Charles, *A General History of Music*, New York: Dover Publications, 1957.

Calef, Scott, 'A Little of the Human Touch: Knowledge and Empathy in the Music of Bruce Springsteen', in Randall E. Auxier and Doug Anderson (eds.), *Bruce Springsteen and Philosophy*, Chicago, I.L.: Open Court, 2008, 223-34.

Carr, David, 'Music, Meaning, and Emotion', *Journal of Aesthetics and Art Criticism*, 62 (2004), 225-34.

Carroll, Noël, *Art in Three Dimensions*, Oxford: Oxford University Press, 2010.

Clarke, Eric, 'Meaning and the specification of motion in music', *Musicae Scientiae*, 5 (2001), 213-34.

Clynes, Manfred and Nigel Nettheim, 'The Living Quality of Music: Neurobiologic Basis of Communicating Feeling', in Manfred Clynes (ed.), *Music, Mind, and Brain: The Neuropsychology of Music*, New York and London: Plenum Press, 1982, 47-82.

Cochrane, Tom, 'A Simulation Theory of Musical Expressivity', *Australasian Journal of Philosophy*, 88 (2010), 191-207.

—— 'Using the Persona to Express Complex Emotions in Music', *Music Analysis*, 29 (2010), 264-75.

Coclico, Adrian Petit, *Musical Compendium*, trans. Albert Seay, Colorado Springs, C.O.: Colorado College Music Press, 1973.

Cohen, Annabel J., 'How Music Influences the Interpretation of Film and Video: Approaches from Experimental Psychology', in Roger A. Kendall and Roger W.H. Savage (eds.), *Perspectives in Systematic Musicology*, Los Angeles, C.A.: Department of Ethnomusicology, University of California, Los Angeles, 2005, 15–36.

Cone, Edward T., *The Composer's Voice*, Berkeley, C.A.: University of California Press, 1974.

Cook, Norman D., 'The Sound Symbolism of Major and Minor Harmonies', *Music Perception*, 24 (2007), 315–19.

Cooke, Deryk. *The Language of Music*, Oxford: Oxford University Press, 1959.

Copland, Aaron, *Copland on Music*, Garden City, N.Y.: Doubleday, 1960.

Cox, Arnie, 'The mimetic hypothesis and embodied musical meaning', *Musicae Scientae*, 5 (2001), 195–212.

Curtis, Meagan E. and Jamshed J. Bharucha, 'The Minor Third Communicates Sadness in Speech, Mirroring Its Use in Music', *Emotion*, 10 (2010), 335–48.

Dahlhaus, Carl, *Esthetics of Music*, trans. William W. Austin, Cambridge: Cambridge University Press, 1982.

Davies, Stephen, *Musical Meaning and Expression*, Ithaca, N.Y.: Cornell University Press, 1994.

—— 'Kivy on Auditor's Emotions', *Journal of Aesthetics and Art Criticism*, 52 (1994), 235–6.

—— 'Response to Robert Stecker', *British Journal of Aesthetics*, 39 (1999), 282–7.

—— *Themes in the Philosophy of Music*, Oxford: Oxford University Press, 2003.

—— *Musical Understandings and Others Essays on the Philosophy of Music*, Oxford: Oxford University Press, 2011.

Dean, Winton, *Handel and the Opera Seria*, Berkeley, C.A.: University of California Press, 1969.

—— *Essays on Opera*, Oxford: Clarendon Press, 1990.

Dempster, Douglas, 'How Does Debussy's Sea Crash? How Can Jimi's Rocket Red Glare?: Kivy's Account of Representation in Music', *Journal of Aesthetics and Art Criticism*, 53 (1994), 415–28.

Dorsey, Learthen, '"And All that Jazz" Has African Roots!' in James L. Conyers (ed.), *African American Jazz and Rap: Social and Philosophical Examinations of Black Expressive Behavior*, Jefferson, N.C.: McFarland, 2001, 35–54.

Dubois, Pierre (ed.), *Charles Avison's* Essay on Musical Expression *With Related Writings by William Hayes and Charles Avison*, Aldershot: Ashgate, 2004.

Dutton, Donald G. and Arthur P. Aron, 'Some evidence for heightened sexual attraction under conditions of high anxiety', *Journal of Personality and Social Psychology*, 30 (1974), 510–17.

Eliot, T.S., *Poetry and Drama*, Cambridge, M.A.: Harvard University Press, 1951.

Ellis, Robert J. and Robert F. Simons, 'The Impact of Music on Subjective and Physiological Indices of Emotion While Viewing Films', *Psychomusicology*, 19 (2005), 15–40.

Feld, Steven, ' "Flow Like a Waterfall": The Metaphors of Kaluki Musical Theory', *Yearbook for Traditional Music*, 13 (1981), 22–47.

Fritz, Thomas, Sebastian Jentschke, Nathalie Gosselin, Daniela Sammler, Isabelle Peretz, Robert Turner, Angela D. Friederici, and Stefan Koelsch, 'Universal Recognition of Three Basic Emotions in Music', *Current Biology*, 19 (2009), 573–6.

Gabrielsson, Alf, 'Emotion perceived and emotion felt: Same or different?' *Musicae Scientiae*, Special Issue 2001–2002, 123–47.

—— *Strong Experiences with Music: Music is much more than just music*, trans. Rod Bradbury, Oxford: Oxford University Press, 2011.

Glarean, Heinrich, *Dodecachordon*, trans. Clement A. Miller, n.p.: American Institute of Musicology, 1965.

Goodman, Nelson, *Languages of Art*, Indianapolis, I.N.: Hackett, 1976.

—— and Catherine Z. Elgin, *Reconceptions in Philosophy and Other Arts and Sciences*, Indianapolis, I.N.: Hackett, 1988.

Gosselin, Nathalie, Isabelle Peretz, Erica Johnsen, Ralph Adolphs, 'Amygdala damage impairs emotion recognition from music', *Neuropsychologia*, 45 (2007), 236–44.

Graham, Gordon, 'The Value of Music', *Journal of Aesthetics and Art Criticism*, 53 (1995), 139–53.

Gregory, Andrew H. and Nicholas Varney, 'Cross-cultural Comparisons in the Affective Response to Music', *Psychology of Music*, 24 (1996), 47–52.

Green, Anders C., Klaus B. Baerentsen, Hans Stødkilde-Jørgensen, Mikkel Wallentin, Andreas Roepstorff, and Peter Vuust, 'Music in minor activates limbic structures: a relationship with dissonance', *NeuroReport*, 19 (2008), 711–15.

Grout, Donald Jay and Hermine Weigel Williams, *A Short History of Opera*, fourth edn, New York: Columbia University Press, 2003.

Hamilton, Andy, 'Rhythm and Stasis: A Major and Almost Entirely Neglected Philosophical Problem', *Proceedings of the Aristotelian Society*, 109 (2011), 25–42.

Han, Shul' er, Janani Sundararajan, Daniel Liu Bowling, Jessica Lake, and Dale Purves, 'Co-Variation of Tonality in the Music and Speech of Different Cultures', *PLoS ONE* 6(5) (2010), e20160. doi:10.1371/journal.pone.0020160.

Hand, Ferdinand, *Aesthetics of Musical Art; or, The Beautiful in Music*, second edn, trans. Walter E. Lawson, London: William Reeves, 1880.

Hanslick, Eduard, *The Beautiful in Music*, trans. Gustav Cohen, Indianapolis, I.N.: Bobbs-Merrill, 1957.

Hari, Riitta and Miiamaaria V. Kujala, 'Brain Basis of Human Social Interaction: From Concepts to Brain Imaging', *Physiological Reviews*, 89 (2009), 453-79.

Hentschel, Frank, 'The sensuous music aesthetics of the Middle Ages: the cases of Augustine, Jacques de Liége and Guido of Arezzo', *Plainsong and Medieval Music*, 20 (2011), 1-29.

Hevner, Kate, 'The Affective Character of the Major and Minor Modes in Music', *American Journal of Psychology*, 47 (1935), 103-18.

—— 'Experimental Studies of the Elements of Expression in Music', *American Journal of Psychology*, 47 (1935), 246-68.

Higgins, Kathleen Marie, *The Music between Us: Is Music a Universal Language?* Chicago, I.L.: University of Chicago Press, 2012.

Honegger, Arthur, *Pacific 231: Mouvement Symphonique*, Paris: Éditions Salabert, 1924.

Hospers, John, *An Introduction to Philosophical Analysis*, third edn, London: Routledge, 1990.

Hume, David, *Enquiries Concerning Human Understanding and concerning the Principles of Morals*, ed. L.A. Selby-Bigg, third edn, Oxford, Clarendon Press, 1975.

Huron, David, 'Why is sad music pleasurable? A possible role for prolactin', *Musicae Scientiae*, 15 (2011), 146-58.

Hutcheson, Francis, *An Inquiry into the Original of Our Ideas of Beauty and Virtue: In Two Treatises*, revised edn, Indianapolis, I.N.: Liberty Fund, 2008.

Jahn, Otto, *Life of Mozart*, trans. Pauline D. Townsend, London: Novello, Ewer, and Co., 1882.

Janata, Petr and Scott T. Grafton, 'Swinging in the brain: shared neural substrates for behaviors related to sequencing and music', *Nature Neuroscience*, 6 (2003), 682-7.

Johnson, Mark, *Body in the Mind: The Bodily Basis of Meaning, Imagination, and Reason*, Chicago, I.L.: University of Chicago Press, 1987.

—— *The Meaning of the Body: Aesthetics of Human Understanding*, Chicago, I.L.: University of Chicago Press, 2007.

Johnson-Laird, P.N. and Keith Oatley, 'Emotions, Music, and Literature', in Michael Lewis (ed.), *Handbook of Emotions*, New York: Guilford Press, 2008, 102-13.

Juslin, Patrik N., 'Emotion in music performance', in Susan Hallam, Ian Cross, and Michael Thaut (eds.), *The Oxford Handbook of Musical Psychology*, Oxford: Oxford University Press, 2009, 377-89.

—— and Petri Laukka, 'Communication of Emotions in Vocal Expression and Music Performance: Different Channels, Same Code?' *Psychological Bulletin*, 129 (2003), 770-814.

—— and Roland S. Persson, 'Emotional Communication', in Richard Parncutt and Gary E. McPherson (eds.), *The Science and Psychology of Music*

Performance: Creative Strategies for Teaching and Learning, Oxford: Oxford University Press, 2002, 19-25.

—— and John A. Sloboda, *Music and Emotion: Theory and Research*, Oxford: Oxford University Press, 2001.

—— and Daniel Västfjäll, 'Emotional responses to music: The need to consider underlying mechanisms', *Behavioral and Brain Sciences*, 31 (2008), 559-621.

Kallinen, Kari and Niklas Ravaja, 'Emotion perceived and emotion felt: Same and different', *Musicae Scientiae*, 10 (2006), 191-213.

Kemp, Stephen W.P. and Gerald C. Cupchik, 'The Emotionally Evocative Effects of Paintings', *Visual Arts Research*, 33 (2007), 72-82.

Kerman, Joseph, *Opera as Drama*, new and revised edn, Berkeley, C.A.: University of California Press, 1988.

King, B.B., *Blues All Around Me*, London: Hodder and Stoughton, 1996.

Kivy, Peter, *Sound Sentiment: An Essay on the Musical Emotions Including the Complete Text of The Corded Shell*, Philadelphia, P.A.: Temple University Press, 1989.

—— *Music Alone: Philosophical Reflections on the Purely Musical Experience*, Ithaca, N.Y.: Cornell University Press, 1990.

—— *Sound and Semblance: Reflections on Musical Representation*, Ithaca, N.Y.: Cornell University Press, 1991.

—— *The Fine Art of Repetition: Essays in the Philosophy of Music*, Cambridge: Cambridge University Press, 1993.

—— 'Armistice, but No Surrender: Davies on Kivy', *Journal of Aesthetics and Art Criticism*, 52 (1994), 236-7.

—— *Philosophies of Arts: An Essay in Differences*, Cambridge: Cambridge University Press, 1997.

—— *Osmin's Rage: Philosophical Reflections on Opera, Drama, and Text, with a New Final Chapter*, Ithaca, N.Y.: Cornell University Press, 1999.

—— *New Essays on Musical Understanding*, Oxford: Clarendon Press, 2001.

—— *Introduction to a Philosophy of Music*, Oxford: Clarendon Press, 2002.

—— 'Another Go at Musical Profundity: Stephen Davies and the Game of Chess', *British Journal of Aesthetics*, 43 (2003), 401-11.

—— 'Critical Study: Deeper than Reason', *British Journal of Aesthetics*, 46 (2006), 287-311.

—— 'Mood and Music: Some Reflections for Noël Carroll', *Journal of Aesthetics and Art Criticism*, 64 (2006), 271-81.

—— 'Moodology: A Response to Laura Sizer', *Journal of Aesthetics and Art Criticism*, 65 (2007), 312-18.

—— 'Moodophilia: A Response to Noël Carroll and Margaret Moore', *Journal of Aesthetics and Art Criticism*, 65 (2007), 323-9.

—— *Antithetical Arts: On the Ancient Quarrel between Literature and Music*, Oxford: Clarendon Press, 2009.

—— 'The Other Shoe: Some Thoughts for Christopher Peacocke', *British Journal of Aesthetics*, 49 (2009), 283–7.

—— *Sounding Off: Eleven Essays in the Philosophy of Music*, Oxford: Oxford University Press, 2012.

Knobloch-Westerwick, Silvia, Yuan Gong, Holly Hagner, and Laura Kerbeykian, 'Tragedy Viewers Count Their Blessings: Feeling Low on Fiction Leads to Feeling High on Life', *Communications Research*, forthcoming.

Konečni, Vladimir J. 'Does Music Induce Emotion? A Theoretical and Methodological Analysis', *Psychology of Aesthetics, Creativity, and the Arts*, 2 (2008), 115–29.

Kreutz, Gunter, Ulrich Ott, Daniel Teichman, Patrick Osawa, and Dieter Vaitl, 'Using music to induce emotions: Influences of musical preference and absorption', *Psychology of Music*, 36 (2008), 101–26.

Krumhansl, Carol L., 'An Exploratory Study of Musical Emotions and Psychophysiology', *Canadian Journal of Experimental Psychology*, 51 (1997), 336–52.

—— 'Music: A Link Between Cognition and Emotion', *Current Directions in Psychological Science*, 11 (2002), 45–50.

Lerdahl, Fred, 'Cognitive Constraints on Compositional Systems', in John Sloboda (ed.), *Generative Processes in Music*, Oxford: Oxford University Press, 1988, 231–59.

Levinson, Jerrold, *Music, Art, and Metaphysics*, Ithaca, N.Y.: Cornell University Press, 1990.

—— 'Musical Profundity Misplaced', *Journal of Aesthetics and Art Criticism*, 50 (1992), 58–60.

—— *The Pleasures of Aesthetics: Philosophical Essays*, Ithaca, N.Y.: Cornell University Press, 1996.

—— *Contemplating Art*, Oxford: Clarendon Press, 2006.

—— 'Musical Expressiveness as Hearability-as-expression', in Matthew Kieran (ed.), *Contemporary Debates in Aesthetics and the Philosophy of Art*, Malden, M.A.: Blackwell, 2006, 192–204.

Lippman, Edward A., *Musical Aesthetics: A Historical Reader*, New York: Pendragon Press, 1986.

Macan, Edward, 'Bring Back the Balance', in Scott Calef (ed.), *Led Zeppelin and Philosophy: All Will be Revealed*, Chicago, I.L.: Open Court, 2009, 187–218.

Mackie, J.L., *Ethics: Inventing Right and Wrong*, Harmondsworth: Penguin, 1977.

Madell, Geoffrey, 'What Music Teaches about Emotion', *Philosophy*, 71 (1996), 63–82.

Martner, Knud (ed.), *Selected Letters of Gustav Mahler*, trans. Eithne Wilkins, Ernst Kaiser, and Bill Hopkins, London: Faber and Faber, 1979.

Masataka, Nobuo, 'Preference for consonance over dissonance by hearing newborns of deaf parents and of hearing parents', *Developmental Science*, 9 (2006), 46–50.

Matravers, Derek, *Art and Emotion*, Oxford: Clarendon Press, 1998.

—— 'The Experience of Emotion in Music', *Journal of Aesthetics and Art Criticism*, 61 (2003), 253–63.

Mendelssohn, Felix, *Letters of Felix Mendelssohn Bartholdy From 1833 to 1847*, trans. Lady Wallace, Boston, M.A.: Oliver Ditson, 1863.

Meyer, Leonard B., *Emotion and Meaning in Music*, Chicago, I.L.: University of Chicago Press, 1956.

Moravcsik, Julius, 'Understanding and the Emotions', *Dialectica*, 36 (1982), 207–24.

Mozart, Leopold, *A Treatise on the Fundamental Principles of Violin Playing*, trans. Editha Knocker, Oxford: Oxford University Press, 1985.

Mueller von Asow, Wedwig and E.H., *The Collected Correspondence and Papers of Christoph Willibald Gluck*, trans. Stewart Thomson, New York: St Martin's Press, 1962.

National Gallery of Art, Washington, *Painting in the Dutch Golden Age: A Profile of the Seventeenth Century*, Washington: National Gallery of Art, 2007.

Neuman, Roland and Fritz Strack, '"Mood Contagion": The Automatic Transfer of Mood Between Persons', *Journal of Personality and Social Psychology*, 79 (2000), 211–23.

Nolt, John, 'Expression and Emotion', *British Journal of Aesthetics*, 21 (1981), 139–50.

Nussbaum, Charles O., *The Musical Representation: Meaning, Ontology, and Emotion*, Cambridge, M.A.: MIT Press, 2007.

Nusseck, Manfred and Marcelo M. Wanderley, 'Music and Motion—How Music-Related Ancillary Body Movements Contribute to the Experience of Music', *Music Perception*, 26 (2009), 335–53.

Pallesen, Karen Johanne, Elvira Brattico, Christopher Bailey, Antti Korvenoja, Juha Koivisto, Albert Bjedde, and Synnöve Carlson, 'Emotion Processing of Major, Minor, and Dissonant Chords: A Functional Magnetic Resonance Imaging Study', *Annals of the New York Academy of Sciences*, 1060 (2006), 450–3.

Panksepp, Jaak and Günther Bernatzky, 'Emotional sounds and the brain: the neuro-affective foundations of musical appreciation', *Behavioural Processes*, 60 (2002), 133–55.

Peacocke, Christopher, 'The Perception of Music: Sources of Significance', *British Journal of Aesthetics*, 49 (2009), 257–75.

Pratt, Carroll C., 'The Design of Music', *Journal of Aesthetics and Art Criticism*, 12 (1954), 289–300.

Predelli, Stefano, 'Platonism in Music: a Kind of Refutation', *Revue internationale de philosophie*, 238 (2006), 401–14.

Prinz, Jesse J. *Gut Reactions: A Perceptual Theory of Emotions*, Oxford: Oxford University Press, 2006.
Putnam, Daniel, 'Why Instrumental Music Has No Shame', *British Journal of Aesthetics*, 27 (1987), 55-61.
Putnam, Hilary, *Reason, Truth and History*, Cambridge: Cambridge University Press, 1981.
Quantz, Johann Joachim, *On Playing the Flute*, trans. Edward R. Reilly, London: Faber and Faber, 2001.
Radcliffe, Philip, *Beethoven's String Quartets*, second edn, Cambridge: Cambridge University Press, 1978.
Radford, Colin, 'Emotions and Music: A Reply to the Cognitivists', *Journal of Aesthetics and Art Criticism*, 47 (1989), 69-76.
—— 'Muddy Waters', *Journal of Aesthetics and Art Criticism*, 49 (1991), 247-52.
Raffman, Diana, *Language, Music, and Mind*, Cambridge, M.A.: MIT Press, 1993.
—— 'Is Twelve-Tone Music Artistically Defective?' *Midwest Studies in Philosophy*, 27 (2003), 69-87.
Reid, Thomas, *The Works of Thomas Reid, D.D.*, third edn, Edinburgh: McLachlan and Stewart, 1852.
Reimer, Bennett, 'The Experience of Profundity in Music', *Journal of Aesthetic Education*, 29 (1995), 1-21.
Rickard, Nikki S., 'Intense emotional responses to music: a test of the physiological arousal hypothesis', *Psychology of Music*, 32 (2004), 371-88.
Ridley, Aaron, *Music, Value and the Passions*, Ithaca, N.Y.: Cornell University Press, 1995.
—— 'Profundity in Music', in Alex Neill and Aaron Ridley (eds.), *Arguing About Art: Contemporary Philosophical Debates*, New York: MacGraw-Hill, 1995, 260-70.
—— *The Philosophy of Music: Theme and Variations*, Edinburgh: Edinburgh University Press, 2004.
Riede, David G., *Allegories of One's Own Mind: Melancholy in Victorian Poetry*, Columbus, O.H.: Ohio State University Press, 2005.
Ringer, Mark, *Opera's First Master: The Musical Dramas of Claudio Monteverdi*, Plompton Plains, N.J.: Amadeus Press, 2006.
Robinson, Jenefer, 'Representation in Music and Painting', *Philosophy*, 56 (1981), 408-413.
—— 'Music as a Representational Art', in Philip Alperson (ed.), *What is Music? An Introduction to the Philosophy of Music*, University Park, P.A.: Pennsylvania State University Press, 1987, 165-92.
—— 'The Expression and Arousal of Emotion in Music', *Journal of Aesthetics and Art Criticism*, 52 (1994), 13-22.
—— 'Startle', *Journal of Philosophy*, 92 (1995), 53-74.

194 BIBLIOGRAPHY OF WORKS CITED AND CONSULTED

—— *Deeper than Reason: Emotion and its Role in Literature, Music, and Art*, Oxford: Clarendon Press, 2005.

—— 'Can Music Function as a Metaphor of Emotional Life?' in Kathleen Stock (ed.), *Philosophers on Music: Experience, Meaning, and Work*, Oxford: Oxford University Press, 2007, 149–177.

—— (ed.), *Music and Meaning*, Ithaca, N.Y.: Cornell University Press, 1997.

—— and Robert S. Hatten, 'Emotions in Music', *Music Theory Spectrum*, 34 (2012), 71–106.

Rousseau, Jean-Jacques, *A Dictionary of Music*, trans. William Waring, London: J. French, 1775.

Rudinow, Joel, *Soul Music: Tracking the Spiritual Roots of Pop from Plato to Motown*, Ann Arbor, M.I.: University of Michigan Press, 2010.

Scherer, Klaus R., 'Which Emotions Can be Induced by Music? What Are the Underlying Mechanisms? And How Can We Measure Them?' *Journal of New Music Research*, 33 (2004), 239–51.

—— and Marcel R. Zentner, 'Emotional Effects of Music: Production Rules', in Patrik N. Juslin and John A. Sloboda (eds.), *Music and Emotion: Theory and Research*, Oxford: Oxford University Press, 2001, 361–92.

Schumann, Robert, *Early Letters of Robert Schumann, Originally Published by his Wife*, trans. May Herbert, London: George Bell and Sons, 1888.

Schweitzer, Albert. *J.S. Bach*, trans. Ernest Newman, New York: Dover, 1966.

Scruton, Roger, 'Representation in Music', *Philosophy*, 51 (1976), 273–87.

—— *The Aesthetics of Music*, Oxford: Clarendon Press, 1997.

—— *Understanding Music: Philosophy and Interpretation*, London: Continuum, 2009.

Sharpe, R.A., 'Sounding the Depths', *British Journal of Aesthetics*, 40 (2000), 64–71.

Shostakovich, Dmitri, *Testimony: The Memoirs of Dmitri Shostakovich*, trans. Antonina W. Bouis, New York: Harper & Row, 1979.

Sizer, Laura, 'Moods in the Music and the Man: A Response to Kivy and Carroll', *Journal of Aesthetics and Art Criticism*, 65 (2007), 307–11.

Slack, Gordy, 'Source of human empathy directly observed', *New Scientist*, vol. 196, no. 2629 (2007), 12.

Smith, Adam, *Theory of the Moral Sentiments*, third edn, London: A. Miller, 1767.

Sonneck, O.G., *Beethoven: Impressions by his Contemporaries*, New York: Dover, 1967.

Sörbom, Göran, 'Aristotle on Music as Representation', *Journal of Aesthetics and Art Criticism*, 52 (1994), 37–46.

Sousou, Shaden Demise, 'Effects of Melody and Lyrics on Mood and Memory', *Perceptual and Motor Skills*, 85 (1997), 31–40.

Spitta, Philipp, *Johann Sebastian Bach*, trans. Clara Bell and J.A. Fuller-Maitland, London: Novello, Ewer, and Co., 1885.

Stecker, Robert, 'Davies on the Musical Expression of Emotion', *British Journal of Aesthetics*, 39 (1999), 273-81.
Steinbeis, Nikolaus and Stefan Koelsch, 'Affective Priming Effective of Musical Sounds on the Processing of Word Meaning', *Journal of Cognitive Neuroscience*, 23 (2010), 604-21.
—— and John A. Sloboda, 'The Role of Harmonic Expectancy Violations in Musical Emotions: Evidence from Subjective, Physiological, and Neural Responses', *Journal of Cognitive Neuroscience*, 18 (2006), 1380-93.
Stinson, Russell. *J.S. Bach's Eighteen Great Organ Chorales*, New York: Oxford University Press, 2001.
Strunk, Oliver, *Source Readings in Music History*, New York: W.W. Norton, 1950.
Tanner, Michael, 'Review of Joseph Kerman, *Opera as Drama*, new and revised edition, and Peter Kivy, *Osmin's Rage: Philosophical Reflections on Opera, Drama, and Text*', *Cambridge Opera Journal*, 1 (1989), 299-306.
Thom, Paul, 'Aesthetics of Opera', *Philosophy Compass*, 6/9 (2011), 575-84.
Trainor, Laurel J. and Becky M. Heinmiller, 'The Development of Evaluative Responses to Music: Infants Prefer to Listen to Consonance Over Dissonance', *Infant Behavior and Development*, 21 (1998), 77-88.
Trehub, Sandra E., Anna M. Unyk, and Laurel J. Trainor, 'Adults Identify Infant-Directed Music Across Cultures', *Infant Behavior and Development*, 16 (1993), 193-211.
Twining, Thomas, *Two Dissertations on Poetical and Musical Imitation* in *Musical Aesthetics: A Historical Reader*, ed. Edward A. Lippman, New York: Pendragon Press, 1986.
Urmson, J.O., 'Representation in Music', *Royal Institute of Philosophy Lectures*, 6 (1972), 132-46.
Västfjäll, Daniel, Emotion Induction through Music: 'A Review of the Musical Mood Induction Procedure', *Musicae Scientiae*, Special Issue 2001-2002, 173-211.
Velten, Jr, Emmett, 'A Laboratory Task for Induction of Mood States', *Behavior Research and Therapy*, 6 (1968), 473-82.
Vuoskoski, Jonna K., William F. Thompson, Doris McIlwain, and Tuomas Eerola, 'Who Enjoys Listening to Sad Music and Why?' *Music Perception*, 29 (2012), 311-18.
Wagner, Richard, *Richard Wagner's Prose Works*, trans. William Ashton Ellis, London: K. Paul, Trench, Trübner, 1893.
Walton, Kendall, 'What is Abstract About the Art of Music?' *Journal of Aesthetics and Art Criticism*, 46 (1988), 351-64.
—— 'Listening with Imagination: Is Music Representational?' *Journal of Aesthetics and Art Criticism*, 52 (1994), 47-61.
Weitz, Morris, *Philosophy of the Arts*, Cambridge, M.A.: Harvard University Press, 1950.

Whissell, Cynthia, 'Emotion Conveyed by Sound in the Poetry of Alfred, Lord Tennyson', *Empirical Studies of the Arts*, 20 (2002), 137–55.

—— 'Sound and Emotion in Milton's *Paradise Lost*', *Perceptual and Motor Skills*, 113 (2011), 257–67.

White, David A., 'Toward a Theory of Profundity in Music', *Journal of Aesthetics and Art Criticism*, 50 (1992), 23–34.

Williams, Bernard, *On Opera*, New Haven, C.T.: Yale University Press, 2006.

Wollheim, Richard, *Painting as an Art*, Cambridge, M.A.: Harvard University Press, 1987.

Young, James O., *Art and Knowledge*, London: Routledge, 2001.

—— 'Resemblance, Convention, and Musical Expressiveness', *The Monist*, 95 (2012), 587–605.

Zangwill, Nick, 'Against Emotion: Hanslick Was Right About Music', *British Journal of Aesthetics*, 44 (2004), 29–43.

—— 'Music, Metaphor and Emotion', *Journal of Aesthetics and Art Criticism*, 65 (2007), 391–400.

—— 'Music, Essential Metaphor, and Private Language', *American Philosophical Quarterly*, 48 (2011), 2–16.

Zbikowski, Lawrence M., 'Conceptual Models and Cross-Domain Mapping: New Perspectives on Theories of Music and Hierarchy', *Journal of Music Theory*, 41 (1997), 193–225.

Zentner, Marcel, Didier Grandjean, and Klaus R. Scherer, 'Emotions Evoked by the Sound of Music: Characterization, Classification and Measurement', *Emotion*, 8 (2008), 494–521.

Index

Abert, Hermann, vii, 70, 143, 166
Aesthetic emotion, 1, 8, 52, 55-8, 79-86, 151, 164
Aesthetic value, 25, 74-6, 78, 86, 115, 140, 149-51, 153, 158, 161, 174-6, 182
Allegri, Gregorio, 17
Anti-formalism, vii, 1-2, 8-9, 87-8, 101, 104, 106, 110, 115, 119-20, 124-5, 128, 131, 145, 150, 156-8, 165-7, 174-5, 180, 182-3
Aristotle, 104-5, 175-6
Arousal of emotion, 8-9, 14, 17, 35-86, 87, 93, 95-100, 104, 122-3, 125, 132, 134-42, 158, 160-1, 174-5, 177-81
Avison, Charles, 2, 101

Bad sad music argument, 73-5
Bach, Carl Philipp Emanuel, 107-8, 111-2, 131
Bach, Johann Sebastian, 25, 34, 88, 166, 170, 177, 180-1
Beardsley, Monroe, vii
Beatles, 74
Beauty, musical, 8, 80-2, 84-6, 110, 151-3, 156, 182
Beethoven, Ludwig van, viii, 108, 111, 116, 166, 178
Bell, Clive, 79-86
Berg, Alban, 126, 129-30, 144, 146
Berlioz, Hector, 108, 111, 181
Biber, Heinrich, 93-4
Bizet, Georges, 123
Brady, Nicholas, xv, 175
Brain reflexes, 59-60, 66-7, 79
Budd, Malcolm, vii, 5, 66-7

Carroll, Noël, 63
Character, viii, 88, 106, 104-5, 109, 130, 132, 143, 174-5, 179-81
Coclio, Adrian Petit, 70
Cognitive content/significance of music, vii, 1-2, 9, 88, 106, 108-10, 113-4, 117, 120, 122-4, 125, 134, 137, 147, 149-50, 158, 167, 177, 179-80, 182-3

Cognitive theory of emotions, 40-2, 80
Composers' intentions, 6, 98, 101-2, 107-9
Consonance and dissonance, 31-2
Convention and musical expressiveness, 26-34
Copland, Aaron, viii, 177
Cross-cultural experience of music, 22-3, 32, 34
Cross-domain mapping, 19, 21-2

Danto, Arthur, 169
Daquin, Louis-Claude, 92
Davies, Stephen, vii, viii, 5, 7, 12, 19, 21, 62, 102-3, 167, 172-4
Dean, Winton, vii, 127, 133, 146
Debussy, Claude, 70, 116
de Heem, Jan Davidszoon, 94, 104
Dickens, Charles, 121-2, 136
Donne, John, 121
Dowland, John, 6, 71
Dryden, John, 2
Dvořák, Antonín, 166

Eliot, T.S., 176
Emotional contagion, 39, 59-2, 67, 69-70, 79, 95-6, 123, 136, 145
Enhanced formalism, 9, 34
Exemplification, 91, 96-7
Expression, musical, 5-7, 117, 176, 180
Expressiveness, resemblance theory of musical, 7, 9-26, 62, 68-9, 98-9, 103, 118

Florentine Camerata, 13, 34
Formalism, vii, 1, 8, 47, 76-7, 86, 87-8, 90, 94, 106, 108-9, 120, 125, 127, 131-2, 137, 143-4, 148-9, 172, 174, 180, 183
Fundamental frequency, 30-1

Geneva Emotional Music Scale, 163-4
Gilbert and Sullivan, 171-2
Glarean, Heinrich, 2
Gluck, Christoph Willibald, 107, 181
Grout, Donald, 176, 181

Hand, Ferdinand, 111
Handel, George Frideric, viii, 17-8, 25, 34, 93-4, 100, 124, 128, 133, 144, 145-6, 148, 176, 181
Hanslick, Eduard, 40, 112, 125, 150
Hayes, William, 14, 18, 34
Hearing-in, 92-3, 99, 115-6
Homer, 121
Honegger, Arthur, 116
Hospers, John, 181
Hume, David, 45, 87
Hutcheson, Francis, 2, 61

Ineffability, 110, 114, 177

Jahn, Otto, 2-3, 179
James, William, 42
Johnson, Mark, 15, 20
Josquin, 2, 78
Juslin, Patrik N., 15-6

King, B.B., 101-2
Kivy, Peter, vii, viii, ix, xv, 7-9, 11-5, 17, 22, 25-7, 34, 36-40, 44-50, 55-9, 64-5, 68-9, 72-3, 76-86, 93-4, 99-100, 110, 117-20, 122, 125-30, 132-3, 143, 146-8, 165, 166-74
Konečni, Vladimir J., 51-2
Krumhansl, Carol L., 43, 48-50, 54-8

Laukka, Petri, 15
Led Zeppelin, viii
Levinson, Jerrold, 9-10, 71, 130-1, 142, 146, 174, 176-7, 179
Liszt, Franz, 179

Mackie, J.L., 45
Mahler, Gustav, 112, 177
Matravers, Derek, 75
Mattheson, Johann, 14, 34, 100, 107
Mendelssohn, Felix, 70-1, 116
Messiaen, Olivier, 113
Metaphor (and music), 3-5
Meyer, Leonard B., 27-8, 63-5, 71
Mirror neurons, 62
Modality, musical, 26-33
Monteverdi, Claudio, vii, 12, 17, 128, 148
Moral characteristics of music, 180-1
Motherese, 18
Motion, 19-20
Mozart, Leopold, 107

Mozart, Wolfgang Amadeus, vii, 2-3, 6, 16, 70-1, 128-9, 146, 166, 179
Musical emotion, 57

Opera, problem of, 125-32, 137, 142, 144, 148

Panksepp, Jaak, 17
Perceptual theory of emotion, 42-44
Pergolesi, Giovanni Battista, 148
Personae in music, 9-10, 111-2, 134, 147, 179
Perspectives, 179, 181, 183
Platonic emotions, 67-8, 72
Pratt, Carroll, 108
Prinz, Jesse J., 42
Profundity in music, 88, 166-74, 182
Propositional theory of literature, 122, 132-4
Psychological insight, vii-viii, 8-9, 87, 98, 124-5, 143, 149, 168, 174-5, 177-8, 181-2
Puccini, Giacomo, 141
Purcell, Henry, 131, 146

Quantz, Johann Joachim, 107

Radford, Colin, 61-2
Reid, Thomas, 14
Repetition, argument from, 120-4
Representation, concept of, 88-93
Representation, musical, 1, 34, 88, 93-4, 97-124, 143-4, 147-8, 165, 174-82
Ridley, Aaron, 126
Robinson, Jenefer, 13, 48, 55, 63, 112, 115-7, 134
Romanticism, 112, 178
Rousseau, Jean-Jacques, 105

Schubert, Franz, viii, 112, 116, 178
Schumann, Robert, viii, 112
Schweitzer, Albert, 166, 181
Scruton, Roger, 112-5
Serialism, 175
Shakespeare, William, 168
Shostakovich, Dmitri, viii, 108
Smith, Adam, 61
Somatic effects of music, 39, 59, 62-3, 67, 79, 123, 135, 153
Song of the Sibyl, 178
Sophocles, 168

Spitta, Philipp, 180
Springsteen, Bruce, viii
Stile rappresentativo, 101, 127
Stimulation model of music, 64–5

Tanner, Michael, 144n
Tchaikovsky, Pyotr Ilyich, 70, 180
Telemann, Georg Philipp, 73
Tennyson, Alfred, Lord, 95–6, 123–4
Tolstoy, Leo, 134

Twinning, Thomas, 105, 147

Verdi, Giuseppe, 127
Vivaldi, Antonio, 93

Wagner, Richard, 101, 147
Wilde, Oscar, 168, 171
Wollheim, Richard, 92

Zangwill, Nick, vii, 3–4, 151

The manufacturer's authorised representative in the EU for product safety is Oxford University Press España S.A. of el Parque Empresarial San Fernando de Henares, Avenida de Castilla, 2 – 28830 Madrid (www.oup.es/en or product. safety@oup.com). OUP España S.A. also acts as importer into Spain of products made by the manufacturer.

www.ingramcontent.com/pod-product-compliance
Ingram Content Group UK Ltd.
Pitfield, Milton Keynes, MK11 3LW, UK
UKHW021249180426
11946UKWH00003B/36